The
Unknown
Judith
Wright

Georgina Arnott is a researcher in the History Program at Monash University. In 2013 she received a doctorate in History from the University of Melbourne for her study of the life of Judith Wright. She holds a Masters in Literary Studies, has taught in that field at Swinburne and Victoria universities, and has had a number of articles and book reviews published in Australian journals.

The Unknown Judith Wright

Georgina
Arnott

UWA PUBLISHING

First published in 2016 by
UWA Publishing
Crawley, Western Australia 6009
www.uwap.uwa.edu.au

UWAP is an imprint of UWA Publishing
a division of The University of Western Australia

National Library of Australia
Cataloguing-in-Publication entry:
Arnott, Georgina, author.
The unknown Judith Wright / Georgina Arnott.
ISBN: 9781742588216 (paperback)
Includes bibliographical references and index.
Wright, Judith, 1915–2000.
Wright, Judith, 1915–2000—Childhood and youth.
Poets, Australian—20th century—Biography.
Women environmentalists—Australia—Biography.
A821.3

Cover design by Alissa Dinallo
Typeset in 11 point Bembo by Lasertype
Printed by Lightning Source

 uwapublishing

Contents

Acknowledgements

I thank the School of Philosophical, Historical and International Studies at Monash University for its support in the publication of this book, and the University of Melbourne and Curtin University for scholarships to write the PhD from which it derived. Through their supervision, Joy Damousi and Tim Dolin have brought more to this book than they know; I am particularly grateful to them for their encouragement. I am proud to be associated with UWA Publishing, and thank them for taking a chance on this category-defying work. Katie Connolly and Kate Pickard approached the production of this book with great care and insight.

Family members of Judith Wright were exceptionally patient in answering my queries. I thank Pip Bundred, Pollyanne Hill, Catherine Wright, Cedric Wyndham, and the very generous Don Seton Wilkinson, for their time and honesty. I would like to pay my respects to Meredith McKinney, who consented to my use of her mother's poetry and papers, provided cover images, and was an interviewee. She engaged deeply with the ideas in this book and demonstrated an intellectual generosity which I hope to learn from. I acknowledge, too, her skilful editorial curatorship, together with Patricia Clarke, of Judith Wright's writing, and the inspiring histories of European settlement which I have drawn on, especially those written by John Ferry, James Miller and Roger Milliss. It may seem odd at this point to thank Judith Wright, but I do, for improving my world.

I am grateful to HarperCollins Publishers for generously allowing me to quote from Judith Wright's *Collected Poems*, to Text Publishing for doing likewise with *Half a Lifetime*, and to the National Library of Australia for permitting me to quote from the papers of Judith Wright, as well as their fabulous oral history collection.

This project has been made possible by the digitisation of many historical and literary sources, particularly the digital indexation of colonial documents done by the School of Comparative Law at Macquarie University. My thanks to the Fisher Library's rare books department, the State Library of New South Wales, the National Library of Australia and the Baillieu Library's cultural collections room.

I have been the beneficiary of advice from Fiona Capp, Robert Evans, David Garrioch, Paul Genoni, Karen Lamb, Sean Scalmer, Andrew Schuller, Susan Sheridan, Chris Wallace-Crabbe, Shirley Walker and Elizabeth Webby. The following magnificent women have fortified me – blessed are they: Marion and Narida Arnott, Jessie Buckley, Catrionadh Dobson, Heidi Golz, Charlotte Greenhalgh, Prue Griffiths, Rosa Holman, Joanne Jones, Anna Kay, Mary McDonald, Clare Monagle, Jeannette Patrick, Amira Pyliotis, Bridie Riordan, and Harriet Turnball. Thanks, especially, to my mother, Jane Patrick, and to my children, Ellis and Saphira, who help me see more in the page. Above all, I would like to acknowledge Nathan Hollier, first mate and lodestar, who tended our flame tree: '...look how gloriously/ that careless blossomer scatters, and more and more'.

All poetry by Judith Wright in this book comes from *Collected Poems 1942–1985* (HarperCollins, 1994), except where otherwise indicated.

It is wise in the young
to forget the common world:

to be lost in the flesh
and the light shining there:
not to listen to the old
whose tune is fear and care —

Judith Wright, 'Age to Youth' (1963)

Introduction

Born in New England, New South Wales, in 1915, it is accepted wisdom that Judith Wright's life could not have been foreseen. Forebears, siblings and cousins became pastoralists; Judith became a towering figure in Australian poetry. Though she received significant accolades, including the Grace Leven Prize (twice), the Asan World Prize and the Queen's Medal for Poetry, honorary doctorates from several Australian universities, fellowship of the Australian Academy of the Humanities, and was once seriously considered as a future Australian Governor-General, perhaps more impressive still is the extent to which her poetry has been read, studied and anthologised in Australia and around the world. In India, for instance, a sizeable body of academic literature devoted to her work has continued to expand since her death in 2000. Other facts underscore how remarkable Judith Wright's life was, and how it seemed to defy the conventions of her upbringing, notably her partnership with the revolutionary but unrecognised philosopher Jack McKinney and her dedicated and high-profile involvement in campaigns for the environment and Aboriginal land rights. The questions 'how' and 'why' such a seemingly inexplicable life came into being have shaped discussion of the woman.[1]

Biographers and literary critics have tended to view Judith Wright as a family aberration; a figure akin to the idealised Romantic poet who is born different, detached from her society, inspired. In a variation of this narrative, others have suggested that Judith's close relationship with nature, as a child, made her unusually reflective and responsive to the world.[2] Some have isolated figures in the family tree who were distinguished by their idealism, drive or empathy for the less fortunate, although their connection to Judith might seem remote.

The woman herself did much to shape her life narrative with the publication of her memoir *Half a Lifetime* (1999), two book-length studies and numerous essays explicating her family background, and through her participation in a series of interviews during the 1980s for the National Library of Australia (NLA). Conceived late in life, much of this material was organised according to her priorities then, focusing on that which she thought was important, skimming over that which was not. Judith had an understandable desire to provide an interpretation of her life, but her letters, written in old age, also reveal a discomfort with others pursuing her biography, and suggest that she wrote her memoir in part, at least, in order to control other interpretations.

For Judith, biographical endeavour was not always virtuous. Why should people presume to look for meaning in her life, or iron out its inconsistencies? Why, when the more pressing issues of environmental collapse and the violation of human rights, particularly those of Aboriginal people in Australia, were so important? Why did it matter just how she travelled her eighty-five years? Such questions seem more pressing now, with the centenary of her birth having just passed, sixteen years on from her death. They reflect the conflicts and compromises that haunt many in the comfortable and polluting 'First World', for the problems that stirred Judith – the destruction of the Great Barrier Reef, climate change, racism in Australia – have arguably only intensified. Perhaps nothing short of full-time activism, such as that in which Judith engaged in the later decades of her life, might be defensible in the circumstances.[3]

Why, then, biography? Why a biography of a person whose legacy seems to resist it? Whose intellectual contribution was, in part, a renunciation of the ego, an ethically rigorous directive to understand the experience and suffering of others, and of natural environments, out of which one's own life has grown?

My engagement with Judith Wright began as a secondary student, as it did for many. Drawn to her uncompromising poetry, I learnt that Judith had been a pioneering modern poet, introducing new themes and stylistic innovations to Australian audiences. The pre-eminent literary critic on her work, Shirley Walker, calculated 'it is difficult to overstate the impact' on Australian writing of her first collection, *The Moving Image* (1946).[4] In poetry, throughout her life, Judith looked for truer means of expression, as in life she looked for truth more generally. Famously, this eventually even meant putting aside poetry for more direct social activity.

Fascinated by Judith's searching for truth in the world, I pursued doctoral studies in her non-fiction in the belief that her contribution as a public intellectual had not been properly recognised. I was impressed by the way that she used her background to highlight broader issues in Australian history and culture. She seemed to provide a personal and honest framework for navigating the conflicts between literature and real life, and one in which White Australians could reassess their own inheritance.

Discussions with Judith's family revealed a necessarily more complex person, alerting me to some of the elisions in public accounts of her life, mostly of an inconsequential nature to my project, but which did suggest a woman comfortable with leaving out certain facts when they seemed to get in the way of a larger or more general truth. Of course, she was human, not an abstracted sense of ethical principles, and she was entitled to represent her personal and family history in the way that best navigated what may have been competing truths.

Things became more complex still as I followed her trail, probing first-hand accounts, local histories, diaries and more-recently published Aboriginal histories to learn the story of her first Australian ancestors, the early colonialists George and Margaret Wyndham, whom Judith had written about in two books: *Generations of Men* (1959) and *Cry for the Dead* (1981). As is well known, the latter was an attempt to fill the gaps created by the former. *Cry for the Dead* emphasised how damaging the colonial project had been to Indigenous people in Australia, and was written with the self-consciousness of a woman who had come to understand that she had been a beneficiary of such damage. Whereas in the first book Judith had appeared largely untroubled by her grandmother May's assessment of George Wyndham as someone akin to the biblical Abraham, whose covenant with God had afforded him a promised land, in the second she was much more critical of such mythology.

And yet, a close examination of even that groundbreaking second history revealed that the Wyndhams were presented as exceptional amongst their peers for their interest in keeping away from colonial conflict. Even if they are presented as having acquiesced to dispossession, they apparently did not directly dispossess. They were better colonialists, in Judith's rendering; in much the way her own grandmother and father were portrayed as benevolent pastoralists of their respective eras. The reader might have concluded that several generations of Wyndham Wrights exhibited, to a greater or lesser extent, the respect for Aboriginal people and care for the less fortunate and the natural landscape that Judith championed in the latter decades of her life.

And then, to my astonishment, I happened upon some facts that seemed to challenge that interpretation. These were not inconsequential facts. The more I looked, the more compelling her family history became. Judith's grandmother May Wright and her father Phillip Wright, hugely important figures within her childhood, were involved in Australian public life and the construction of a rural conservative politics to a much greater extent than current literature on Judith showed. Their values were strongly informed by the colonial Wyndhams, but not in the way I had understood. Such revelations only seemed to take me further away from Judith Wright as I met her on the page. The gap between background and public figure seemed larger, and at the same time I could see how she had tried to downplay that gap. What was the missing link between her life and theirs? How should one understand her?

There has been only one full biography of Judith Wright: *South of My Days* (1998), written by literary academic and nun Veronica Brady, and its approach and findings have dominated discourse on the woman. Brady looked to the poet's latter-day understanding of her life for its coherence, afterwards reflecting: 'I thought that my task was to tell the story of her life as she would have told it herself'.[5] In doing so, she relied heavily on the pre-publication manuscript of *Half a Lifetime* (1999) and interviews with her subject. On even mildly controversial subject matter, Brady asked Judith whether she should include it, or how exactly to do so. Judith seemed to anticipate this, explaining why she agreed to Brady above other biographer candidates: 'my publishers at Collins warned me of various aspiring biographers and told me to get one at least under control before I can't argue with their interpretations'. She did not want a biography, but if one were to be written she would rather be on friendly terms with the author. Brady would at least not be a 'constant problem', living as she did on the other side of Australia, in Perth.[6] A warm and considerate rapport developed in their correspondence. In an irony instructive to sympathetic biographers, Judith took issue with Brady's interpretative framework and, post-publication, attempted (unsuccessfully) to have her corrections to the biography printed by the publisher. She told family and friends that Brady gave the wrong impression of her upbringing and that she did not agree with the book. But would Judith have agreed with any biography? In fact, in the wake of Brady's book, Judith hoped another would be written, modifying its impression. 'Everyone assures me there will be other biograph[ies]', she told one friend.[7] Brady's pioneering work made her more open to the endeavour.

As a way of understanding the woman, Brady argued that Judith came to her unconventional world views through a process of emotional, intuitive realisation which had marked her from birth. 'The saying has it', she wrote, 'that poets are born not made'.[8] Describing episodes from Judith's early childhood which showed a particularly acute response to injustice, Brady said that by the age of three she 'resisted the emotions of the crowd, implicitly understanding that life ought to be based on relationships between people'. Though she was 'born into privilege', as a young child she began to understand that 'her "place in the sun" might be at the expense of others'.[9] Brady argued that Judith's grandfather Albert had been a profound influence, for his diaries indicated a unique interest in and sympathy for Aboriginal people: his 'intuition was to be at the centre of his granddaughter's sense of herself'. Though Judith never met her grandfather, who died when her father was one, and only began reading his diaries when she was thirty-one, for Brady, Albert was an example of the 'unseen presences' which filled Judith's childhood. Others included trees, flowers, birds and animals – 'all instinct with some mysterious life'.[10]

In recent years there has been increased discussion of Judith's biography, prompted especially by revelations of her two-decade long affair with H. C. 'Nugget' Coombs by Fiona Capp in *My Blood's Country* (2010). Capp, a writer who had known Judith personally, used her own correspondence, interviews with relatives, Judith's poetry and descriptions of the natural landscapes Judith lived within, to argue that she was principally shaped by these landscapes. Capp substantiated Brady's depiction of Judith as intimately connected with nature, which was alive to her from her very earliest years. Charting the main interests in Judith's life, and how these were reflected in her writing, Capp gave a rich sense of Judith's emotional and physical landscapes.

And yet, I still could not quite believe, I suppose, that broader cultural and historical forces, and her parents and family, whose influences were downplayed in these biographical works, had not also fundamentally shaped Judith. Poets, like all of us, are partly made, not wholly born, I might have ventured. The new material I was unearthing about Judith's family members, compared to her portrayal of them, seemed, if anything, proof of their hold over her into old age; that they had 'made' her much more than had been recognised.

Existing accounts moved quickly from moments of trauma or illumination in her childhood years to early encounters with Jack McKinney at the age of twenty-eight, compressing Judith's actual upbringing and maturation, and giving the impression that she was self-realised from a young age. What's more, there seemed a significant absence in almost all accounts: Judith's undergraduate career at the University of Sydney in the mid 1930s. In biographies of writers, authors tend to dwell on academic years, in the belief that such periods are intellectually formative, and that first encounters with other writers and publishing enterprises usually shape the writer's work. But in the public telling of Judith's life these years had been left almost completely unexamined.

Basic facts about them have been provided. Judith's daughter Meredith McKinney, and editor of *Half a Lifetime*, Patricia Clarke, introduced sections of *With Love and Fury: Selected Letters of Judith Wright* (2006), with biographical summaries, which included the following:

Then, in 1934, she moved to Sydney to begin life on her own terms, as a student at Sydney University. Judith later remembered her three years at the university, studying English Literature, History, Psychology and Philosophy, as a time of happiness, friendships and freedom.[11]

Describing the years preceding and following in some detail, there is nothing in these letters from which McKinney and Clarke might have drawn to extend their discussion beyond those few lines. The collection skips from the letters Judith wrote as a child to those she wrote in her mid twenties, a period of fifteen years. In Meredith's personal collection there are no letters from the period either, something she describes as 'a mystery', but one which may, in the end, simply be the result of Judith being less scrupulous about such matters during these years – a normal enough occurrence at that time of life.[12] In Judith's extensive archive at the NLA there are no diaries, poems, or transcripts from her time as a university student, and no letters at all from her life before the age of thirty-three. Though biographical accounts have grappled with the relative dearth of primary material relating to Judith's years immediately preceding the publication of *The Moving Image* (1946), of her three university student years in the mid 1930s there appears to be precisely nothing.

Judith did provide two limited accounts of the period, to which others have referred. In *Half a Lifetime* she dedicated seven out of 296 pages to her time as a student, mostly as it transpired outside the lecture halls, giving the impression that it was a fun and simply frivolous period of her life. Her NLA interviews offer a similar emphasis. In both, Judith indicated that neither her lecturers nor her peers had aided her intellectual development or poetry in any significant way. She did reveal that she had written numerous poems as a student, none of which she was prepared to identify.

For her part, Brady regarded the university years essentially as an intellectual non-event, through which Judith's pre-existing worldview and intellectual approach emerged unscathed by academic and social encounters. Accordingly, a mere eleven of her biography's 500 pages are devoted to this time. Brady largely restated Judith's impressions of this period, but also produced a number of inaccuracies that have led other critics to make unsubstantiated claims.[13] For Capp also, the university years did not represent a significantly affecting period in Judith's life; she mentions only in passing that Judith studied and lived in Sydney.

There have been two major literary studies of Judith's work, Shirley Walker's *Flame and Shadow* (1991) and Jennifer Strauss' *Judith Wright* (1995), both of which have considered the years immediately prior to the publication of Wright's first collection *The Moving Image*. Walker and Strauss affirmed Judith's own conviction that the most important influences on this book had been World War II and intellectual encounters with Jack in her late twenties, with the period before barely mentioned. Walker summarised the influence of Judith's university career in a sentence and Strauss argued that the 'first fruits of Sydney writing were not spectacular'; that without her return to New England, in the early 1940s, 'nothing good might have come' of her girlish desires to write accomplished poetry.[14] None of the poetry or intellectual concerns of her student years were expanded on. Similarly, Brady remarked of Judith's university poetry that it was of too poor a quality to be considered relevant to her later work.[15]

Nonetheless, over the past two decades, there have been strengthening calls for Judith's life and work to be examined as one would those of a public intellectual; for her life beyond the boundaries of her successful poetry career to be considered, on the basis that it might tell us something more broadly about Australian cultural and intellectual history. Strauss initiated such discussion by stating, in 1995, that there had been a 'relative neglect of Wright in works with some ambition to present Australia's cultural history', and pointed to her omission from Brian Head and James Walter's influential edited work *Intellectual Movements and Australian Society* (1988).[16] Similarly, in the wake of Brady's biography, literary academic Philip Mead lamented that the intellectual networks which aided Judith's development, and which she in turn helped shape, had not been seriously explored.[17] Partly, this was due to the fact that the influences and allegiances in her career formed an 'intense, contradictory matrix', he ventured; however, such a discordant life might illuminate something of Australian culture over the same period. Judith's evolving stance on nationhood, for instance, meant that she 'contributed as powerfully to the critique of national identity as she did to its construction', and that this is in itself a powerful expression of the 'bi-polar politics of Australian white identity'.[18] Mead championed paying attention to the contours of Judith's thinking, shaped by other figures and social contexts, rather than searching for an intellectual unity within it. It became a provocation for this book, and other studies on Judith Wright.

In 2009 literary academic Brigid Rooney appeared to take up Mead's challenge, documenting Judith's interactions with other literary intellectuals and demonstrating how such pairings explained her intellectual development, in doing so undermining depictions of her as 'public prophet' and 'unworldly' figure. Rooney argued that Douglas Stewart's response to Judith's early work, in which he assumed that she 'had emerged suddenly, without precedent, from the obscurity of the private realm', had been formative in shaping a patriarchal framework for reading her work.[19] Around the same time, Susan Sheridan, a scholar in postwar women's writing, added that the lives of Australian women writers, including Judith's, had been routinely misconstrued by both patriarchal and feminist readings. 'Subtler instruments', she wrote, 'are needed to analyse the varying degrees of recognition that this cohort of women experienced when they began writing'. Of their early publishing experiences – which constitute that crucial make-or-break period – we should be asking: 'how did she come to see herself as a writer? How did she get started?...Who and what helped or hindered her?' The focus of Sheridan and Rooney's work, however, was on the years leading up to *The Moving Image*, which they considered the defining apprenticeship.[20]

There was that gap, a period which to me seemed as potentially rich as (and possibly more experimental than) her late twenties. For, we knew, this was the time in which she first encountered innovative figures who did much to shape the intellectual landscape of Australia in the twentieth century; men such as the philosopher John Anderson, anthropologist A. P. Elkin, and the literary critic and inaugural editor of Australia's first literary publication, *Southerly*, R. G. Howarth. What did she learn from them? Make of them? She had told us that her early poetry and attempts at journalism had been largely rejected by her peers. On what grounds? Was she already writing and thinking differently to her peers at university? How did such rejection affect her writing? What was the influence of other students, especially other more dominant figures within the writing scene there? What was the effect of her encounters with such figures? I wondered if an explication of this relatively unexamined period, and what may have been intricate and strongly affecting networks – going beyond the existing few sentences published on these – might enable a better understanding of her life course and the formation of her intellectual approach.

As I began researching Judith's three years at university I saw how this evidence, like that relating to her family history, challenged established understandings of her life and her work. Immersing myself in the world of mid 1930s Sydney University, hunting student publications, lectures, the published works of her lecturers, first-hand accounts, university transcripts, records and official histories, I came to see that Judith's emphases sometimes did not fit with the 'facts'; that she was, for instance, not quite the 'shunted' poetess she had remembered, that in fact she had a presence as a writer at the University which has never been acknowledged. I came across thirteen columns Judith had written for the student newspaper which revealed a feisty and talented young writer and not one who, to put it mildly, was always sympathetic to society's victims. I learned that she could be frivolous and judgmental when discussing others, in ways that were perhaps, after all, not all that remarkable for a woman of her time and place. Such material demonstrated that Judith, as we met her in *The Moving Image*, and especially in current biographical accounts, was not born, but developed out of her interactions with the social world. I began to see, too, how challenging the lectures Judith attended must have been for her, and that in fact her reflections on them in later years showed this, though not in ways that had been properly understood. It became increasingly clear that the preoccupations of her early poetry were also those of the lecturers and students she spent three years with.

And then I wondered about her university poetry, the stuff which critics and biographers had dismissed as amateurish and unworthy of consideration, while identifying very little of it. Judith had said that she had used numerous pseudonyms, but would reveal none, while Walker and literary critic Hugh Anderson had connected her with two, albeit in an unpublished source and a short review published in the 1960s. I found more poetry under these signatures and another two signatures which I thought might have been Judith's, and considered all that poetry – indeed all the poetry published in student journals at the University between 1934 and 1936 – in light of the poetry Judith published under her name in the decade after university, and its aesthetic, linguistic, formal and thematic interests. Eleven poems, under four signatures, stood out. I gathered evidence to convince the reader of what I was convinced: that these were Judith Wright's first published adult poems.

One poem, to me, felt astonishingly familiar. When I returned to *The Moving Image* I concluded it was an early draft of perhaps her most famous poem, 'Bullocky', published a decade later. I now began to believe that Judith's thinking and craft must have been more developed before she met Jack McKinney in the early 1940s than has been acknowledged; and that much intellectual and poetic development had occurred while she was at university. Of these three years, as of her family background, there was in fact so much relevant primary material that a book quickly emerged from my attempts to piece it together.

This book does not offer a complete account of Judith's first twenty-one years. Instead, it focuses on a number of events and figures to provide greater understanding of her intellectual and creative development. Chapter 1 describes the lives of Judith's first colonial ancestors, George and Margaret Wyndham, and argues that this history formed an enduring and very powerful mythology within her family. Contrary to established understandings, I argue that that mythology was something which she never fully abandoned. Chapter 2 examines the legacy of May and Phillip Wright, Judith's paternal grandmother and her father. I argue that their lives maintained the family mythology established by their colonial forebears but also provided a framework for Judith's unconventional thinking and public activism. Chapter 3 considers the influence of Ethel Wright, Judith's mother, and her allegiance to conventional femininity, particularly as it related to

Judith's early interest in poetry. These three chapters provide the background to Judith's young adulthood.

The remaining five chapters focus on the years 1934 to 1936, when Judith attended the University of Sydney, and are given the greatest weighting because this period has attracted such little attention to date. The aim of these chapters is to provide a clearer understanding of the link between Judith's early life and her later, more public life. Indeed, I will argue, the 'contradictions' of her life are less apparent when we examine this period. Chapter 4 outlines the cultural stimulations of Sydney and describes how Judith's time there was informed by modern ideas about the identity and sexuality of young women. Chapter 5 examines the ideas that were circulating outside the lecture halls, primarily as they were expressed by student publications. This chapter identifies and discusses student journalism written by Judith herself. Chapter 6 considers the influence on Judith of academic figures, texts and curricula in the disciplines of History, Philosophy and Anthropology. Chapter 7 examines the influence of the English department on Judith's poetry and on her understanding of what was possible within the field.

Chapter 8 presents eleven pseudonymous poems from student journals and argues that on the basis of the evidence now available they can be identified as having been written by Judith. Not only do these poems show that Judith was engaged by the intellectual concerns of her lecturers and peers while at university, but they reveal that some of the preoccupations and stylistic approaches of that monumental collection, *The Moving Image* (1946), were in place a decade earlier. These poems help explain how it was that she came to be that poetic figure of such significance. Like this book as a whole, they also prompt us to consider other influences in Judith's life which have been neglected.

Why write biography? Why write a biography of a woman who, according to her daughter, preferred to 'express herself on the level of truths rather than mere facts', believing a strong distinction existed between the two.[21] Judith's emphasis, throughout her life, on emotional perception as an undervalued but highly significant way of determining 'truth', sits at a philosophical distance from the usual methods of biographical enquiry, which rely on general histories, archival material and interviews. For Judith, such an endeavour might produce facts, but these should not be confused with 'truth'. Certainly, too great an emphasis on facts might do so, but to date there has been too little an emphasis on and explication of facts relating to Judith's background and early adult years to judge whether they could lead us closer to truths.

In biography, most of us are drawn to lives which appear to have been lived outside of expectation, and thus have changed our understanding of what is possible. That public figures, especially prolific and high-profile writers, leave a catalogue of sources, makes us feel that their lives might be grasped to some special degree. Judith's life story offers particular intrigue because it suggests that conservative and conventional upbringings can sometimes produce the most radical of thinkers. This book might add that, by extension, in some cases at least, even the most radical thinkers do not necessarily 'shed' the conservative traces of their heritage.

This biographical story is foremost a work of history. The two forms of knowledge, as scholar Barbara Caine shows, have for centuries been in a dance – sometimes intimate, sometimes haughty. In 1967 cultural historian Donald Horne was being bold when he claimed that his autobiography showed 'what social history can look like when told through *people*'.[22] Today, writes Caine, this is meat-and-potatoes stuff. Subjects are busy illuminating their 'social and political' worlds in biographies, and there is a widespread recognition that 'traditional biography, with its intense focus on the life of one individual' is no longer adequate. Caine observes that biography today often seeks to define 'the complex ways' that individuals relate to these worlds. And, she adds, within biographies of prominent individuals, there is an increasing concern with how they emerged into public life, for this reveals something crucial about 'public life' itself.[23]

These developments have encouraged me to reach beyond my subject. Judith's background and early life, after all, tell a history of Australia which prompts us to consider vital matters in new ways. Her life story reveals much about colonial race relations; the gulf between expectation and reality experienced by early European migrants; early attempts to develop a distinctly rural politics; the difficulties faced by women on isolated properties; and historical relations between the city and the country. The final five chapters, which centre on Judith's time at the University of Sydney between 1934 and 1936, and the work she produced there, tell of the class and gender distinctions embedded in Australian tertiary education; of the birth of modern Australian cities; the rapid social transformation which took place in 1930s Sydney; the liberties this transformation afforded to young women; the origins of Australian historiography; and, most forcefully, the birth of modern Australian poetry – a birth largely brought about by this woman. Lists of equal import might be made in regards to the final sixty-five years of Judith's life. Hers was a life of special significance, both for what she made happen, and for the milieu she occupied.

I cannot believe that I could have convinced Judith of the value of biographical research or of my particular approach to her life, which challenges aspects of *Half a Lifetime* as well as other autobiographical material. But, in the end, a person's desire to read their life according to their present-day interpretive framework is one thing. The duty of the literary critic, biographer or cultural historian may be to resist this desire, even when their subject is held in such high and deserved esteem as is Judith Wright.

This book then is an unapologetically historical study of Judith Wright's first twenty-one years, which presents a very different version of her life from those oft-repeated narratives recounted in the opening paragraphs of this introduction. Like any life, Judith's was of course impossible to foretell. But, when we look more closely at her family background, at her early and her young-adult years, her life course appears less implausible. As with any human being, she did not stand impervious to all of those things, good and bad, that took place around her. She was in fact made through her experience of and responses to them.

CHAPTER 1

The Wyndham World

I feel more and more, as far as creative writing is concerned, everything important happens to one before one is born.

Patrick White, 1958.

Not only my parents, but their own forebears, have influenced my life.

Judith Wright, 1992.[24]

In April 1945 Judith Wright wrote to her lover, Jack McKinney, from her family's pastoral station in New England, telling him of its 'nineteenth-century atmosphere'. She added: 'there's no doubt about it, looked at from this angle you and I are queer and sinful fish!' Most of Judith's family did not know of Jack and must have wondered that their thirty-year-old daughter, sister and niece was not already a pastoralist's wife. Jack, far from being a pastoralist, was a homeless, sometime garden-hand, twenty-four years Judith's senior. And though separated, he was married with children. To Judith, he was a philosopher whose work was nothing short of revolutionary. His lack of formal training and institutional recognition served only to bolster this belief: these allowed him to perceive the world more clearly, unencumbered by standardised thought processes. In his reply, Jack acknowledged 'how strange *our* life would seem by contrast', reassuring Judith that 'we of course are *right*, but it's difficult being the only people who are *right*'.

Jack was not referring to moral or social codes but to something much larger which separated them from her familial society. He suggested a way of rectifying this: could a philosophical article he had written 'make your folk realise that that good old world of theirs is now a fiction'?[25]

Was it right that Judith's family's world had become obsolete? This chapter and the two that follow chart this world of the Wrights, beginning with Judith's colonial forebears and with the period where she joked that her family remained stuck: the nineteenth century. Although these quotes hint at some of the complexities of Judith and Jack's relationship, and their relationship with her family, this book does not deal with these matters directly, which are illustrated in other biographical works and in the selected letters of Judith and Jack, *The Equal Heart and Mind* (2004), instead focusing on the period in Judith's life that came before, in order that we might, amongst other things, more fully comprehend that relationship when we come to it.

Judith's comment about the significance of her forebears to her life was profoundly true. Much of her creative and intellectual life was shaped by a desire to comprehend the value of their lives and legacies. Yet the results of this often uncomfortable pursuit have not been treated with adequate rigour. Her biographical studies have been accepted as authoritative by many literary critics and historians, who have not conducted their own enquiries.

Much of this stems from the great and deserved esteem in which Judith is often held. When, as an adult, her principal commitments became the protection of natural environments and the return of them, where practical, to Aboriginal people, she publicly disclosed the actions of her ancestors with a degree of honesty many would not. Her family was one which had dispossessed Aboriginal people to occupy and cultivate great acreages of land, which employed dozens of workers who had little control over their working conditions, garnered significant social power from its wealth and connections with ruling-class England, and which fought desperately for the maintenance of these privileges.

Judith's reappraisal of her family history represented, for professional historians and general readers alike, a benchmark in historical revisionism, an example of how White Australians could, and should, interrogate their own 'inheritance'. Where *The Generations of Men* (1959) gave a largely positive account of her family's history, in which Aboriginal people were almost entirely absent, *Cry for the Dead* (1981) emphasised with sometimes apocalyptic atmospherics the devastation caused to Aboriginal people by the pastoral invasion of Australia. At its core Judith's revisionism centred on two figures, George and Margaret Wyndham, her first colonial ancestors. From them sprang the family's pride, borne out in numerous histories; from them sprang the greatest potential source of shame.

Judith shifted discussion of Australian colonialism in the 1980s. This feat was laudable, even monumental. Yet, if we are to properly understand the woman and the degree of influence this history held over her, and have a fully informed discussion of the ongoing effects of colonialism on White Australians, it is important to examine closely Judith's representation of her family. The point of this is not to undermine Judith; she was, I believe, as rigorous a historian as was possible. Where family loyalty influenced her interpretation, it was not conscious, and it did not necessarily lead to a misrepresentation of truth; it was simply Judith's attempt to synthesise two different versions of history that had influenced her life and thinking. Though, as mentioned in the introduction to this book, we expect public figures to uphold exemplary standards, Judith was human and her engagement with a history that was both extremely personal and of public significance produced complex results.

Researching Judith's family history, I gradually developed the view that the Wyndhams directly dispossessed Aboriginal people, rather than only occupying and cultivating areas already 'settled', as Judith suggested. And although Judith deals with evidence which suggests that, on at least one occasion, they did this with the force of ammunition, I could not agree with her conclusion that this amounted to the Wyndhams' sixteen-year-old son simply 'pursuing' Aboriginal people. Her interpretation suggested to me the enduring strength of a family loyalty that she was not always fully aware or in control of.

Unhappily, there is not enough evidence to give a complete picture of her family's engagements with the original inhabitants, despite a huge amount of primary material relating to other aspects of their lives. There is, however, circumstantial evidence to indicate that these early encounters were unlikely to have formed as peaceful and tolerant a relationship as Judith suggested. A number of Wyndham friends, some of whom were very close, had views on the best ways of dealing with

Aboriginal people which were considered extreme, inflammatory and intolerant even by the standards of colonial society. Such associations sit uncomfortably alongside portrayals of the Wyndhams in family histories, including Judith's.

As I read on, it became harder to accept that Judith had fully escaped the nineteenth century of which she spoke, that she was indeed as much that 'queer and sinful fish' — that rebel of the family — as she perhaps would have liked to have been. It is a conclusion, however, I approach with caution; for, as much of this chapter also bears out, Judith was in so many ways an exemplar of good scholarship, who found ways of telling a colonial history that few others had, and in which evidence was often scant.

In all societies particular narratives become dominant; they are retold and re-imagined in order to affirm the fundamental beliefs of the group. Growing up in Judith's family one story loomed larger than all of the others. It was that of her great-great-grandparents George and Margaret Wyndham, her father's first colonial ancestors, who arrived in Hobart in 1827 and embarked on the creation of a colonial dynasty. In time they would help form the original Australian 'squattocracy'. The term was derived from combining 'aristocracy' with the word 'squatter', used to describe a person who moved animal stock to 'unoccupied' land where there were fresh reserves of grass and water.[26] Squatting suggested an opportunistic approach that sacrificed safety and permanency for potential wealth. By the twentieth century those families who had done well from the practice were regarded as well established. As the term suggests, they formed a social elite.

Down the generations George and Margaret were regarded as 'figures of serene achievement'.[27] In retellings, their lives became lordly, dignified, momentous. Prefacing a collection of George's correspondence, granddaughter May Wright compared him to the biblical Abraham, that 'father of a multitude of nations' whose covenant with God enabled his descendants to possess the land of Canaan.[28] So foundational, so germinal, did the story become, it was as if it marked the beginnings of time. By the era it reached Judith Wright, it had 'something of the atmosphere of the Book of Genesis'.[29] Growing up, she felt as if the Wyndhams' lives resembled the 'first years in human growth in their rapid and spectacular development'.[30] Judith explained in her family history *The Generations of Men* (1959) that the Wyndham story offered an authoritative cultural tradition, in the absence of others, complete with instructive moral codes for her grandmother May:

> It was not necessary to look further for a tradition, or for an aim that she should set herself. Accordingly George and Margaret, their lives and their achievements, took on for her an authority that made them, for their grand-daughter, a point of reference which she retained all her life.[31]

Judith forgave May for encasing her grandparents' lives in an impossible reverence. After all, May's life was full of terrible hardships, as well as triumphs. It was only human to search for a purpose in them, such as that produced by grafting her life onto ones of such obvious import. But, at age forty-four, when she wrote *Generations*, Judith wanted to assert her distance from that family tradition and understand it in critical terms. Over the years her critique of the family legend would become stronger, as she connected it with a larger story that White Australia told itself. Judith's 1985 poem 'For a Pastoral Family' was a bitter meditation on the way such narratives conditioned generations of Australians to ignore brutal aspects of their nation's past: 'a certain consensus of echo, a sanctioning sound,/ supported our childhood lives. We stepped/ on sure and conceded ground'.[32] By 1993 she concluded there was something 'terribly wrong' with such stories. *Generations* was not 'good' or worthy of republication.[33]

And yet the family story was a lifetime preoccupation for Judith too, albeit from a perspective that shifted over time, its significance for her, ironically, encapsulated in her description of its importance to her grandmother May: it was 'a point of reference which she retained all her life'. In the 1970s Judith sought to make amends for *Generations* by writing *Cry for the Dead* (1981), placing greater emphasis on Aboriginal experience.

Late in life, in her memoir *Half a Lifetime* (1999), she opens with the Wyndham story again, stating that the answer to the question 'who am I?' lay in the past. It was as if her life began there, a hundred years before she physically entered the world; as if, like Patrick White, she perceived that 'everything important happens to one before one is born'. And so she took up the family narrative, that lifelong touch-stone: 'the first two of my forebears to arrive in Australia...'[34]

Judith and May Wright were far from alone in their genealogical preoccupation. Judith's father, Phillip, opened his memoir with an account of the Wyndhams, stressing that their story deserved to be told to a greater extent than it had been. Other Wyndham descendants, including Judith's brother Peter, have taken up this task. In 1986 a number of Wyndham descendants formed the Dalwood Restoration Association (named after the Wyndhams' estate), which Judith had an ambivalent attitude towards.[35] Since then, Association members have published several books on the history of their forebears, including an edited collection of George Wyndham's diaries. In the afterword to Phillip Wright's memoir, descendant Bruce Mitchell said that he had 'respect for family links, and for the traditions and achievements passed down from earlier generations'.[36] It was a family trait shared by many. And while Judith would be distinguished within the family and within Australian society at large for her revisionism, a closer look at the Wyndham story, and Judith's readings of it, reveal that she never surrendered her respect for those 'figures of serene achievement'.

The Wyndham narrative began on Christmas Day 1825, in Rome, when George Wyndham, recovering from a fever caught on the Continent, met Margaret Jay. A union was forged. George's father owned a large property named Dinton, in Wiltshire, and, according to great-grandson Phillip Wright, belonged to 'one of the ancient families of England'.[37] Margaret's father had been a successful Dutch merchant in England before losing money in the South Sea Bubble affair. This drove him to Brussels, where he became a schoolmaster. Margaret's Scottish mother died while she was young.

As the third son, and with no land entitlement, George was expec-ted to become a clergyman in the Church of England. But from his time at Cambridge things went awry.[38] There he encountered theories of equality and joined the growing call for systemic discrimination against Roman Catholics to be removed. Against his family's interests he became a proponent of the Reform Bills and an exponent of the Corn Laws. He became friendly with John Galt, who would later critique political corruption in his novels. Galt was friends with another radical, Lord Byron, and wrote his biography. 'All these symptoms of advanced Whigdom', Judith wrote, 'had an alarming ring to the family at Dinton'.[39]

After Cambridge, the Church held little appeal for George. When his father offered to use his influence to get him a government posting George refused, Judith wrote, 'in a high-stand against becoming one of the "hangers–on, one of the eaters–up" of his country'. Around this time George reflected: 'my habits and inclinations, and the sources of my enjoyments, are very different from those of the world around me. There I cannot alter, but I can live in retirement, and avoid the contest of the world, which annoys me'.[40] The colonies beckoned.

Much less is known about Margaret, as is so often the way. Family histories record that she 'enjoyed a reputation as a most charming and cultivated young lady'.[41] She spoke French, Italian and English fluently. Granddaughter May declared that her 'sympathies were all English' though she was 'very French in many ways', having been raised in Brussels. On one occasion May recalled a French scientist visiting, at which Margaret turned 'into a vivacious French woman'. Sewing and piano performances were lifelong activities. May marvelled at her grandmother's ability to balance European refinement with colonial frontier-ism, noting that though she was not brought up for an Australian pioneering life, she 'acted her part like a heroine'.[42]

Four months after their marriage the Wyndhams set sail for Hobart. The boat was named *George Home*, presumably in honour of the vessel's principal passenger. On it they spent three–and–a–half months, travelling in cabins alongside the boat's commander, its owner, and a surgeon. Below travelled twelve steerage passengers, including two children; the Wyndham's staff; and the ship's crew. The newlyweds did not travel lightly. Across the world they took Merino and South Down sheep, Hereford cattle, horses, pigs, hounds and an assortment of agricultural implements. On arrival there remained more than 500 casks of ale, beer and rum amongst their cargo, plus a £3,000 loan from George's father. Hobart Town was shocked to learn news carried by the *George Home*: Tory Prime Minister George Canning had died just four months into his term. But George had travelled across the world, and was prepared to live 'in poverty', to get away from British politics. Years later he wrote: 'your emigrant is not a rich man, the fact of his being an emigrant shews him to be a man of small means'. Noting the advantages with which they travelled, Judith quipped: 'poverty was a relative matter among the county families'.[43]

Just why they embarked on that journey is a subject of contention. Family accounts have tended to intimate it was George's idealism and sense of independence, rather than economic exigency, that drove them from England. May said her grandfather was full of 'the spirit of adventure' and that he 'wanted somewhere where there was more elbow room'. Similarly, in *Generations*, Judith described George as a 'rebel' with 'Shelleyan dreams' who had a better chance of realising them in the colonies than amongst 'Dinton's county conservatism'. In the colonies, perhaps, he could help mould a society along more rational principles. In her 1947 poem 'G. W. Australia 1827', Judith wrote: 'they say you thought then of a second Rome,/ and of new helmeted legions moving out/ under a wiser discipline and law'. That George left because of political frustration is supported by a letter from his sister to Margaret in which she explains that George 'will be quite charmed with Mr Peel's conduct, and now that the Catholic question is likely to be carried, we may almost expect George's coming back to England'.[44]

Other evidence indicates George was gripped by intellectual curiosity. A sketch taken the year of his arrival depicts him as a learned man, his eyes fixed on a book held high. While it was common for gentlemen to surround themselves with symbols of wealth in portraiture, this was a soft-backed pamphlet. The text must have been contemporary, read not so much to indicate refinement but out of intellectual curiosity. His pose is one of intense concentration.[45] In the introduction to his diaries, Wyndham descendant Frances McInherny describes her forebears' building of a house in the colonies as 'the creation of a dream'. It was, she wrote, 'a Greek revival structure meant to encapsulate...a tradition of liberalism, freedom and aesthetics'.[46]

There may well have been something rebellious and independent about George's decision to emigrate to Australia, and both his and

Margaret's persistence in staying there, but such an explanation overlooks the bleak alternative they faced by staying in England. The gentleman was no longer necessarily afforded a gentrified lifestyle and land was becoming increasingly unaffordable to buy.[47] England was economically strained by its recent wars with France, a factor that Judith acknowledged in her 1999 memoir. The usual professions of gentlemen were becoming 'overcrowded', she writes in *Cry*. Such economic pressures were keenly felt by the Wyndhams of England. George's two elder brothers emigrated to Canada, but George did not like its climate. The Australian colonies, although further, were becoming more established, less a frontier. And in choosing them George was able to ride on an early wave of land occupation. Whereas during the 1820s almost all free emigrants of the British Isles chose the United States of America or Canada, by 1839 a quarter preferred Australia. In 1827 it was still an unusual choice but not without clear advantages, which others would increasingly recognise.[48]

The Australian colonies wanted gentlemen settlers and duly enticed them with an abundance of land that could be secured at a low cost. Folk such as the Wyndhams could afford to be picky. Although arriving in Hobart, they decided against settling there. On the 18th of December 1827 they once again boarded the *George Home*, bound for Port Jackson.[49] In Sydney they arrived to an offer of 640 acres in northern Sydney, but this they declined too. George was interested in positive reports he had heard of the Hunter Valley and in 1828 travelled there on horseback to inspect conditions. Things looked good. Back in Sydney, he responded to an advertisement promoting the sale of over 2,000 acres of land adjacent to the Hunter River, securing it on a 1,000-year lease for £1,200. With the sale came twenty convicts, one for every hundred acres.[50]

George was not alone in seeing the economic benefits of conducting large-scale agriculture and pastoralism in the Hunter Valley. In fact, he was part of a rush to secure tenancies in the area after exploratory expeditions in the late 1810s and early 1820s, led by John Howe, resulted in reports of as 'fine a country as imagination can form'.

Whereas in 1822 the valley housed no Europeans, by 1826 almost all of it had been allocated, mostly to men of wealth or connection, and was largely occupied by stock.[51] John Ferry, observing the behaviour of early settlers to New England, an area with a similar history to the Hunter Valley, notes that nearly all arrived 'for what were clearly and primarily economic reasons'. Despite what people said, 'there were no idealists seeking to establish a brave new order in the wilderness'.[52]

Indeed, it was difficult to be completely idealistic, to maintain theories of equality, when one was entangled in a labour system heavily weighted in your favour. Large-scale projects such as the Wyndhams' required a very substantial labour force. Of the 2,000 acres they leased from the government, a mere sixty had been cleared by the one previous tenant. On this stood a stockyard and some fenced paddocks.[53] Judith described the Wyndhams arriving to 'almost untouched forest over all their land'.[54] If this land was to become profitable in the way they hoped, the Wyndhams required large-scale tree clearance, plotting and sowing of the land, and assistance in animal husbandry, the construction of a house, stables, sties, folds, yards and cellars.

The colonial administration, at least at the beginning, was on their side, ensuring the ready supply of free and cheap labour. As well as twenty male convicts, an unspecified but large number of female convicts were also supplied. George's diaries describe a steady flow of women from the prisons, called 'Female Factories'. Often, within a few months, the women were returned when it was discovered that they were pregnant or had committed an offence, such as stealing.[55] The diaries, which cover a ten-year period, also record several incidents in which George sent workers to the cells, presumably those at the local Maitland police station, where he was a magistrate. On only one occasion did George record flogging a worker, for stealing melons.[56] Given that the practice was common amongst Hunter Valley landowners, perhaps he was, as family histories have unanimously concluded, a 'kind master', as Judith put it in 1999.[57] And yet George may have underplayed such incidents; his granddaughter May seemed to incorrectly believe he had never flogged a convict.[58]

Of course, convicts alone were not enough, given the job at hand. Aware that landowners were having difficulty finding sufficient numbers of workers, the colonial administration adjusted land regulations in 1825. Previously grants of up to 30 acres had been issued to immigrants without wealth or connection. This enabled ex-convicts and freemen without capital to start up their own plots instead of working for someone else. The 1825 reforms abolished these small land grants, forcing large numbers into the labour market. They also made the purchase price of large land-holdings refundable, after ten years, to those who 'maintained' a number of convicts.[59]

This was just the start of a series of laws beneficial to George, and of which he took advantage. An 1828 law allowed him to lease adjacent runs at a cheap price. In 1829 he secured 640 acres.[60] In 1831 he secured a further 2,500 acres of land adjoining the family's Mangarinda grant, on the upper Hunter Valley.[61] By 1840 the Wyndhams had claimed almost 11,000 acres of land throughout the Hunter Valley, each parcel under its own conditions from the administration.[62] It was behaviour typical of a New South Wales pastoralist. Attempts to confine them appeared as futile, Stuart Macintyre writes, as bounding 'the Arabs of the Desert'. In land there was money. By all accounts George was satisfied, telling his family in England that he was not disappointed in his expectations of the country. A characteristic diary entry, made in July 1837, reads: 'rain all day. Very steady. Abundance'.[63]

Economic prosperity may have inspired George to assume aristocratic forms of behaviour and attitudes. Maybe he would have anyway. As his great-grandson remarked, though George's 'personal inclination was to break away' from his cultural traditions, 'all of us are indelibly influenced by our early upbringing'.[64] So obviously true in its absolute sense, harder to determine is the extent and manifestation of such influences. This book asks the same question of Judith's life that she once asked of her great-great-grandfather's: is it possible, or even desirable, to escape the influences of our early social world? And can apparently 'negative' influences inspire more 'positive' ways of being in the world? Judith believed that, over the years, George's 'innate conservatism' reasserted itself, as if early influences are an untameable force that lives within, sometimes latently.[65]

There is, however, evidence that even from the start George was keen to recreate something of the gentrified English life he had left. In 1830 the Wyndhams moved into their house built from stone quarried in the nearby Black Creek. Naming it 'Dalwood', it was modelled on George's father's house, Dinton, which was itself late Elizabethan or early Jacobean, according to Wyndham family history. A visitor to Dalwood told George's proud mother in England that it was 'far the most comfortable domicile' that he had seen in Australia.[66]

George experienced commercial advantages created by inequalities in the British economic structure he had initially sought relief from. Dalwood's greatest source of wealth, large-scale animal husbandry, required large land holdings to move stock around. Such holdings were a direct result of inherited privilege because they were reliant on borrowed capital. Social status and pre-existing capital were crucial in determining loan conditions, or whether commercial loans were even required. May Wright acknowledged that George received loans from his family, also clear in the letters, presumably on more favourable terms than banks could offer.[67]

Animal husbandry became especially profitable if one could secure the stock of a valued breed, traditionally guarded by members of the English ruling class, for whom ensuring an animal's exclusivity was a sign of cultural distinction. George brought out the colony's first purebred Hereford cattle, held by his family in England. Down the generations the animals facilitated wealth and honour. The first volume of the *Australian Hereford Book* (1885) listed a number of prized Wyndham cattle. Later, May Wright purchased half of the family's famous Leconfield stud, enabling her to buy up several more properties on the profits. Phillip Wright, president of the Australian Hereford Society for fourteen years, boasted that the family stud had become 'famous for its good qualities throughout the country'. When Phillip retired, his son became president.[68]

Other agricultural activity helped maintain the Wyndhams' prestige and prominence. Of the South Down sheep they imported, George's mother commented in 1828 that 'your father was delighted to hear [they] were so highly prized, and is almost tempted to think that you will make a fortune by their progeny'.[69] The English Wyndhams were always on the look out for rarefied beasts they could send. Although uncommon in the Australian colonies, George also oversaw the construction of a vineyard. In 1867 recognition came in the most splendid form with a gold medal at the London International Exhibition. By 1886, the vineyard had expanded to 78 acres, making it the second largest in the world.[70] Today known as Wyndham Estate, and owned by an international conglomerate, it is Australia's oldest commercial vineyard.

Back in the nineteenth century, inside Dalwood an air of stately, English country life dominated. There was the 'continual soft murmur of voices as the women of the household sat stitching', a productive buzz muted by the Wyndhams' refinement. Margaret would speak 'discreetly' and 'low-voiced', recalled May. 'Everywhere was order, business, the pleasantness of cool whitewashed stone', Judith reported in *Generations*.[71] On return from expeditions Margaret always yearned to go 'home to civilization and a piano'.[72] She taught the children music, Italian and her native French. In his spare time George would go hunting, 'very much the English squire in his leggings and his uncompromisingly well-cut clothes'. Margaret would send wild lilies and possum skins home to her aunt's 'wonderment'.[73] The stone, the piano, the leggings: such details formed a pleasing oral history down the ancestral line.

Indeed, Judith grew up to understand that her family's estates, which she was raised within, were much more than their physicality; they were a statement of assertion, a symbol of power and control. To 'innocent eyes', she recalled, they were 'examples of settled beauty and success'.[74] Certainly they represented a victory. The house and the order established within served to tame a triple-headed danger: that posed by the strange wilderness, by the convicts and labourers, and by the local Indigenous people. The house meant everything. Dalwood, she wrote in *Generations*, 'smiled triumphantly over its vineyards and cattle, secure of its serenity'.[75] Many early pastoral families conceived of their presence as a kind of battle. The New England Everetts, friends of the Wyndhams, described their struggle for refinement in letters back home. They keenly anticipated the erection of a 'more gracious house, a more feminine house, [that] would mark their success in taming the wilderness'. They coveted 'petticoats and pianos'.[76]

This way of life – English, refined, productive – which the Wyndhams came to embody, helped forge the term 'squattocracy' in Australia. It was as if there was something so vitally English and civilised about these squatters that they were able to re-create the rural life and traditions they had known. As if their pre-eminence was, as the English aristocracy understood theirs, the result of a divine sanction. For the following generations, Judith said, it was as if an aura of 'supernatural descent clung to them'.[77] Historian George Farwell, writing approvingly of the Hunter Valley squatters, said they came into 'this provincial society of ours, spiritually impoverished', lacking in civility, and 'showed other men how to live with style and flair'.[78] According to Judith, George felt something of this. Depicting his emotions late in life, she surmised: 'it was reassuring, in this wild undisciplined colony, to be surrounded by sons brought up in English traditions of family duty, in English views of the rights of property and the responsibilities of children to their parents'. It was a sense passed down the family. May was always comforted by the knowledge that her offspring would 'carry a certain stamp'.[79]

There is another aspect to the Wyndham story which has received little attention in family histories, but which would become intensely important to Judith over the course of her life. The land that the Wyndhams began cultivating in 1828 was already owned by a group of people known as the Wonnarua. Although identifying traditional borders is an ongoing and contentious project, the Wonnarua Nation Aboriginal Corporation has defined the borders of their territory as forming a triangle, on the points of which stand today, roughly speaking, Singleton, Maitland and Wollombi.[80] The northern edge of this border, connecting Singleton and Maitland, is the Hunter River. Dalwood sat south of this natural border, about halfway between Singleton and Maitland, just outside Branxton. The borders of this triangle total a modest 160 kilometres, whereas other estimations of Wonnarua boundaries have included much larger areas.[81]

Although Wyndham family histories differ in some ways, the universal consensus amongst them has been that, by 1828, there were few Aboriginal people in the southern region of the Hunter Valley where their ancestors settled, and that those that were there sought no conflict. The very first family 'history', May's introduction to the *Extracts from the Dinton–Dalwood Letters, 1827–1853*, written in 1927, mentions Aboriginal people when describing the Wyndhams' expeditions north of Dalwood. It was only when they left this area that they went 'in fear of the blacks', and armed themselves.[82] In her 1987 introduction to George's diaries, McInherny concludes that his entries suggested 'at least a working relationship with the aborigines: they bring him a "plant of nails" and assisted pulling corn'. Such cordiality was 'documented elsewhere', she said.[83]

Judith's first family history, *Generations*, acknowledged the presence of Aboriginal people in the Wyndhams' lives but presented this as a largely subliminal one. Any threat the Aboriginal people posed was never realised. For Margaret they represented a danger on a par with others in nature: 'the orchids and parasite plants that flowered on the tall trees were all strangers; the blacks, the animals, and particularly the insects frightened her'. For George the Aboriginal people were another undependable element which required taming: 'the country, he could not trust it…"We should have left the place to the blacks!" his old friends would sometimes burst out, half-seriously, at news of droughts, bushrangers, speared cattle, rust in the wheat…' *Generations* gave the impression that Aboriginal people had already been displaced in the Hunter Valley. They had become a manageable nuisance. The only confrontation between Aboriginal people and Europeans in that book occurs further north, where there were 'hostile' and 'treacherous' tribes.[84]

But, as mentioned, Judith would come to regret the impression of pastoral colonialism she gave in *Generations*, and would write her second family history, *Cry For the Dead* (1981), to 'fill in some of those gaps'. The book described conflict that occurred between European migrants and the land's original inhabitants from pre-contact years to the early 1900s in New South Wales and Queensland, focusing on the Wadja, whose land Albert and May Wright had spent the most gruelling years of their lives on. The immense archive generated by Judith's research for *Cry*, and housed with her papers at the National Library of Australia, shows most of her sources related to Queensland. The depth of this research underscores the tenacity and commitment that propelled the epic project, a fact which many reviewers recognised.

Tom Griffiths, writing almost three decades later, in an essay entitled 'Judith Wright as historian', observed that 'she shows that the whites were as human as the blacks', a simple statement, for a seemingly simple feat, and yet a lack of appropriate documentation in fact made achieving it achingly difficult.[85]

Only one chapter of *Generations* was devoted to George and Margaret Wyndham, and so it would be in *Cry for the Dead*. Chapter 2, 'The Breaking of the Bounds', examined the impact of Europeans in the Hunter Valley during the 1820s and 1830s. The Wyndhams, as mentioned, arrived there in 1828. The chapter does not directly state that encounters between the Wyndhams and the Aboriginal tribe whose land they occupied will be examined, but the overall context of the book, its claims to fill the gaps of an earlier family history, leave the reader assuming this. The chapter focuses on the impact of pastoral settlement on the Kamilaroi, a tribe which some studies have argued was in fact the dominant Hunter Valley tribe, the Wonnarua a component tribe of them.[86] Early and recent accounts have convincingly argued otherwise; that they were distinct tribes, the Kamilaroi situated well north of 'Dalwood'.[87] But Judith did not claim that the Wyndhams were on either Kamilaroi or Wonnarua land.[88] Who her first Australian ancestors dispossessed, or her ancestors' role in that dispossession, is not described, a fact that was not widely acknowledged in the critical reception of *Cry*. Judith did not shy away from the horrors that followed the pastoral invasion of New South Wales, but she did not seem able to forensically examine her family's role within them.

It might be countered that the reason why the Wyndhams did not receive much attention in *Cry* is that they had very little contact with Aboriginal people, a defence which Judith hinted at: 'by the time George arrived, those who refused to tolerate Aboriginal presence on their land grants felt justified by high authority in driving them off into the hills and in using whatever measures they thought fit to keep them there'. Some Europeans did 'tolerate' their presence; those that did not were now so sure of their ownership that they 'drove' them northwards with 'measures'. Where the Wyndhams sat within this schema, Judith did not make clear. Some clarification is achieved by her account of how the Wyndhams chose, as the location for their home,

Dalwood, a part of the Hunter Valley which was 'tamed in comparison with the wild frontier land of Smith's Rivulet at Mahngarinda', where they had been offered a free grant by the colonial administration. Mahngarinda, Judith explained, George would only use for surplus animals. In *Cry*, there is one single mention of conflict occurring in the vicinity of Dalwood; Judith explains that at times, in the area, 'hungry Aborigines' were found by the roadside, dead, hanging from trees, with corncobs stuffed in their mouths, as a warning to other hungry, would-be thieves. Significantly, these victims were from neighbouring tribes, having 'descended from the sandstone hills'. In contrast to those Europeans, mainly shepherds, living in parts of the Hunter Valley further northwards, the Wyndhams lived in 'safety in the settled country'. *Cry* suggests, but, crucially, does not state, that when the Wyndhams arrived in 1828 there was no tribe of local Indigenous people on or around Dalwood, and that they chose it precisely for this reason.[89]

A lack of conclusive evidence continues to make it difficult to discern the precise ways European pastoralism impacted on the Wonnarua, but there exists a significant amount of primary material which suggests that the Dalwood plot was not 'settled' or 'tamed', with the degree of finality suggested by those terms; that George and Margaret could not have avoided encountering the Wonnarua, who continued to live on their territories, or being directly implicated in the ongoing dispossession of these people from those territories. The Wonnarua were not destroyed by the influx of settlers that followed John Howe's exploration around Singleton in 1819. Newspaper articles throughout the nineteenth century refer to the 'Maitland Aborigines', a society whose members were involved in violent conflict with other tribes, were subject to the zeal and benevolence of missionaries, were offered blankets. The only uplifting aspect of the Wonnarua's lives recorded in these newspapers is the occasional cricket match between 'Maitland' and 'Aboriginals', beginning in the 1860s and exciting the interest of newspapers throughout the colonies.[90] One anthropological study conducted in the late nineteenth century estimated that there were between 500 and 600 Wonnarua living on their territory in 1850. Various factors contributed to a further reduction in their numbers; the study asserted these 'almost wiped them out altogether'.[91] In fact, although the first decades of invasion were devastating for them, they survived, continued to live in communities on their land and have been represented by the Wonnarua Nation Aboriginal Corporation since 1999.[92]

When George and Margaret arrived in the Hunter Valley in 1828, Europeans had been living there for just six years. In 1823 the colonial administration surveyed the 2,000 acres which would become Dalwood; that same year the plot was granted to merchant David Maziere, who named it 'Annandale'. Between 1823 and 1828 six convicts cleared and cultivated 60 acres of the land. It is unlikely Maziere spent much time at Annandale before he became insolvent in 1827 and had to sell.[93] During this period, the land, in all likelihood, continued to be inhabited by the Wonnarua, though not as Englishmen like George understood the meaning of the word 'inhabit'.[94] The Wonnarua moved around their territories, camping on the same grounds that generations before them had, which were chosen for their proximity to fresh water and a food supply. The Wonnarua considered the Hunter River, alongside which Annandale sat, their 'keeper of life'; from it they collected fish and water; around it they collected leaves for food and medicine.[95] On all but 60 of the 2,000 acres that constituted Annandale, there remained native wildlife and flora, forests and swamps, providing the Wonnarua with shelter and a source of food at the same time as they were experiencing a radical dwindling of such sustenance elsewhere in their territory. Roger Milliss has shown that the 'full impact' of the invasion of the Hunter Valley was not felt by its original inhabitants when Europeans first arrived, when they began buying and selling land, or even when they introduced hundreds of cattle to the area. The full impact of invasion, writes Milliss, was felt when settlers 'with the means and manpower to clear [and] fence' embarked on 'large-scale cultivation'.[96]

And so it was that from 1822 to 1825 there was very little overt conflict between Europeans and Wonnarua. James Miller, a Wonnarua historian whose *Koori: A Will To Win* was published just four years after *Cry*, argues that this peace was also the product of a resolution, reached by the Wonnarua internally, that they would not actively resist the invasion of their lands, having been horrified to hear of the devastation befalling other tribes who had done so. And yet problems arose, especially around the mistreatment of Wonnarua women, the spread of disease, the loss of native plants and animals, and the hostility of some Europeans to the Wonnarua's use of their waterways. Writes Miller: 'it was time for more talking amongst the Wonnarua. Something had to be done'.[97]

For the Wonnarua, 1826 was a decisive and tragic year. In response to an increasing number of violent incidents in the Hunter, the Mounted Police were deployed to the Valley, on their first mission in 'frontier warfare', writes John Connor. They arrived in Maitland, which sat on the highest point of the river, and was about 20 kilometres from Annandale. Meanwhile, the Wonnarua had decided to join with several tribes in the Hunter Valley to mount a coordinated attack against the Europeans. 'For several months', writes Milliss, 'the valley was in turmoil'. Aboriginal people and Europeans murdered one another in ones or twos, in perceived revenge for an earlier attack. Violent incidents occurred close to what was then Annandale. Miller characterises the murder of Wonnarua in 1826 as 'a drawn out and cruel affair'.[98]

One rampage, conducted by Singleton magistrate Robert Scott, stood out. In August that year, with a group of soldiers and civilians, he oversaw the murder of eighteen Aboriginal people in revenge for the death of two European men, according to *The Australian*. A formal investigation into the incident, partly conducted by Scott himself, found Scott had committed no crime. It was not so difficult to conduct a 'whitewash', as Milliss termed it, in a constitutional environment where crown sovereignty had not been firmly established. Individual acts of retribution did not halt the violence. Eleven prominent Hunter Valley landowners sent a petition to Governor Darling that year describing the 'very disturbed state of the Country by the incursions of the numerous Tribes of Black Natives, armed and threatening death to our Servants, and destruction to our property'. They wanted greater military assistance. Perhaps, like Scott, they believed they were at war with the Aboriginal people. He told his sister in England: 'if the Governor had acted as he was advised by persons on this river, and as he ought to have done, the natives would have been quiet in a very short time'. As it was, frequent violence occurred on Wonnarua land until around 1830.[99]

Robert Scott was perhaps the central figure in what took place on Wonnarua territory between 1825 and 1830. He is also central to *this* story, for he was the man to whom the Wyndhams had the strongest ties and was the reason for their being in the Hunter Valley in the first place. Judith acknowledged in *Cry* that Scott was George's 'closest friend' and had told him about the Annandale plot when it came up for sale. But she did not detail the extent to which Scott was implicated in the murder and dispossession of Wonnarua. She did not surmise anything much from the friendship between the two men, born just a year apart.[100]

George and Robert Scott had known each other for years when they were reunited in the Australian colonies. Scott and his brother acquired Glendon, just out of Singleton, in the early 1820s, becoming stud masters of valuable horse breeds. Scott was one of the district's earliest magistrates. When George purchased Annandale, just over 20 kilometres from Glendon, making them close neighbours by the terms of a pastoralist, George's father wrote: 'I am glad to hear that you have made an eligible purchase of land, and in a good neighbourhood too, and so near an old acquaintance, which must be a great comfort to you'.[101]

Soon after the purchase, in 1829, Scott travelled to England and met George's family. There he stayed for two weeks, describing George's new life to his family using maps and sketches. Scott never married, which made travel easier, but George's sister Charlotte thought he seemed to 'envy George his domestic happiness'. Charlotte also reported: 'we liked him very well'. George appears to have too; his diary, which covered the years 1830 to 1840, shows many visits between their estates. The English Wyndhams, who hosted Scott again, encouraged the friendship. George's mother suggested George set up a house at Newcastle, as Scott had done, giving him 'comforts such even as are enjoyed by few English gentlemen'. George was inevitably influenced by his friend. As Scott had done, George became a magistrate, invested in the controversial Bank of Australia, acquired northern plots, and championed the introduction of 'coolie' labour. Indians, Scott believed, would not only be a cheap workforce but could assist in 'civilizing the Aboriginal natives'.[102]

When, in late 1827 or early 1828, Scott told George about the sale of Annandale, he must also have told him of the violence occurring in its vicinity. The frontier war was on his mind; in official correspondence from 1826 Scott declared himself 'a man so deeply interested in this topic, that I cannot by any means be an unprejudiced witness'. That same year he predicted, in a letter to Attorney-General Saxe Bannister, that the 'disturbances on the Hunter's River district are likely to continue', and that the military was 'in activity' but experiencing 'difficulty'. He was right and the hostilities continued into 1827, when twelve Wonnarua were killed by shepherds. Several letters from 1827 show Scott despairing after a station manager named George Claris, who lived on a neighbouring Singleton property, received a threat from an Aboriginal man known as 'King Jerry' concerning an Aboriginal man they called 'Bit o Bread'. Claris wrote to Scott:

> King Jerry told me that if Bit o Bread was hurt by the white men that he would assemble a thousand Black fellows, and spear every white man they fell in with that the Soldier were all gone away, that they were not afraid and desired me to inform white man at the plains so one showed me how they would surround the huts of the Settlers, and with a frying pan handle how they would spear us …

Scott believed King Jerry was serious and that his countrymen would inflict 'indiscriminate vengeance' if Scott and his men were to capture Bit o Bread. He requested a 'vigilant and strong armed power' from the colonial secretary. Did Scott tell his old friend about the prospect of a war of this scale developing around Singleton, which itself sat 20 kilometres from Annandale, in the year before they bought it?[103]

Perhaps Scott conveyed to George, as he did to his sister, his belief that peace could be achieved by the imposition of extreme pressure on the Wonnarua. Being by then an active participant in this 'pressure', perhaps Scott had reason to believe that more would be inflicted on the Wonnarua in the following few years. In 1838, giving evidence before the Committee on the Aborigines Question, Scott spoke about his sixteen years of experience in the colonies. He explained that the only thing that pacified the Aboriginal people was 'force, and the certainty of instant retaliation'. The best method he had observed had been adopting 'so imposing an attitude as to prevent even the attempt at resistance'.[104]

Had Scott assured George and Margaret in 1828 that the Wonnarua would soon be 'tamed', despite the violence of the last two years? They had, after all, only agreed to the Annandale plot, according to Judith, because it was tamed 'in comparison' to the more northerly Mahngarinda, on which they kept animal stock, and to where George 'could not ride' without being armed. George's diary shows that he went to Mahngarinda regularly, and for overnight visits, though it does not show what occurred on these visits.[105] Miller believes it was not until 1830, two years after George and Margaret's arrival in the Hunter Valley, that conflict between Europeans and Wonnarua became less overt.[106] These were the years in which George and Margaret lived in a slab hut. From 1828 to 1830 the European population in the Valley was still small, with relatively few women willing to live there. How George and Margaret dealt with the Wonnarua is not relayed in any of the available primary material. While letters from English relatives convey George's interest in British politics and farming machinery, they do not refer to the arguably more pressing issue of his role in a frontier war. It is impossible to know whether this is because such references were edited out.[107] And it was not until 1830 that George began keeping a diary, or one that has been preserved.

That year the Wyndhams moved into their house. On only three occasions in his decade-long diary did George refer directly to Aboriginal people. In 1830 he mentioned 'the Blacks' trading in stolen nails, in 1832 to them destroying a crop of his wheat, and in 1833 to them getting 'saucy' on a nearby property, after which the police were sent in their pursuit. There was of course no incentive to document conflict with Aboriginal people (either one's own conflict or others'), and certainly a disincentive to, given that in 1820 a European man had been hanged for killing an Aboriginal man. Certainly George was conscious of the diary being read by others; he wrote in code when discussing taboo subjects, such as insanity or domestic violence. Alward Wyndham, who edited the diaries, observed that 'poor Pat was treated to French in ancient Greek Script so scribbled that experts were somewhat baffled'. And then there was 'that other mystery', George's repeated use of the word 'Evoke', the meaning of which Alward never discerned.[108]

One 1833 incident, described by Scott in a letter to the Colonial Secretary, suggests George had greater contact with the Wonnarua than his diaries imply, and that he shared at least some of Scott's approach in dealing with them. According to Scott, an armed Aboriginal man was attacked by a bushranger on his property. The Aboriginal man's gun had been provided by George Wyndham.[109] On at least one other occasion Scott had armed Aboriginal people, and this had led to a fight 'amongst the Aborigines', according to a newspaper report.[110]

There were hundreds of Wonnarua living along the Hunter River in the 1830s. Many of them now had no reliable food source and were living with debilitating diseases.[111] Throughout the 1830s their resistance to the invasion of their lands was weakened but they were still involved in 'spasmodic outbreaks of violence'. In 1839 George Bowman told Scott that on and around his Hunter Valley properties, some of which sat around 40 kilometres from Dalwood, Aboriginal people were 'more daring than ever', killing men and sheep. In 1843, just 20 kilometres northwest of Dalwood, one European hut keeper recalled two Wonnarua men stopping to enquire whether he was a former convict or free settler. When told that he was the former, the Wonnarua men replied that he was lucky: 'because he was forced to come to their lands' they would leave him alone. How did George avoid such encounters?[112]

In what was effectively her final family history, her memoir *Half a Lifetime* (1999), Judith concluded of George: 'Aborigines he seems to have viewed with a kind of amused tolerance, once the first battles were over'. Yet George, like Scott, was not a disinterested man by nature. He was an outspoken advocate for the political and financial interests of his class. He opposed the establishment of juries, representative government and a dilution of British power. One diary entry from 1833 shows George working together with his closest friend on a political issue: 'To Scotts. Agreeing on a petition'. It may have been the lengthy appeal, reported two months later in the *Sydney Gazette*, that no greater leniency be given in existing prison sentences.[113]

When George was invited to join William Wentworth's Australian Patriotic Association, he replied that 'he was opposed to those privileges being granted to the Colony, which it was the object of the Association to solicit'. The Association noted in its minutes that

George's was the 'only letter of the kind that has yet been received' and 'Mr. W., we believe, is nearly isolated in his opinion'. In fact there were many others who held George's views, but these tended to be his neighbours. Land grants, those pivots on which the squatters' fortunes often turned, were approved by governors, whose power was endowed by the Crown. Diary entries for 1831 show George socialising at length with Governor Ralph Darling, Wentworth's most bitter enemy; that same year Darling approved further land grants to George.[114]

George had strong views on land that further challenge the notion that he could have been 'tolerant' of Aboriginal people. He believed in the legal right of squatters to assume exclusive dominion over land once they had occupied it. In the lead up to an 1847 meeting to discuss Edward Wakefield's suggestion that squatters should be charged more for land, George distributed a twelve-page pamphlet. In it he highlighted sections of *Blackstone's Commentaries on the Laws of England (1765–1769)*, the basis of English property law, that seemed relevant to squatting, such as Blackstone's understanding that, for reasons of practicality, occupancy 'confirms that right against all the world besides'. Blackstone defined occupancy as permanent and unceasing occupancy, indicated by alterations made to the land in the tradition of European pastoralism.

Any land was up for the taking, provided it was found 'unoccupied by any one else'. George asked: 'when did the crown thus occupy, and acquire ownership?' and concluded with the question: 'whose is the land?' George was not contesting the right of Englishmen to occupy and control the Australian colonies; he was contesting the right of the Crown to do so. Nowhere did he consider that it was owned or even occupied by another group of people. George believed, strongly, that land in Australia belonged to the individual who first cultivated it, and that such individuals should not be charged for their use of the land. Elsewhere he referred to 'rent' as that 'hateful word'. 'Who are the fools?' he asked in his Blackstone pamphlet. 'They who, neglecting Blackstone, make Wakefield their oracle upon squatting', he wrote. In the 1860s, when Wakefield's system had been taken up in some colonies, he wrote again, stating that the 'evil results of the Wakefield system are manifold'. According to George, keeping large numbers of animals extended a sacred tradition that stretched back to ancient

Greece and the Bible, and it should be protected. Through their attacks on people and property – by their very presence – the Wonnarua defied the squatters' claim that they were entitled to practise their tradition on this land.[115]

Cry for the Dead set out to describe, as Judith termed it, the 'hurried' and 'ruthless' 'pastoral invasion' that spread north and westerly from Sydney. A distinguishing feature of this process was the colonial administration's continuing redrafting of boundaries within which they would permit land grants. Many squatters pushed beyond these boundaries. George Wyndham, as Judith emphasises in *Cry*, did not – at least initially. In the absence of evidence indicating George's attitude towards Aboriginal people, Judith depicts George's original commitment to stay within the boundaries as a reflection of his good character. She notes that to usurp the boundaries would have involved conflict with the colonial administration: 'George himself had not joined the illegal exodus and the squabbles and battles', instead taking his usual 'prudent course' to remain free of the 'brawls and contests of the world', a stance of which his family in England approved. But as historians have also noted, these boundaries were completely arbitrary morally, and even perhaps legally. There was no permission given by the land's original owners for these boundaries, so in what sense, for a historian working within Judith's framework, was staying within them any better?[116]

Judith considered George moderate, careful and cautious, in contrast to those squatters around him who recklessly spurred 'lawlessness'. The conviction with which Judith repeatedly uses the words 'lawless' and 'illegality' in these passages is anomalous given that *Cry* contests the very basis of the occupation, and demonstrates that British law was, more often than not, an instrument of that occupation. Even when advocating continuing invasion George can be benevolent in Judith's hands: the English Wyndhams, she explained, often obtained from George 'sage advice on where to look for land', that could be passed on to would-be colonialists.[117]

Presented with material that seemed to confirm that George's views on land occupation were predicated on an unfavourable understanding of Aboriginal people, Judith interpreted it in the best possible light. In his reply to an 1839 questionnaire, sent by the Legislative Council to Hunter Valley landowners to ascertain their attitudes towards employing Aboriginal people, George responded that the best way to encourage them to work would be 'to cut off their great toes. They could not then climb the trees for opossums'. George reasoned that Aboriginal people could 'live without labour' since they could subsist on food collected in two hours each day. Judith, who recalled his responses in *Cry*, contended that George's response demonstrated an 'insight' into 'the Aboriginal way of life [which others] dismissed as little better than that of the beasts that perish, as well as nasty, brutish and short…it at least indicated that George's contacts with the Aborigines had not been unobservant'. It was an upbeat interpretation of statements that only barely concealed an aggression towards Aboriginal people and a lack of interest in their welfare. At least one prominent colonialist advocated similarly violent schemes in all seriousness; in this context, such 'humour' was not benign. Given that George viewed the cultivation of land, within European terms, as a proper basis for securing exclusive occupancy, could he really have been sympathetic to the 'Aboriginal way of life' to which Judith refers?[118]

As Judith would note, George's views on Aboriginal people and the rights of squatters were shared by 'the valley's gentry'. Amongst them was some difference in opinion. Visitors to George, William and Mary Ogilvie, 'were noted for their good relations' with Aboriginal people, as Alward Wyndham observes in a footnote to George Wyndham's diary. Alward Wyndham did not observe that Scott, whom George exchanged visits with more often, was not known for having good relations, nor was any comparable notation offered for both men's friend Peter Cunningham, who ferried George's letters to the English Wyndhams on one of his regular trips home and, like Scott, socialised with the family once there. George's mother told him: 'I hope we may have the pleasure of seeing Doctor Cunningham, as we shall then be able to compare the accounts of Australia with that given us by Mr. Scott. No doubt the Doctor's will be the one most tinted with the couleur de rose…' But between Scott and Cunningham, the English Wyndhams may not have received radically different reports when it came to discussing Aboriginal people, for Cunningham believed that they sat 'at the very zero of civilization, constituting in a measure the connecting link between man and the monkey tribe'.[119]

The views of the Valley's gentry towards Aboriginal people can be glimpsed further elsewhere. One month before the 1838 Myall Creek massacre trial, in which seven European men were put on trial for killing twenty-eight Aboriginal men, women and children on the Liverpool Plains, a group called the Hunter River Black Association was established to support the defendants. The group was semi-clandestine, with most members unwilling to publicly declare themselves, aware that they risked their freedom and reputation in advocating stronger 'measures' against Aboriginal people. Its spokesman was Robert Scott. Other members were made up of Hunter Valley landowners who sought greater control over the Liverpool Plains, as the Wyndhams would shortly do. Members were wealthy; so successful was their fundraising that they were able to retain the 'colony's foremost barristers' for the Myall Creek defendants. Scott visited the men in prison, assuring them that 'they had little to worry about in the prosecution case' as he 'had personally arranged for evidence to be produced' showing that the only witness against them was insane. As Milliss writes, it was an 'extraordinary and outrageous thing for him', a magistrate, 'to do'.[120]

Judith acknowledged George must have been under pressure to join the association but did not dwell on the point, nor detail the extremity of their views. In newspapers, Scott gave voice to these:

> We say to the Colonists, since the Government makes no adequate exertion to protect yourselves; and if the ferocious savages endeavour to plunder and destroy your property, or to murder yourselves, your families, or your servants, do to them as you would do to any white robbers or murderers – SHOOT THEM DEAD, if you can.

The *Australian* newspaper took a tough stand against rumours of a 'Black Association brotherhood', declaring 'that if there be such a thing as a regularly organised association for protecting the whites in their collisions with the blacks (which can have no other result than to encourage bloodshed), that it will be forthwith disbanded'. It was not disbanded, for members ensured there was no record of their band.[121]

Many Hunter Valley association members ventured northwards to the Liverpool Plains in the late 1830s and 1840s in search of new frontiers, where they could make up the losses brought on by a depression which had reduced produce prices and increased costs. Forced sales in the Hunter Valley became common. Judith believed that George carefully considered whether or not to go beyond the established boundaries during this period, and only did so in light of his family's needs: 'Margaret, that cornucopia of children, had produced six sons and two daughters and the question of their future was becoming ponderable'. Though letters show that George found venturing into dangerous regions exciting, Judith does not acknowledge that this may have been a motivation. Everything indicated moving northwards would involve violent encounters with Aboriginal people. Scott had been one of the first to move northwards and by 1837 allowed that his overseers on the Plains were understandably likely to murder Aboriginal people in order to hold his land. George was not deterred; in 1839 he took his flocks beyond territorial boundaries. During these same few years, George contributed £5,000 to the construction of Robert Scott's house: the men were as close as ever.[122]

In 1844, when Scott was only forty-five years old, he died; according to George's family, it was the result of 'too active' a mind, and 'constant anxiety'. In 1845, with debts mounting, George rounded up his large family, a string of house servants, workers and stock, and disappeared into the bush, following in the steps of his old friend once more and escaping his creditors. Where some talked of 'abandoning the whole colony', Judith reported in *Generations*, George's clan set out 'through virtually unknown country, and among hostile tribes'. As they travelled northwards, they claimed thousands of acres on the Liverpool Plains, Macintyre and Clarence rivers. The land they moved into was the scene of the worst violence in New South Wales history. As R. H. W. Reece writes: 'such records as there are indicate that between 1837 and 1846 the colony experienced the worst racial clashes in its history, the squatting districts of Portland Bay and Liverpool Plains being the most severely affected'.[123]

Letters from George's family offer an account of their expedition. In 1845, George's brother John wrote:

I have lately read a letter of yours to Ella, in which you speak of shooting the unhappy blacks. There is something in shooting down a brave though savage foe which I cannot at all reconcile to my ideas of fair play. I suppose it is justified under the plea of self-defence, but surely the settlers should be very careful that they are not the aggressors, otherwise I think in the eye of Heaven it will approach nigh unto murder.[124]

It was hardly surprising that George used violence to secure land around the Liverpool Plains. There was, after all, a territorial war taking place. Other family members were less perturbed than John. George's sister Ella looked forward to the family ceasing their roaming: 'when will you find a location?...I fear you will not be able to get land enough for your sheep and herds'. Another sister, Charlotte, acknowledged the possibility of more conflict: 'I hope your next letters may arrive speedily, and tell us you have recovered all your live stock, and that the natives are decamped from about you and your encampment'. John, less optimistically, gave the impression that violent conflict had continued: 'I am sorry to find by it [your letter] that your black neighbours are so hostile, and rather fear that you have got into a hornet's nest, where you will find it difficult to hold your own'.[125]

Nonetheless, George remained convinced that he was doing the right thing. Perhaps by way of justifying his actions to an apprehensive John, he offered what John then referred to as 'your arguments in favour of colonisation'. Acknowledging 'your wild mode of life' would be 'by far the most exciting, especially as a little profit is mixed up with it', John declined George's suggestion that he should join them, for he had to think of his 'delicate' wife and children. Shortly afterwards, George's brother Alexander referred to another violent encounter George had had with the Aboriginal people:

Your other letter mentions the blacks having speared and eaten some of your cattle. When reading it I longed to have been with my nephew Alward; we would have had another turn for the cattle next day, and, if lawful, would have treated the blacks with a little powder and ball. I should have liked to have sent whistling among them, when they set up their shouts, a few balls with holes bored through them, the same way that we frightened rooks. I would answer for it stopping the shout for the time, but you know how to deal with them, which I do not.[126]

The whole family did not see it in the same terms, which George perhaps anticipated when he wrote again, explaining the incident in greater detail. John, who had used the word 'murder' the year before, wrote back: 'I have received yours…you enter into a lengthened defence of shooting the blacks, which was needless. I never imagined you went out for the express purpose, as we would to destroy rabbits, or had recourse to the rifle till every other argument had failed'. In such a blatant invasion of territory what argument could possibly succeed?[127]

In *Generations* Judith did not acknowledge the letters. In *Cry* she did. Her reading of them reveals a complex response. Acknowledging no additional sources, Judith reported: 'in Wyndham's absence, they [the Widjabal] came out of the heavy brush forests with cries of defiance and drove the cattle off. Young Alward Wyndham, now sixteen, pursued them with his English rifle, a present from his grandfather'. In fact nothing in the letters suggests that George was not there and that it was only his son Alward who fired shots. To add that the firearm came from England, and was a present from the sixteen-year-old's grandfather, seems intended to allay blame. Yet the Wyndhams frequently carried guns. May reports that the Wyndhams went armed into the Clarence River country, 'in fear of blacks'. Elsewhere Judith acknowledged that Margaret carried a revolver whilst carrying out her house duties. Judith's summation of the letters, covered in one page, suggests that there was only one incident, whereas the letters indicate that there were at least two incidents, and that some form of hostility continued for about one year.[128]

Perhaps Judith did have other information that led her to conclude that George was not involved in these incidents. And yet her calculation of the letters' significance suggests a wilful disbelief in what they so categorically reveal: 'it is not clear from the letters whether Wyndham was defending the actions of his neighbours or those of Alward and Wyndham himself'. In one letter, John clearly refers to 'you', George, 'shooting the blacks'; in another to 'you', George, going 'out for the express purpose…' Perhaps it was natural that Judith would view George's actions in the best possible light, but she did not extend the same generosity to more distant family members: 'the English Wyndhams, who by this time themselves had considerable capital invested in the success of the Australian branch, were for the most part tolerant of the difficulties of so distant a colony'. At the same time, she questioned why John, who did challenge George, felt justified in doing so: 'his younger brother John, now a cleric, thought it his duty to remonstrate, though mildly'. For George there was no such interrogation.[129]

By 1850 the George Wyndhams, as well as securing vast acreages, had established a house on the Macintyre River, about which English relatives, on seeing a picture of it, remarked: 'what can a man want more?' Such properties were passed down the family line and secured the family's rank as one of the most successful in New South Wales pastoralism. They were central members of the squattocracy. As Judith so painfully knew, these privileges came at an immense cost to others, but perhaps she could not fully accept the extent to which George and Margaret, those 'figures of serene achievement', were implicated in such tragedies.

Why did she not consider more closely George's close relationship with Robert Scott, and what this implied about George's beliefs and actions? When Judith wrote, in her final statement on George, that he viewed Aboriginal people with an 'amused tolerance, once the first battles were over', this can only be seen as enigmatic and elusive. She did not state, after all, whether George was involved in these first battles. For one who would set out to fill the silence, the gaps of Australian history, it was a notable lacuna.[130]

In the years following the publication of *Cry for the Dead* (1981), Judith lamented that a lack of resources and time meant she could not pursue more fully her family history. Filling the gaps held special potential: 'a bit more education in history wouldn't come amiss for most Australians'. In *Half*, published almost twenty years on, she acknowledged those gaps again, knowing she would never be able to fill them. Judith quoted from the obituary of an ancestor who had lived in a part of Queensland where massacres had taken place: he 'never found occasion to pull triggers with fatal effect'. Commenting, 'I hope the obituarist was right about the trigger-pulling but in any event most of the job had been done before the Biggs reached Queensland', Judith occupied a similar emotional posture to that she had held in *Cry*; that deep sense of fear and sorrow about what the gaps in her family history contained and, at the same time, a kind of wishfulness – bordering on wilfulness – that such gaps might have been harmless after all, as if her ancestors were lucky, possibly providential, actors who seemed always to cross the stage just after the drama had taken place.[131]

Since it is hard to fault Judith's intentions, the gaps that I have identified in this chapter might suggest that the telling of Australian history is hamstrung as much by deficiencies in source material as emotional strain. It must also be acknowledged that the digitisation of vast quantities of original sources in recent decades makes it far easier to pursue colonial history today. Many of the documents I have used to understand Robert Scott's actions and beliefs, for instance, were digitised in the years immediately preceding the publication of this book. Other illuminating histories were published in the years after *Cry*. If Judith could have written *Cry for the Dead* in 2016 a different history would have been produced, very possibly one which considered the mythology of George Wyndham in a more sceptical light.

What do we learn about Judith's familial culture from the Wyndham story? At its core the story told of the Wyndhams' claim to the land. There were no Aboriginal people living on Dalwood, nor any in the vicinity who might have contested the Wyndhams' right to be there. Apart from *Cry*, family histories depicted George's northward ventures as a triumph and tended to downplay the very real advantages the Wyndhams assumed.[132] They confirmed that he, like Abraham in the Bible, gained possession of the land through self-sacrifice, courage and ingenuity, and with every moral sanction. Down the generations Wyndham descendants, such as May Wright, used this model to explain their own lives, leading them to feel a sense of entitlement and triumph when they achieved success. It was an interpretation Judith's biographer was happy to support, even if her subject was less certain of it. Brady claimed that although Judith's family were prosperous, it was a 'prosperity won against the odds'.[133]

In 1945 Judith described her life, in the context of such a family history, as queer, strange and even sinful. She had no intention of being a pastoralist's wife. In fact she would be a poet. But could what Judith suggested in her letter to Jack be true? That her family, in 1945, retained the values set down by her nineteenth-century forebears? And was it really the case that Judith, in acting against family convention, wholly overcame the blind spots and elisions of that world? The following two chapters will consider how the generations immediately before Judith upheld and extended the Wyndhams' story of success, even when struck by family tragedy, before we follow Judith to Sydney to see how she became that 'sinful fish'.

CHAPTER 2

The New England Wrights

The Wyndham story loomed large over Judith's childhood. As an adult she challenged its fundamental bases – that wealth was a testament to one's strength of character and that the Hunter Valley was peacefully settled – but she never disputed its central lesson for her family: that George and Margaret were exemplars of noble achievement. This was an unshakeable knowledge, a guiding assumption, that in others might have devolved from a religion or political ideology, continuing even when its more fanciful elements had been cast aside. As a child, George and Margaret's story explained the material circumstances of Judith's life – how she came to be the daughter of successful pastoralists – and the circumstances of others around her, helping to make sense of the gaping difference between her life and those of the workers' children, for instance: the congruity of this.

How exactly did George and Margaret's story, and its meaning, get conveyed to the young Judith? In this chapter I argue that two remarkable characters most strongly connected Judith to her Wyndham ancestry. Judith herself, as an adult, testified to the powerful influence of these two: her grandmother May Wright and father Phillip Wright, both Wyndham descendants. By force of their example she became roughcast as an Australian Wyndham. Both were models, much more so than Judith's mother, Ethel Wright (nee Biggs). Ethel provided a strong example of what Judith did *not* want to be. The reasons for this were not straightforward, as we will see in Chapter 3. Nonetheless, a pattern emerged: it was successful Wyndhams whom Judith took as role models, ones who proudly upheld many of the ambitious Wyndham values and practices, as George and Margaret had pioneered them.

When applied to most of us, this acknowledgement of being profoundly influenced by one's family would hardly be controversial. In a biography of Judith, there are certain facts and standing interpretations which make it appear wildly capricious. Even before she was ten Judith wanted to be a writer. May and Phillip spent their entire lives as graziers. Looking back, Phillip expressed amazement that he could have 'fathered a person with Judith's academic, creative and literary capabilities'.[134] There is also the matter of their different political positions. As an adult Judith embodied two defining left-wing causes of late twentieth-century Australia: environmentalism and support for Aboriginal land rights. Her family, on the other hand, she described as 'dyed-in-the-wool' conservatives. May and Phillip, staunch monarchist backers of Empire, were early supporters of the Country Party, a political organisation not known for preserving environments in their natural state. Although, during Judith's teenage years, Phillip campaigned for the establishment of a National Park in New England, arguing that the area constituted a 'national asset', and investigated problems of soil erosion, this was not his most common response to nature.[135] Phillip was, like his mother, a large-scale pastoralist and saw land as an opportunity to produce – for the betterment of humankind.

Recognising the disjuncture between Judith and her immediate forebears, some writers have emphasised other influences in Judith's early life. Biographer Veronica Brady referred to the role of 'unseen presences', and Fiona Capp, Judith's natural environment. Both explanations are premised on the belief that Judith was, from a young age, quite fundamentally different from her family – not so much a black sheep as one out of the box. Even Judith portrayed her family in ways almost completely at odds with her own adult identity, leaving the reader somewhat confused when she also testified that her father was the biggest influence in her life and her grandmother a 'great influence'.[136]

Without dismissing any of these readings, or trying to resolve the questions they raise, there exists space for more closely examining the familial environment in which Judith grew up, especially the dominant, adult figures within it. Such an endeavour aims to understand Judith in her original context, so to speak, rather than viewing her through the prism of herself as an older adult, when she put her life on the public record.

Though the biographical enterprise encourages us to seek unity in the subject, a straight trajectory of self-realisation from childhood to adulthood, or at least to discern an order in their development, it could be that the identities most commonly applied to Judith – a poet with an emotional connection to the landscape and the body, a left-wing activist, a public intellectual who encouraged Australians to critically examine their lives and heritage – developed in a more haphazard and slower way than we have recognised, partly as a reaction to her upbringing but partly in accordance with it. It could be that, at least before she was thirty-one, when her first collection was published, dedicated to her father, Judith was more a product of her upbringing than biographers and the woman herself have let us believe.

May and Phillip's lives take us back to the bigger story, a partial retelling of which is already underway in this book, of the pastoral settlement of New South Wales and the coterminous creation there of an agrarian politics. May and Phillip were persistent and single-minded actors within it. Phillip, from a young age, had a clear, bold vision for a better society, with pastoralism at its core, economically and culturally. His life was a demonstration that determined effort in public matters made a difference. It was an attribute he seemed to inherit from his mother. May Wright, observed her granddaughter, might even have been termed 'dogmatic'; many were surprised at the lengths she went to to uphold and advance the Wyndham legacy.[137]

First, to a new setting. After half a century in the colonies the Australian Wyndhams formed a sizeable mass, albeit one spread widely, beyond the original confines of the Hunter Valley. Some said George and Margaret's most favoured grandchild had been May Mackenzie. By the 1880s she had made her own lines in the family tree after becoming married to Albert Wright and leaving the Hunter Valley to take up land in Queensland. Within a decade May and Albert returned to rural New South Wales, this time in the north, not far from Armidale. Their decision to settle in New England would have as great an impact on the lives of their descendants as any.

Even now, but certainly in the late nineteenth century, to speak of New England culture is to speak about something distinct and very different from that of Sydney, pastoral Queensland or even the Hunter Valley. Geographically, the borders of New England have always been less certain. In the late nineteenth-century New England was generally regarded as the area north of Hastings River, about 500 kilometres north of Sydney, up to the Queensland border. Its east–west span was approximately 200 kilometres long, beginning at an indefinite line where the tablelands meet the plain, and ending another 200 kilometres or so inland. Here rests an elevated tableland with soil rich from ancient eruptions in the earth's surface, eruptions that had formed hills, gorges and cracks that became creeks.

The European invasion of New England took place in a similar fashion to that of the Hunter Valley. During the 1830s and 1840s squatters seeking large land holdings rushed to the area. The land seemed to speak a language they understood. It was hilly, green and fertile. It reminded them of home. Or at least until breakfast, when the sun assumed its force, quips New England historian John Ferry. Most agree it was this group of squatters who invented the term 'New England', first recorded in an 1836 edition of the *Sydney Herald*. In 1839 its 'capital', Armidale, was formally created. Shortly afterwards, the colonial government defined the pastoral district around it as New England, sending a Commissioner of Crown Lands to manage the society.[138]

Before this abrupt invasion several Aboriginal tribes occupied the New England region. Language groups identified include the Anaiwan, Dhunghutti, Gumbaingerri and Kamilaroi. Given this, R. B. Walker's estimation in the mid 1960s that the area's Aboriginal population was very sparse when Europeans arrived, probably totalling no more than 600, seems doubtful. A smallpox epidemic between 1829 and 1831, though its exact impact remains unknown, is estimated to have killed half of the region's Indigenous population. More fully documented is the rapid European pastoral expansion of the 1830s and 1840s, which severely depleted the Indigenous population's food source, and which the Wrights joined towards the end of the century.[139]

The pastoral settlement of New England was distinctive in one sense, a sense which continues to generate the identity of the place today. Much of the land taken up was by wealthy English and Scottish men, more so even than in the Hunter Valley. New England developed a reputation: one nineteenth-century gentleman, Thomas Tourle, remarked that New England was 'considered by far the most Aristocratic Part of New South Wales.' This he put down to the fact that 'almost all the young settlers are either Oxford or Cambridge'; they came from money and an education. William Gardner, a New England school teacher during the 1840s, recorded that there 'people were names'. Though it was clear that this colonial class had, in effect, shipped their wealth, along with their servants and possessions, from Britain, a narrative developed around them, much like the Wyndham narrative, which suggested their fortune was self made; that it was the result of effort. Historian Alan Atkinson argues it is a mythology which the squatters themselves invented.[140]

The distinct geography and climate of New England was also said to have strongly influenced the culture of the place. Summers in New England are cool by Australian standards, and winters frosty. Rain is consistent but not torrential like that seen in Queensland. Adjectives rarely used to describe the Australian landscape, such as 'crisp', 'temperate' and 'gentle', sprinkle New England literature. Even from the start, it was said, these conditions affected the temperament of the people. They did not fall prey to the hot 'hedonism of the subtropical life' experienced directly eastward.[141] They were not lazy. Effort was rewarded but rewards were responsibly managed; they did not corrupt. Regional historian J. S. Ryan believes that the crisp mornings and space gave people a 'clear-sightedness in the moral sphere' and enabled them to interact with others respectfully. The whole 'social atmosphere of the Tableland was more elevated than that of the city', writes Ryan, 'a place still pungent with convict and ex-convict life'. Ferry, on the other hand, considers this part of a fantasy which knew no limits, and that New Englanders considered themselves a second race within colonial Australia.[142]

By the time the Wrights arrived in New England, in the mid 1880s, its aristocratic reputation was confirmed by the substantial presence of a squattocracy. As the decades drew on the Wrights would form a large block within it. Like her grandfather George, May basked in the notion that her family was an 'important' group, which formed something of a 'fortification'.[143] Against what, she did not say. Born in 1915, Judith grew up largely within these walls. Describing how it felt, she said it was as if 'everyone in New England was somehow related to me, with the exception of course of the labouring classes and the Aborigines':

> Wrights, Biggs, Mackenzies and other cousins crowded my horizon. The land appeared to be owned largely by people my parents knew, the households I visited seemed to have been established forever, and prosperity seemed the norm.[144]

In the early twentieth century people spoke of 'the Wrights, the Whites, and the Not-Quites', the Whites being Patrick White's extended family. The same architect built part of their family estates. Of her upbringing Judith recalled: 'snobbery was such an entrenched factor in life'. The Wrights had little contact with smaller farming families in the area, who had mostly gained their land through the Soldier Settlement program and other government schemes, and almost no contact with the townspeople of Armidale.[145] Donald Horne, born six years after Judith, described life from the other side, as a middle-class townsperson in Muswellbrook, New South Wales.

> It is hard to convey the sense of special consideration with which an Australian living in a country town could then regard the large landholder whose property was developed (even if not by his own family) before the town itself began to form...There was something of the Norman about them: in the original land seizures from the natives, and in the massive indifference of some of them to the townspeople...[146]

The Wrights, like other large-landholding families, sat at the top of a feudal-like society, known as a pastoral station. On these self-contained, isolated properties, dozens of people were employed throughout the year, many of whom lived there. Stations produced food and supplies that workers could purchase from a shop. Since it was costly for workers to travel into town, station shops existed with little competition, setting their own prices. With a largely non-unionised workforce, bosses were at liberty to set wages and conditions. At times, such as during harvesting or shearing season, the balance of power shifted in favour of heavily in-demand workers, giving them greater bargaining power. But with most workers bound by the necessities of family life to stay in one place and provide a year-round salary, this was an exception to the rule. Conditions among New England stations varied but the better ones were always conditional on the benevolence of the boss.[147]

For Phillip Wright, who managed and owned stations for most of his life, the system produced benefits for everyone. Judith said of her father: 'he had a reputation in New England for being a very good employer, and he was'. It was a reputation he sought to explain in his memoir, *Memories of a Bushwhacker* (1972), where he argued that he never owned land 'merely for the purpose of personal gain'. He saw his role as encouraging positive lives amongst those who had less wealth. Phillip cultivated relationships with workers whose entire working lives, and sometimes those of their sons, were spent in his employment. He singled out Tom Diamond for praise, for Diamond refused to take a salary throughout the year so that he would accumulate savings, all the while feeding and clothing his children. Diamond was the model employee and proof that those at the lower end of the hierarchy could benefit from it.[148]

While Phillip acknowledged that some considered him a 'selfish landgrabber, accumulating large areas when thousands were seeking land in vain', he felt vindicated by his principled management of the land:

> While I have undoubtedly always been in the large landholder class, I have felt justified in the position, because I never held land that I did not do better with than the original holder, and on principle I never bought land from small holders who had any chance of making a success of it. Moreover, in a number of cases, I leased small holdings from the owners and, after improving the land, returned it to them, thus enabling them to carry on.[149]

This was a self-conscious form of *noblesse oblige*. Perhaps it was another instance of the New England squattocracy fashioning itself as an

Australian aristocracy. But it also indicated that Phillip believed he had a responsibility to improve society, a value he inherited from his mother.

May Wright fulfilled an important function in Judith's childhood. She was a woman to admire. She showed that being smart and independent was more important than being 'womanly', according to the standards of the day. Judith grew up on a station just 14 kilometres from her grandmother. Visits between the two properties were frequent. In the epilogue to Judith's family history *The Generations of Men* (1959), which followed May from girlhood until the end of her life, Judith said May was 'entitled to her triumph'.

> No one can rob her of her conquests, of the awe that she is held in, of the love that is rendered to her by right. She may expect, perhaps she does expect, that not only her children but her grandchildren and their children too – for who knows how far ahead the ripples of her influence may travel? – will all carry a certain stamp, a mark that singles out even the most distant or rebellious of them for her own.[150]

Perhaps Judith was thinking of herself, for she had been the rebellious grandchild who still respected her grandmother's influence. She was not the first in the family to do so. In the introduction to 'Extracts from the Dinton-Dalwood Letters: From 1827 to 1853' (1927), May had written reverentially of Margaret Wyndham. Both Judith and May took their respective Wyndham grandmother as a figurehead, both sought her out through her diaries and letters, creating books in her memory. Both grandmothers embodied the family's resilience, its pride, the self-assured belief that it could confront seemingly dire situations and make good of them.

May's life was a lesson in perseverance. Unlike the Wyndhams a generation before, May's parents, Weeta and Arthur Mackenzie, did not emerge triumphantly from their pastoral misfortunes. For most of May's childhood they lived in a small house on George and Margaret's property, poor by Wyndham standards. Amongst the Wyndhams – 'at least in the eyes of Weeta's female relatives', family historian Cedric Wyndham explains – theirs was not regarded as a 'successful marriage'. So it was that May, by the time she reached adulthood, had little financial capital to bring to a union. As a Wyndham, however, she was part of what Judith described as the Hunter Valley's 'strict list of "gentlefolks"', and was invited to social events amongst the squattocracy. She became friendly with one Mary Wright, whose brother Albert was achieving pastoral success in Queensland. He was a remote figure, and the Wrights built a 'somewhat Byronic legend' around him, perhaps for the benefit of potential wives – perhaps for May – who reported experiencing love at first sight on their eventual meeting.[151]

Things did not go smoothly. May and Albert first settled in the Dawson Valley in Queensland, about 150 kilometres south-west of Rockhampton, where they spent a decade working to establish pastoral runs. Phenomenal toil was countered by drought, floods and endless bouts of tropical fever. In the end they discovered it was their unreliable water supply which had led to the death of their first child, at the age of four. In 1885 they sold up and bought a much smaller, ill-reputed parcel of land in New England. May, happy to have escaped the exhausting northern climate, named it Wongwibinda, which she understood meant 'stay here always' in the language of a Dawson Valley Aboriginal tribe. Albert died five years after they migrated southwards, of a fever on one of his return trips to Queensland. May was left with five children, the youngest of whom was Phillip, then just thirteen months old, who had been born in 1889.[152]

Though life had been slowly improving before Albert's death, it was May's determined management of the station that radically improved her family's fortunes. May's decision to assume control went against the dictates of the time. Her family strongly encouraged her to sell the land and raise her children in town. To May, as Judith recalled, the prospect of becoming a station master excited the 'head-shaking of the world...it could not be done, they had said; impossible to manage a station, bring up a growing family, and remain womanly'. The plan could have easily failed. Though by then her major assets were sheep and cattle, when Albert died the overdraft on her bank loan was greater than the value of the land. But May's management was not half hearted. She made the daring decision to sell her entire sheep stock and focus on cattle, concluding that the New England landscape was much better suited to them. Reducing this risk was the fact that May still had access to the Wyndham Herefords, which she began buying up. Eventually she would own half of the herd. By 1896, so successful had her strategy been that May received accolades at the Armidale Show, where her cattle fetched staggering prices.[153]

Judith devoted one of twelve chapters in *Generations* to May's success that day. Later, she became less enamoured of May's glory, noting that good fortune played a major part in it. Her grandmother's reputation as a good stock manager depended, she concluded, 'more on the vagaries of the market than on her skills and knowledge'. Though this made good sense, wealth nonetheless couched May in a mystique enhanced by her Wyndham ancestry. In 1901 May added two more stations to the family's portfolio: nearby Wallamumbi, where Judith grew up, and Jeogla. In 1909 May bought a car, which was so exceptional for the times that the local newspaper wrote an account of the family's drive to Sydney. By the time Judith Wright was born, in 1915, May and her sons owned thousands of acres of profitable grazing land in New South Wales and Queensland. The Wyndham legend lived on, in yet another family branch.[154]

Culturally, May extended the Wyndhams' reverence for English, upper-class values. Judith said that she grew up to understand from her grandmother that everything that was English was good. Many products, such as farming machinery, clothing and even preserved food came to them through mail order from London. In 1902 May took Phillip and his sisters to England, partly to collect George and Margaret's letters, which she thought remained there, and partly because the girls were then at an 'impressionable' age. Phillip was sent to grammar school in England, a confusing experience because his classmates 'could not understand how I was so white in colour and could speak English so fluently, albeit with a different accent'. It was as if the Wrights sought an Englishness that no longer existed. When May wrote to the school asking that Phillip be allowed to attend King Edward's coronation her request was declined. When he snuck out May was, Phillip later reflected, 'secretly pleased'.[155]

In Australia's new England it was still possible to be English in a way they knew. May, like her English grandfather George, had a sense of civic responsibility, a felt obligation to guide the less fortunate. She also thought that hard work could improve people. Judith remembered that her grandmother was 'beneficent', but intolerant of a lackadaisical attitude: 'you had to do things right'. She recalled: 'if you were given a job of polishing you had to use real elbow grease, none of this flicking dusters about'. After witnessing a vast number of homeless orphans in England, May transported several girls, and companion English families, to her properties in Australia. There they were trained by her daughters as domestic servants. In an inversion of the colony's ranking as a penal settlement, they were sent to colonies to be civilised. Perhaps there was an element of snobbery to it; perhaps May thought the English poor would, once improved, make better workers than their colonial counterparts. Improved they were, according to son Phillip, who noted that they grew up to become 'very good citizens'.[156]

But May hardly conformed to the English upper-class feminine ideal. Though her granddaughter recalled her having a good library, and 'a great respect for books', she did not have much time for reading them. Even before marriage she was unconventional. A photo taken on May's wedding day shows a beautiful, confident woman looking directly at the camera, a smile creeping across her face. Whereas portraits of May's mother and grandmother show the women looking into the distance, modestly unaware of the camera, May regarded it confidently. Even her daughter-in-law's wedding day photograph shows a woman looking downwards. With her long hair flowing May displayed little of the meekness the times, and her class, expected of her.[157]

In *Generations* Wright tells the story of her grandmother attending a party at which guests played a game of writing frank, anonymous notes about each other's character. Of May someone had written: 'irritable temper and disposition; inclined to be vain and fond of flattery, but pleasing in manners and kind hearted. Inclined to gossip and be sarcastic. Good hand at business and shrewd at making any bargain'. May kept the note, even into death, for family members to discover, suggesting a woman unintimidated by criticism. Judith said May found the description buoying after her husband's death and it gave her the confidence to manage the family stations. To her granddaughter it seemed that May 'scarcely paused to wonder whether her powers and strength would be sufficient' to do what was considered a man's job.[158]

By performing the role of breadwinner and station master, May gave her family an unconventional perspective on gender. Around May the word 'unwomanly', wrote Judith, 'was not exactly spoken' but nonetheless implied. She associated May with the world beyond the small domestic space occupied by women and girls. 'My grandmother May', she wrote, 'whose mind was keen with an Outside quality I respected, nevertheless knew dozens of nursery rhymes...' This must have delighted the girl who struggled to admire what were considered the female tasks of sewing and cookery. Judith wrote about her grandmother with an affection she did not use for her own mother, a more typically feminine woman. She 'respected her terribly deeply'. She 'loved her very warmly indeed'.[159]

It has been suggested by May's female descendants that her legacy was a mixed blessing, especially for a girl like Judith. Though May demonstrated that women could take charge of the land, her will maintained the family tradition of leaving it to sons. Judith's half-sister Pollyanne Hill believes Judith wanted Wallamumbi and felt 'disadvantaged somehow' that she only received money, not land, as her brothers did, as part of her inheritance. Perhaps, if she had not grown up witnessing a woman manage the land, she would never have expected to have done so herself.[160]

May's life achievement was re-establishing her family's place within the colonial squattocracy. She demonstrated to her children and grandchildren what hard work and determination could achieve, even from a woman. She was bold and this boldness changed things. But she also adhered to the strictures of her cultural tradition, and she used the advantages she had been given – her social position, her access to the Wyndham Herefords – to great effect. May was conventional and conservative in that she sought to maintain, and leave intact to her descendants, the station life George and Margaret had pioneered in Australia, with its English aspirations and its clear delineations of class power. To May, the alternative to this, life in the city, working for someone else, would have been 'humiliating'.[161]

Yet as the twentieth century unfolded it seemed that this squattocratic tradition was becoming increasingly marginal to Australian political and cultural life. Phillip's life became a battle against the trend. Though by temperament less verbal, perhaps even less 'dogmatic', than his mother, he was as single minded in preserving the family traditions. Phillip's youngest daughter, Pollyanne Hill, explains that her father 'didn't philosophise', but that he was a 'visionary' nonetheless, with a 'strong sense of public duty'. Judith said of her father that 'he was a very impressive person' and that 'everyone regarded him pretty highly', not least his mother May. This led him to regard 'himself as quite an important person, and he was', she said. Phillip's grand-daughter Catherine Wright believes that Phillip's 'powerful sense of community spirit and public duty influenced my family enormously'. To the generations below he became a role model like May, Margaret and George.[162]

But what kind of influence did Phillip have on Judith? On her early life, she said, he had the greatest influence.[163] Hill agrees, stating that he was the biggest influence on Judith, 'followed by school and university'. Although many would see their causes as diametrically opposed, Hill insists that Phillip's values were 'with her all her life'. For Phillip, it seems, being independent and performing one's public duty, however one conceived of it, was essential. Hill remembered: 'as soon as I left school he suggested I join the Country Party and I became a secretary. He would have suggested the same thing to Judith'. When it became clear that Judith would not, Hill believes it is unlikely that they would have had an open disagreement, being disinclined to discuss 'serious stuff' in the family home. For Hill, Judith became involved in politics in the same way that her father did: reluctantly, perhaps even resentful that it was taking them away from their real interests (agriculture and poetry), but with a profound sense that something needed doing. Hill said of Judith: 'that was where it all started, her duty'.

Phillip, from his early adult years, believed something needed doing. From the start he was aligned with the conservative side of politics, which in early twentieth-century Australia meant the anti-labour side of politics. In issues-based campaigns Phillip sided with monarchists and avowed patriots, and favoured the employer. His first active involvement in public life occurred during World War I, though not in a predictable form. Phillip became involved in the 'Yes' campaign in the 1916 and 1917 referenda on conscription. This put him at odds with his neighbours (who were mindful that conscription would take workers from the area), but on the Right side of politics. Despite Labor Prime Minister Billy Hughes' support for conscription, the 'No' campaign was associated with the labour movement. Amongst its most vocal supporters were socialists, radicals and feminists, 'all of whom', writes Stuart Macintyre, 'challenged the assumption of a unified national interest in war'.[164] It was not surprising that Phillip opposed such challenges. What might be surprising is that he did not enlist himself.

Phillip's decision not to enlist was a difficult one which pitted against each other two deeply held commitments: one to the British Empire, and one to his family. His was not a unique dilemma. But he must have felt that the stakes were higher for his family. At the time Phillip was managing approximately half of May's business, with the other half controlled by his brother Cecil. Phillip was also newly married. Referring to Phillip (Arundel Wright) as 'P. A.', relative Bruce Mitchell wrote in the afterword to Phillip's memoir: 'depending, then, on P. A. were his wife, his mother and two unmarried sisters, to whom were soon to be added P. A.'s children, the first two of whom were born during the war'. As war broke out Phillip may have felt the family empire to be under threat. Between 1914 and 1915 the Australian economy contracted by 10 per cent. Difficulties in shipping created a stockpile of rural produce at ports. Things did, however, quickly improve when Britain agreed to underwrite Australian primary production.[165]

The episode is a tense moment in the family narrative, recorded in Phillip's memoir, Mitchell's afterword and Judith's memoir. Conscious that he could be accused of hypocrisy, all emphasised Phillip's commitment to duty and self-sacrifice in other areas, and the difficulty with which he made the decision not to enlist. Phillip acknowledged the shame he felt as his friends signed up. It made him feel his position was 'almost unbearable'. But by staying at home he was able to provide vital primary goods for the war effort. There was also the matter of his 'stiff leg', acquired during a school football incident, which would have prevented him from active service. Explaining his involvement in the 'Yes' campaign, Phillip stated that he wanted the decision to be taken out of his hands, to sort out his dilemma once and for all. Mitchell, on the other hand, framed Phillip's decision in more heroic terms. At risk, he said, was 'the survival of the very properties which had been built by generations of sacrifice and effort'. He was maintaining a family tradition of self-sacrifice, paved by Margaret and George, continued by May. Judith dealt with the issue briefly (typical of her when discussing difficult topics): 'my father, torn two ways, stayed to look after the stations under his management and his mother, sister and wife'.[166]

For Mitchell, one demonstration of Phillip's 'strong patriotism' was the support he gave his two sons for their participation in World War II. Another was his involvement in breaking the 1917 Sydney general strike. For Phillip, becoming a strike-breaker was the closest thing to enlisting. He, like many countrymen, volunteered his labour to weaken the position of the strikers, whom they regarded as unpatriotic for undermining Australia's war efforts. It was heavy toil, performed willingly, and in the face, Phillip remembered, of crowds who became 'more and more menacing' towards them.[167] Verity Burgmann makes the point that though the NSW government sought to position the strike as a tactic by anti-conscriptionists and Bolsheviks to sabotage the war effort, its scope reached much further than could have been mustered by either of these relatively marginal movements. Almost 100,000 workers went on strike throughout Australia, mainly in New South Wales, over a period of eighty-two days. For most, it was a clear case of the workers versus the bosses. The strike, after all, originated in Randwick repair and maintenance workshops when employers proposed a 'card system' enabling them to record the time taken to complete tasks. And yet the NSW government declared: 'the Enemies of Britain and her Allies have succeeded in plunging Australia into a General Strike...at the back of this strike lurk the IWW [Industrial Workers of the World] and the exponents of direct action'.[168]

For Phillip it was no coincidence that the strikers were mostly city dwellers and the breakers mostly countrymen. A distinction between the populations became increasingly important. 'From my early years of maturity', wrote Phillip, 'the political and economic growth of Sydney, and indeed of all the mainland capitals, has been a matter of deep concern to me'. Coinciding with Phillip's maturation was a growing movement of countrymen, particularly in New South Wales and Queensland, who believed that 'only a political party which placed its emphasis on rural needs could reverse growing policies of centralisation'. It was not the first time such a party had been envisioned. From 1893 various manifestations had risen and fallen, including the Progressive Party, which Phillip had been involved in. By the time he was thirty-one, in 1920, something more solid had been established: the Country

Party. Judith explained that May had been consulted on the formation of the party, with founder Earle Page visiting her 'often' to discuss it.[169] Looking back, Phillip described himself as the Party's 'stalwart supporter'. Within New England, he was amongst the most active of its members. Judith believed that her father's involvement in politics was at the behest of his mother, May: 'Dad was so often away outside or at a meeting, doing Ninna's bidding on politics and the Country Party'.[170]

The promotion of that original 1920 Country Party vision was, after all, a way of preserving the Wyndham family tradition. The outcomes it sought, the philosophy it promoted, aligned with those of the Wyndham Wrights and their pastoral enterprises. Country Party historian Don Aitkin has expounded what he sees as the organisation's original 'farming vision': it was strongly anti-collectivist and individualist, hierarchical where necessary, and celebratory of an individual's integrity and independence. Other historians have referred to this as 'countrymindedness', implying it holds widespread rural support.[171] But as Aitkin observes, this particular farming vision, this ideology which the Country Party helped forge, did in fact favour the economic interests of the large-scale farmer. That the Country Party was particularly popular amongst the New England squattocracy might be proof of this, for they were a group with unique economic needs. As Ferry notes, the average wealth of pastoralists in New England 'far exceeded any other group in the region', but they relied on a large workforce, were usually heavily indebted and their income came at long intervals.[172] For pastoralists like Phillip the prospect that wages could spiral out of control seemed ruinous. And yet this was only likely to happen if his workforce became unionised.

The Country Party's opposition to labour unions may have been its defining cause. It does, after all, seem more than coincidence that the movement gained momentum during the labour disputes of the 1890s, which also spawned the labour movement in Australia. The Country Party's unofficial historian, Ulrich Ellis, maintains it was the divide between city and country, not worker and employer, which distinguished the Party. Aitkin, more sceptical, notes that it was a characteristic of the Party that it refused to acknowledge that it had a position on labour politics. Drawing on a relatively small population for its electoral support, it could not afford to alienate employees by doing so, he argued. But, as suggested by Phillip, many in the Party believed that what was good for bosses was good for employees, at least in the country.[173]

Whether out of political strategy, philosophical commitment, or both, the Party sought widespread rural support by developing a version of Australian history where British pastoralism was the hero; not the boss, not the worker. Ellis reprised it in his 1958 history:

> When the first British convoy anchored in Sydney Harbour in 1788 less than half a million aborigines [sic] occupied the Australian continent. These stone age primitives were scattered in small tribal groups throughout 3,000,000 square miles of territory. Husbandry and agriculture were unknown to them.

The British planned the Australian colonies as evenly populated spaces, well suited to the production of primary goods, with most administration occurring in Britain itself. But problems gradually arose, Ellis argued, throughout the nineteenth century, as colonial administrators became more powerful and channelled funds into growing cities. With time, rural infrastructure, especially transport infrastructure, became neglected and rural populations became economically disadvantaged and isolated. Such changes were compounded by a rapid transformation in Australia's population, around the turn of the twentieth century, which saw a mostly rural population become a mostly metropolitan one.[174]

Australians as a whole embraced industrialisation and the growth of cities, providing the Country Party with many battles and a sense of marginalisation. Ellis argued that after forty years the Party's greatest achievement was survival, given the 'war of attrition waged by larger, wealthier and more numerous parties who regard it as a nuisance'. Always pursuing decentralisation, Phillip worked on tangible projects, such as the creation of a shipping port in Newcastle to allow primary goods to be exported without entering Sydney. Phillip met with brokerage firms, wrote letters to government, and even provided the 'necessary finance' to keep the struggle going. By 1957 his determination proved successful, with seven of the nine major Sydney broking houses conducting operations at Newcastle.[175]

Another campaign sought the establishment of a rural university in New England. At an Armidale Chamber of Commerce meeting in 1928 Phillip moved a motion to convene a meeting to discuss the idea. 'This move', he later reflected, 'could be said to have been the genesis of the University of New England'. More than a decade later, Phillip became Vice-Chairman of an advisory council set up by the University of Sydney to establish a University of New England College. When an independent university was eventually created, in 1954, after almost thirty years of lobbying, Phillip became Deputy Chancellor. Fellow Country Party member Earle Page was its first Chancellor, a post which Phillip succeeded him in. It was an acknowledgement of Phillip's role in the university's creation, rather than any scholarly qualification, since he had not studied beyond secondary school. Being an 'uneducated' University Chancellor caused Phillip 'quite a lot of anxiety', remembered Judith.[176]

But Phillip's most public legacy was arguably his reinvigoration of a movement to establish a seventh state out of northern New South Wales. Originally launched in 1915, the year that Judith was born, the movement drew on a similar vision to that of the Country Party, believing that regions should govern themselves and allocate taxes towards ends they approved of. Phillip claimed that the Country Party owed its formation to the movement, as many of its principal protagonists, such as himself, emerged from the New States lobby determined that they needed a larger platform to support their push. And, indeed, during its early years the Country Party actively sought a new state. To Phillip, the Country Party betrayed its founders by letting the issue of a new state go into 'cold storage' in the 1940s. During this time, Phillip became an agitator within the Party – a rebellious, even undiplomatic figure who would not be appeased by appeals to pragmatism. The Party lacked 'statesmanship and vision'. In his memoirs he reflected that there seemed to be something corrupting about political power:

I often wonder whether country Parliamentarians are not the victims of centralization…the fearsome monster challenged by their predecessors has become familiar and inoffensive. In fact they seem to have been indoctrinated by the very conditions they were elected to fight…[177]

He wrote with a fearlessness and frankness that appeared to be familial.

Remaining true to their original vision, Phillip and high-profile conservative politicians Earle Page and David Drummond got together to 'cook up' a scheme after World War II, remembers Pollyanne Hill. In 1957 Phillip was crowned president of this new New States movement and commissioned Ellis, also aligned with their organisation, to set out their tenet in a pamphlet entitled, *New England, the Seventh State*. It maintained that 'an undue proportion of public money' was devoted to the city and that 'present legislatures are subservient to city needs'. The pamphlet captured fears circulating as a result of the Cold War. Because rural populations were so small, and the country's infrastructure so centralised, 'a few well aimed bombs directed against Sydney alone could virtually immobilise the whole system of Australian defence'. The construction of a new state was a matter of 'national survival' given the 'southward thrust of Communist world conquerors'. Phillip presumably approved of the threatening, gloomy conclusion Ellis drew: Australia's chances of survival are 'none if we fail to populate the continent and develop our resources'.[178]

The culmination of Phillip's decentralisation mission was arguably the 1967 referendum on secession. By championing Liberal and Country members of parliament who privately supported him, when a Coalition government was elected to New South Wales in 1965 sufficient support was obtained for a referendum on the issue. Change seemed likely; a 1954 poll of New Englanders had already shown that 77 per cent supported a new state. Indeed, the 1967 referendum revealed around 72 per cent supported it in northern New South Wales. But things were not so good in Newcastle, a district which had only been included because of its existing infrastructure. There, the vote for a new state was so low that it swung the outcome. 'But for the inclusion of Newcastle', Phillip lamented, 'the result would have been overwhelming'. Rural populations had been thwarted by the metropolis once again. It must have been a blow. In its wake, and after decades of agitation, Phillip passed on the baton to son Peter, whom he hoped would have better luck in advancing the family's rural vision.[179]

But what of daughter Judith? She would not have any direct involvement in pastoral operations or causes, and certainly none in organised conservative politics. The 'Pastoral Aristocracy of the Country Party', as she put it, had vested interests in her not succeeding, politically, in campaigns on behalf of Aboriginal people and the environment.[180] And yet, strangely, many of the positions she took throughout her creative and political life, and indeed the way she framed and pursued them, were premised on the same values as those which drove May and Phillip. It was, though not always, a case of individuals from different generations interpreting the same values according to their times.

The most striking resemblance Judith bore to her grandmother and father was her uncompromising, utterly tireless commitment to what she regarded as her public duty. Whether championing Australian literature, the rights of authors, the environment, or the rights of Aboriginal people, Judith spent decades writing letters, travelling, meeting, speaking publicly, and providing moral support to her kindred spirits. She was a fearsome fighter who gathered troops around her in much the way her forebears socialised with, and protected, their political friends. When Judith was a teenager, Phillip brought local politicians and other associates camping with the family in New England, as part of his campaign to have a National Park declared in the area.[181] We learn from the archive of Judith's letters, if we learn nothing else, that Judith worked remarkably hard on campaigns and movements for many decades, sometimes yearning for a little peace – a gap where poetry might spring – but mostly resigned to their centrality within her life. It was the way it was, in much the way Phillip accepted his public duty. At seventy, she said, 'I'm a slave as usual to Causes and don't really want to escape'.[182]

It has become a cliché that the greatest advantage class privilege affords is the confidence to extract such privileges from society oneself. Yes, money and connections and schools matter, but it is the example of a parent, grandparent, aunt or uncle moving confidently into an arena which makes the child believe they can too. And so it was for Judith. For what May and Phillip modelled was a belief in their own convictions and, because such convictions and interests were regarded as increasingly marginal to Australian society, a consequent suspicion of figures of authority and dominant social expectations. These Wrights would not acquiesce to ideas described as progress just because so many others did. They had an understanding of the way power works and that social change is not something which occurs naturally, or simply as a function of people exercising their free will in a democracy. They understood that there is space for wrangling if one can wield that power.

Judith, like May and Phillip, was determined. She was confident. And, like them, much of her thinking was premised on a belief in the value of a life lived close to the land – even if the conclusions she came to were different. The commitment to country living, the disdain for life in the city, endured down the generations. Throughout her work, both creative and intellectual, the natural landscape sits in contrast to the city, a force which corrupts environments and people. At age twenty-four, years before she was widely known as a poet, she had a poem published in *The Australian National Review*, which attested to the way cities corrupted people, inflating their sense of importance and impeding an appropriately respectful relationship with nature. 'City Rain' accused the city dweller of trying to evade the power of the natural world. The natural world would assert itself, she warned: 'the sun, the earth, the rain,/ we are the trinity,/ the final reference of all that is or can be./ You, within your roof,/ think you to withdraw?/ Beware; the shells you build/ we are the fatal flaw'.[183] It was, of course, the thinking of an early environmentalist. But it was also that of a woman who had known, from a young age, how it was to feel marginalised by an impervious, self-confident majority.

Judith remained uneasy about cities, and avoided pausing in them for any length of time throughout her life. They could make you sick, physically and morally. In 1987 she said, 'I think cities have a great deal to do with wickedness', when describing how she was raised in the company of male workers but never experienced 'any approaches that I would regard as out of the way'. Natural environments did not just enable a creative life, they enabled life. Reflecting on her family's commitment to rural living, Judith said in her eighties that it wasn't so much 'for love of the land and its characteristics' that her family stayed there but that 'they felt at home there'. It might be a metropolitan conceit to talk of passion for the land and its aesthetic virtues. For Judith, though she was nature's most devoted lover, she spoke about her reason for living in the country in a similarly straightforward, perhaps rural way: 'I prefer the country and that's my background'. She was a Wright after all.[184]

CHAPTER 3

A Childhood Unravelled

The Wyndham Wrights, mighty as they were, were not the only familial influence on young Judith, of course. What of Judith's mother, Ethel Bigg? What kind of example did she set? Ethel was her daughter's first model, yet as a child Judith did not seek to emulate her mother's conventional, upper-class, rural life. In fact, she watched it nervously hoping her fate would not be similar. This did not lead to a happy childhood. Other dramatic happenings turned it into something of a trial. Judith's childhood took place within a household marked by both extreme order and disorder. A period in which everything had its place was followed by a time when there was no good place for anything. It was something of an unravelling of childhood. And whether in times good or bad, Judith observed that being female was about suffering constraint and isolation. Books, however, provided a possible way out. In this way, Judith's childhood follows the generic conventions of a writer's biography.

Indeed, that bookish love affair helps explain the modern young woman who we meet in Chapter 4, who would confidently step onto the streets of Sydney, already set on becoming a poet. But her relationship with books, and the landscape, singled out as formative by Judith herself, are only part of the story. Here, in this chapter, Judith's relationship with her mother is examined in greater detail than in any previous biographical discussion. Defining episodes in Judith's teenage years, including her experience of gaining a stepmother and half siblings, and of enduring boarding school, variously completely ignored or barely mentioned in other published accounts, are brought to life with new primary evidence. And poems Judith wrote as a child, also only very briefly examined elsewhere, are considered in light of these trials. For Judith's relationship with her mother was a kind of trial, at times, since her mother did not, perhaps could not, always act in ways that were predictable, intentional or pleasant. This experience had a profound impact. Ethel, conventional, long-suffering, acquiescent even, might be the ultimate reason Judith would turn out to be none of these things.

How did the union of Ethel and Phillip come about? Like his forebears, Phillip looked to the close knit, land-owning families of New South Wales and Queensland for a wife. One such New England family was the Biggs. No known description exists of how Phillip became engaged to 'Ethel Bigg of Swallowfield, near Armidale', as he put it in his memoir. But it cannot have been an extended courtship, the two having met each other only once or twice as adults before marriage. Patrick White reported of the New England squattocracy, of which he was a part, that they were 'not known for impulsive or passionate marriages'. Ethel, for her part, put no first-hand accounts on the public record. Of her life, and background, we do not have the vast literature of the Wyndhams. Yet because the Biggs also came from wealth, their lives, travels and transactions were the subject of both private and public record. Henry Edward Bigg, Ethel's great-grandfather and her first known colonial ancestor, who arrived in New South Wales in 1856, thoughtfully left a personal diary, giving us some insight into Ethel's background and another illuminating colonial story.[185]

Henry Bigg came from the original Swallowfield house in Sussex, England. The house was surrounded by woods, gardens, greenhouses and conservatories, according to Judith, who stayed there in 1937. At that time, she recalled, 'gardeners, domestic staff and farm tenants supplied a background of settled Englishry'. In this respect, little may have changed in eighty years. Upon leaving this comfortable life, Bigg ventured much of his inherited wealth on the newly 'opened' country along the Isaac River in Queensland. Susceptible to flood and drought, the area was also scene to violent clashes with Aboriginal people. He was one of many who returned to New South Wales virtually penniless. Moreover, to what must have been his family's immense embarrassment, he married a woman, Annie, of unknown lineage – Judith suspected convict – after she became pregnant. The Biggs were saved by the death of Henry's aunt, by suicide, whose inheritance was substantial. They bought a property called Thalgarrah, near Armidale, and oversaw the construction of a grand estate modelled on the English Swallowfield. There they had two children, Amy and Alfred, the latter becoming Judith's maternal grandfather. Alfred would marry Mabel Spasshatt, the daughter of a doctor and a headmistress, who gave birth to six children, including Ethel, at Swallowfield. She was friendly with one May Wright, from nearby Wongwibinda.[186]

Life at Thalgarrah tended to be more lively than at Wongwibinda. When Ethel's sister came out into society, and her brothers returned from war, Thalgarrah became 'one of the social focuses of Armidale', holding parties and dances. Privately, May told her granddaughter that all that gaiety relied on English money, as distinct from their own wealth, which was accrued in Australia, at least in recent generations. That the Biggs gained a 'certain prestige' from this annoyed May. But it was not enough to deter her from joining forces with the Biggs. Perhaps it was the mothers who arranged Phillip and Ethel's marriage, which took place in 1913 at the Anglican Cathedral in Armidale.[187]

A photo from the day shows Ethel wearing a spectacular dress, intricately constructed from lace. In her hands she holds a large bouquet of roses which cascade beyond her knees. She looks in that same direction with a serious, even mournful expression. In Judith's poem, 'Wedding Photo, 1913', a separate wedding photo is described, but it must have been similar for Judith noted her mother's 'downward conscious poise of beauty'. She always thought of her as very beautiful. In contrast there was her father, his 'awkward faun-look, ears spread wide'. Addressing her parents, Judith saw them 'surrounded, wished-for, toasted by your clans'. The couple honeymooned in Japan and China. May provided them with a home on nearby Wallamumbi, making additions to the house that existed there. Together they had three children: Judith in 1915, Bruce in 1917 and Peter in 1919.

Judith Wright's entry into the world occurred on the 31st of May, at Thalgarrah, about 50 kilometres from Wallamumbi. It was tradition for children to be born in their mother's family home. Wright described

Thalgarrah as gracious and warm. Of all those in her extended family she loved it most. Apart from the property's garden of wattles, in full bloom when she was born, Thalgarrah was a picturesque, English scene. Beyond the English-looking house there was an orchard of fruit and nut trees. These were framed by oaks, poplars and a lake with a small island and swans. Further afield lay a chapel. Yet even this pocket of serenity was troubled by events occurring on the other side of the world. Australians had entered a world of horror just one month earlier by landing at Gallipoli. Though her own father's internal battles had led him to stay at home, two of Ethel's brothers had joined the Light Horse, and one of them was captured at Gallipoli. Ethel had sombre things on her mind before the birth of her first child. It was not until Judith was three-and-a-half years old that Germany signed an armistice and the Great War was over. It must have provided for a gloomy infancy. For Judith, smart and sensitive even then, understood that danger might be close, digging an air-raid shelter, not much deeper than her knees, in case she needed to shield her family from bomber planes. She remembered the end of the war, when her family burned an effigy of the Kaiser. But even this was not a completely joyous occasion, the small child wondering to herself: 'surely somebody will save him?'[188]

And yet, the Wrights had much to look forward to. After all, their immediate lives took place within a prosperous and orderly universe. Paddocks, full with cattle and sheep, surrounded the Wallamumbi homestead and stretched far towards the hills. An orchard and vegetable garden supplied the kitchen with fresh produce. Meat was butchered from the property's animals. Dairy came from the same source. Pastry, jam, cakes, biscuits, preserved fruit – all food, except bread, which was delivered two or three times a week – was made in the kitchen by an army of servants the family referred to as 'the girls'. 'All this production', Judith wrote, 'with almost everything we ate pouring into the house in a steady rhythm…underpinned our existence so that even when the Depression later cut deep into most people's lives, we were unconcerned and well-fed'. Outside, myriad activities, revolving around animal rearing, were undertaken by men. When describing Wallamumbi, Judith emphasised its structured quality. Every creature had its place:

...the dogs and their kennels and chains, the fowls in their high netted yard, the pigs in their sty, the woolshed on the hill, the cattleyards and cowyard, the trees and the blue of the faraway mountain range...[189]

The boundaries of this world were hazy, for Judith's observations of what was beyond indicated that even there Wallamumbi asserted its influence. In the nearby township of Wollomombi, Wallamumbi cattle and sheep grazed freely. Beyond this, of which Judith for the most part could only read or hear about, was much of the same. Reports indicated that the life at Wallamumbi was replicated all over the country. 'Even the *Sydney Mail* and the other newspapers we took', she wrote, 'gave me little notion that there were places in which the life of the land which supported us had little importance. For in Australia, in my childhood, the pastoralist ruled the roost'. While this economic and power structure was gradually coming undone, Judith grew up thinking of it as indestructible. Perhaps it is the inclination of all children, but Judith saw this apparently self-sustaining world as 'immemorially unchanged and permanent'.[190] The isolation of Wallamumbi gave Judith little opportunity for thinking otherwise. She left the place rarely. Visits to May's were relatively frequent but petrol usage in the Summit car was always a consideration. To the Biggs' they only went 'in a crisis or for Christmas or a birthday or something'. Armidale, some 50 kilometres away, was a real town by 1915. It boasted 'well-ordered roads, council water supply, gas lights, picket fences, stately buildings', writes John Ferry. But Judith went to Armidale rarely.[191]

Even the presence of Aboriginal people gave no indication of the impermanent nature of life at Wallamumbi. As an adult Judith learned that Wallamumbi existed on what had been an important gathering place for the Anewan people.[192] But as a child she witnessed nothing more than 'a few dark shadows' who, together with itinerant rabbiters and fencers, gypsies, drovers and other wanderers, made up the 'lowest level of the New England community'. Another class of Aboriginal people worked on the family stations, especially on Judith's uncle Cecil's station Dyamberin. At May's Wongwibinda the Cohens, an Aboriginal family of well-regarded stockmen and domestics, became the family's primary interface with the land's former occupiers.[193]

Phillip's experience of and views on Aboriginal people must have reinforced this dual image of Aboriginality. For Phillip some Aboriginal people were reliable, albeit remnants of a dying race. In his memoir he discussed their 'passing' in the same passage as changes to the native bush and wildlife. The proliferation of kangaroos, he explained, was a result of the passing of its 'natural enemies like the aborigines [sic] and the dingo…' As a child he remembered Aboriginal people who would walk in groups and come begging for food 'in a wheedling voice'. Most did not work, he continued, though there was the exception, such as Paddy Ross, 'a full blood…in many ways he was my father's, and afterwards my mother's, right-hand man'. Phillip also had an Aboriginal nursemaid, whom he 'loved very much'. She married Paddy. Apart from naming their properties after Aboriginal words, a squattocratic tradition, the Wrights made no acknowledgement of the presence of Aboriginal people on the land.[194]

It must have seemed to Judith in her early years that all that was dangerous could be tamed. All that lived was controllable. Her father exerted complete authority over his station, which to her meant the world. 'As a child', she wrote, 'I believed him to own and manage everything and everyone'. Behind him stood the authority of May, and the Wyndham legacy of triumph. Judith noticed that her father consulted her grandmother on a daily basis on the running of the station. May was, after all, the owner of Wallamumbi. Against this might, all counterforce succumbed. Forests of trees were torn down to make wood for the stoves, pigs were slaughtered despite their heart-rending cries, and all day 'the girls' rolled pastry, scrubbed, polished and plunged their hands into boiling water to ensure the family's silver cutlery shone.[195]

But all that order began to unravel. The beginning of the downfall, which as an adult Judith playfully described as her fall from Eden, was the birth of her first brother when she was two-and-a-half years old. The appearance of a sibling seemed to affect her more than most, especially given that she was unlikely to have remembered much about the time before. However, there was, in the end, good reason for Judith to resent the arrival of her brothers. Though she did not know it as a young child, she came to realise that they would inherit the land that she, as a female, could not. May, in a little protest against patriarchy, arranged her will so that her granddaughters would receive money for their education. But, as mentioned in Chapter 2, they would not inherit land. Judith recalled, even as a young child, recognising her inferiority; Bruce was 'fair-haired, brown-eyed, happy and cooed over by everyone, while I was dark-haired, greenish-eyed and female'. 'He', she wrote, 'had supplanted me'.[196]

If Bruce's birth changed Judith's world in a manner that was fairly normal for a child, Peter's changed it beyond recognition. While pregnant with Peter, Ethel caught the first wave of influenza to hit Australia. After his birth ill health plagued her.

> Influenza left my mother with what were known as 'complications' and, as time went on, asthma, coughing and kidney trouble turned her beautiful face a shade purple and her hands and ankles became swollen.

Ethel frequently became breathless and avoided going outside. She shuffled around the house and woke in the night with terrible 'choking fits'. Her migraines were so bad they were 'legendary'. The family tried all manner of cures, including 'asthma cigarettes', which produced a heavy smog in the house. When the 'Anglican God' did not respond to her prayers by curing her, Ethel stopped believing in him; it must have been isolating, and perhaps heartbreaking, for a woman whose whole society believed. But Ethel had always been open to less orthodox metaphysics; she was in no doubt her family had, for generations, been living under a curse. At one stage Ethel turned to Christian Science, at another to the French psychologist Émile Coué de la Châtaigneraie, who recommended autosuggestion. Ethel went through a stage of faithfully repeating the mantra, 'every day and in every way I am getting better and better'. May believed that tuberculosis began in warm climates so Ethel sometimes sat shivering on the verandah, covered in blankets.[197]

Judith wrote about her childhood in letters to friends, in a book of recollections entitled *Tales of a Great Aunt* (1998), and in her memoir, *Half a Lifetime* (1999). And in 1987 she recalled her childhood in a series of interviews for the National Library of Australia archives. In all of these accounts, Ethel is always sick. Judith said: 'I can never remember my mother other than ill'. What she recalled most frequently were the symptoms of her mother's illness and the dominating effect it had on the household. As a child she began to view the house as her mother's prison, where she was 'locked in her illness and despair'. Judith described the ambiance of the house as, variously, 'mournful', 'sickly and impractical' and 'poisonous'. Ethel's despair sometimes manifested in nervousness and irritability. She became impatient with 'noise, difficult and persistent questioning and loud conversations, and even to being touched suddenly, which perhaps caused her actual pain', Judith reflected. Judith said the illness 'affected her kidneys and affected her mind, I think, a little too'. She cried or got angry without warning.[198]

Of all the accounts Judith gave of her mother the most illustrative one is fictional. In her little known, thin volume of autobiographical reflections, Judith confessed to having represented herself and her mother in a 1966 short story entitled 'The Colour of Death'. It casts a sepulchral light on her childhood. In that story the child protagonist, Isa, is alone and lonely. Her only sibling, Benjy, is away at boarding school. Her father works late on the farm. Her mother is confined to a bed with illness. Isa takes consolation in the companionship of a cat and a secret garden. Planting the bud of a violet plant she decides that in order to grow it needs a 'spell of some kind' and settles on the comforting words uttered by 'the pensioner odd-job man and gardener'; 'there ye are now, snug as a bug in a rug', she tells the bud. The violet, like other details in the story, came from Judith's childhood.[199]

Isa's search for comfort is a response to the coldness of home life, dominated by her aunt who has come to look after her while her mother is ill. Judith did have an aunt Weeta whom she saw regularly, especially when her mother became sick. But Isa's aunt is called Ethel. Aunt Ethel and Isa's mother are a united force and respond similarly to Isa. The two characters appear to represent different phases of Ethel's illness: before and after she was well enough to look after her daughter. Neither manifestation of Ethel was happy. Both treated Isa harshly.

'There you are,' said her mother softly from the bed. Lately she had had a new look, strained like a running hare, her skin too tight for her large starting eyes. 'And where's the big kitchen tablespoon, I'd like to know? You don't think Aunt Et didn't see you at the drawer?' Isa pulled it out of her pocket and threw it on the table. Crumbs of dust fell from it, and her mother exclaimed 'Spoiling the polish on the furniture! Wash it, child, and put it away. And your hair! You're as bad as the wind itself, annoying me all day. Go and brush it, clean yourself for tea, wash the spoon, I say!' And the long curtains at the window came bulging and flicking in another gust of wind. 'And it's after sunset!' cried Aunt Et, putting down the tray crossly and tying back the curtain from where it hung askew on the corner of the mirror. 'Your tea's on the kitchen table, Isa, and don't let the cat in, even if she *is* mewing round out there.'[200]

Through Isa, Judith likened herself to the wind, upsetting and destabilising anything that was not grounded. Her mother was one such thing. Ethel's response to her vulnerability manifested in a preoccupation with controlling her environment, perhaps with the aim of controlling her illness. Judith reflected that in her childhood 'there was always this pain, this sense of being cut off from her [Ethel] in a way because often when I wanted to talk to her she was just not available'.[201] When Isa begins to tell her mother about her secret garden they are interrupted and her mother does not ask about it again.

In describing her mother Judith often used the word 'lonely': 'an immense loneliness enclosed her'. For Ethel had little adult company. This was partly a product of her illness. Tennis parties, for instance, a fashion amongst the New England squattocracy, and a primary form of social interaction, became too difficult to host or attend. Even visits to family were a physical challenge. But perhaps, more than anything else, it was the social structure of daily life as one of New England's social elite that intensified her loneliness. It was a structure that Judith observed with horror, and promised to herself that she would never grow up to operate within. Roles within the home, between husband and wife, parents and children, boys and girls, master and servant, were clearly prescribed and, according to laws of respectability, inelastic.[202]

Though Ethel lived amongst many people, including female and male servants, and farmers on small neighbouring plots, none were considered appropriate social companions. Her social milieu was made up of the large-landowning families of New South Wales and

Queensland who were, by dint of their land, set at great distances apart from each other. Judith observed: 'one of the chief factors in the loneliness of the women of the "New England aristocracy" was just this refusal to admit any outsider even to afternoon tea...' She explained: 'my mother spent much of her time in solitude. It was not done to talk to the house "girls" and a housewife who was not well enough to do much work about the house or in the garden was doubly isolated'.[203]

During the late nineteenth and early twentieth century the home increasingly figured as a private sphere governed by women. In her account of the ideology informing the architecture of the modern Australian home, Kerreen Reiger describes the early century, middle-class ideal of 'a peaceful home in which a clear-cut sexual division of labour existed between husband and wife [and where the] children were orderly, "well-governed"'. In the Wright household Ethel spent almost her entire time inside the house and Phillip spent most of his time outside it, including at Country Party meetings.[204] This Judith registered to the extent that all of her childhood memories were arranged accordingly: 'I find it all falls into inside and outside for me. Inside was women...My brothers used to follow the male side, which I always thought of internally as the outside'. Phillip did have an inside presence as well. When the children did something wrong they were sent to Phillip's study to describe their misdemeanour and explain why they had committed it. Then Phillip would select one of his straps, pinned to the wall, and administer it. But he had a warm and loving demeanour too, reading imperial adventure stories to the children from his armchair most evenings.[205]

The ideal of familial privacy assumed a ferocity for Ethel. She missed her family, whom they rarely saw. Visits to her more proximate mother-in-law May, and sister-in-law Weeta, must have done little to relieve her loneliness. May and Ethel were suspicious of one another. Every day Phillip and May spoke at length on the phone, which were both on the same line, allowing easy communication between the homes.

I can't remember how this phone was connected, but my mother was convinced that, even when she telephoned her own family, my grandmother would pick the phone up stealthily at Wongwibinda and listen in – I think she was quite capable of this.[206]

Phillip could listen as well, without Ethel knowing. It must have compounded her loneliness.

Judith resented that it was up to her, as a girl, to ease her mother's loneliness. Being female seemed to offer nothing and take so much. That she felt this way made her feel guilty: 'her loneliness...must have been worsened by my own inability to be a good, normal little girl with an interest in domestic matters. Sewing, knitting, dolls and scrapbooks soon bored me...' Judith was also conscious that her appearance did not match the feminine ideal, and that this was a problem. After all, her life's purpose appeared to be marriage and children. The alternative was embodied by her aunt Weeta, who remained unmarried and lived with her mother, May, reportedly always under her thumb. To achieve power, Judith perceived as a child, a woman had to get married, 'and for marrying it seemed one had to be pretty'. When she asked her mother if she was, Ethel replied: 'you will always be pretty to me, darling'. According to Judith, her mother was intensely disappointed by her appearance. Persistent thumb sucking until the age of six left her with 'buck teeth', something which drew her mother to tears. She felt her knees and ankles disappointed her mother too, not to mention her 'greenish-brown and triangular eyes', only partially hidden by unflattering glasses. Even her cuticles, which her mother furtively pushed back, could not be tamed.[207] Girls sometimes perceive that their lack of prettiness is their own fault. Barbara Falk, born five years before Judith into a well-off middle-class family, recalled feeling as if she had committed the 'crime of being...ugly and a girl'. Intelligence was not regarded as a worthy substitute in either Falk's or Judith's families.[208]

Escape beckoned. 'Most of the time', Judith remembered, 'partly because of my mother's illness, I went as much outside as I could'.[209] Another mode of outbreak was reading. When it was too wet to go outside she took to 'sliding under the beds to read in dusty privacy'. Searching for another option to marriage, Judith came upon Miles Franklin's novel *My Brilliant Career*. It told the story of wilful country girl Sybylla who decides against marriage in favour of being a writer. She read it over and over.

> My mother was somewhat shocked to see me reading it, for (and I don't know how the book had entered a respectable household) it was very much condemned by society, or so I gathered. I could understand that. It seemed a little over the odds to use a stockwhip to assert your refusal to give in to a man – but if you had to? At least it was possible to say 'No' to marrying and to find a way of living outside the household. I already wanted to be a writer. Those poems I wrote to please my mother...might offer a way out.[210]

But Judith must have forgotten that Sybylla's 'way out' was hardly exemplary. She did avoid marriage, but ended up poor and working on her family station, not a writer. It seems Judith confused Sybylla with Franklin, whose success as a writer was, ironically, most likely predicated on her novel's ending, which did not ultimately offer women and girls a happy alternative to marriage. That the novel even broached the subject of rebellion must have worried Ethel. Indeed, she frowned upon Judith's compulsive reading, not considered ladylike, and told her that it would ruin her eyes.[211]

Still, as Judith said, one highly valued 'feminine' trait in which she did excel was writing poetry. Poetry was different to fiction. From the age of six, poetry became 'central to what I am and do', she reflected late in life. Judith's interest in poetry pleased Ethel; it was territory they were both happy in. Ethel created a scrapbook of poems from the *Sydney Mail*, wartime magazines and the *Ladies' Home Journal*, which came from England. Judith described them as 'rather sentimental verse about men going to the war, and babies, and flowers, and eternal love'. By the age of seven or eight she was mimicking them, filling out her own scrapbook with highly sentimental, formulaic poems. These poems, wonderfully, have been preserved. Judith's archive at the National Library of Australia contains two exercise books of juvenile poems and short stories. One contains eighty-seven finished poems, with titles listed in an index at the back. The poems are written in a neat hand, with very few corrections. As well as reflecting a notable degree of focus for a child, the poems reveal Judith's sensitivity towards words and tone at a young age. She reproduced her mother's favoured styles, typically creating pleasing rhythms with regular metric and rhyme structures in short stanzas.[212]

Poems in the first part of the book express a cheerful innocence. Authority figures, such as God and parents, alleviate negative experiences. In 'The Flickering Candlelight', the sense of danger a child feels going to bed is depicted as a little game: 'isn't it fun to go to bed/ in the flickering candlelight?...For who knows what horrible beasties might stop/ in the flickering candlelight!' The final stanza concludes with an image of maternal comfort: 'isn't it fun when mummy comes/ in the flickering candlelight?/ For the bogies fly when they hear her tread/ as she stoops to rumple my little head,/ and tucks me up in the nice warm bed/ in the flickering candlelight!' Other poems promote a gentle and contented femininity, such as 'My Own Self', in which the young Judith wrote: '...I'd like to be a robin, and preen my soft red breast – / But still I think I'd like to be my own self best!' From other poems emerge dramatic narratives involving nature and supernatural beings, such as fairies.

Yet Judith's early poems also espouse an unconventional femininity, one that places value on being adventurous. 'Two Little Girls' tells of two girls who each take a different path. One chances upon some fairies, but 'fled, for she wasn't bold'. The other girl stumbles upon the doors of Elfland: 'she knocked, and they let her in,/ when they saw that she wasn't frightened/ they asked her to be their queen.' The lesson is clear: the bold girl becomes deliriously happy, the shy girl is reduced to eating bread and milk.

Many of Judith's childhood poems depict flight and spontaneous movement as pleasurable. In 'My Own Self', for instance, she writes: 'I'd like to be a magpie, that flies around and sings...I'd like to be an eagle, and soar away aloft'. While this was in keeping with popular poetry which favoured drama and striking imagery, we might also read other desires into Judith's choice of subject. In poems such as 'The Kite' and 'The Eagle', where wind creates excitement, and in 'The Black Horse Thunder', there is a clear will towards freedom and escape, perhaps even sexual. In her short poem 'The Wind', we find an even more explicit connection between desire and wind. Here the wind excites and satisfies the feminised wheat, prompting it to croon in a muffled tune.

The wind sang through the creamy wheat,
Soft and low, gentle and muffled,
Crooning on a lullaby soft and sweet
Through the tall grain with its green plumes ruffled.

In 'White Sheets', too, bedtime and dreaming, that daily, mental escape from reality, is laced in sensual pleasure. The lavender scent of bed 'fills me with delight' and 'thrills me through', purifying and pleasuring simultaneously.

In poetry Judith found an early and socially acceptable realm for expression. That the tone of Judith's poems changes so markedly over the course of her exercise book, along with the script — indicating several years duration — that they become darker, and that they become preoccupied with a lost figure, all confirm that Judith's poetry reflected her experience of the world. For on the 3rd of September 1927, when Judith was just twelve years old, her mother died from complications arising from influenza. Her dying happened over several years, during which time she became practically immobile. Judith said it was a 'process that horrified and deeply marked me'.[213] The final day of her life was bright but cold. Judith remembered reading in the sun.

> When her nurses found me, she had already died as I could see at a horrified glance. My father and brothers were in tears beside her. I think I had known for so long that she would have to die that I had shut off the knowledge. When at last she died — on a day I can never remember without a shudder for her — the end of my childhood was final. Apart from grief, I had guilt to contend with. I knew I had not been able to comfort her or help her through those dreadful days at all, though I was the eldest and the girl, facts always emphasised when I failed in my duties. I could not even comfort my father and brothers, though I did what I could to keep myself from crying as they all stood together in tears in her bedroom.[214]

Ethel's death confirmed Judith's worst feelings about herself, derived from her experience of being female. Whereas her brothers could openly grieve for their mother, Judith was left with the guilt that she had made Ethel's suffering worse, and a sense of unfulfilled responsibility. She was also on the cusp of puberty, now more aware of her gender.

In response, Judith threw herself into being female in the manner her mother had modelled. She darned her father's socks, took to knitting and crocheting. She became overly protective of her brothers, especially towards rival mother figures, such as governesses. But Judith's performance of a mother was clumsy and impossibly inadequate. When she sensed that her father looked to the governesses – 'helpless and not particularly intelligent…desperate for marriage to rescue them from their unhappiness' – as potential wives, she became intensely possessive towards him. Grandmother May tried her best to soften the blow, singing her grandchildren to sleep in the aftermath of Ethel's death.[215]

When Phillip escaped on a holiday to Queensland, Judith and her brothers stayed at Wongwibinda, where their aunt Weeta resumed their schooling through the Blackfriars correspondence course that Ethel had previously overseen. On return, Phillip introduced his children to a city woman named Dora, whom he was engaged to marry. In November 1928, fourteen months after Ethel's death, Phillip remarried. He had two children with Dora: Annette (now known as Pollyanne Hill), born in 1930, and David, born in 1933. The same month that Phillip was married Judith won first prize in the senior section of the *Sydney Mail*'s children's poetry competition. It seemed it was the only thing female she could successfully do.

Judith never felt an affinity with Dora. Even at the age of eighty-one Judith spoke about her resentfully, though acknowledged that it must have been difficult for Dora too. Her father, she reflected, in the way many loyal daughters imagine of their fathers in instances of such apparent disloyalty, was a well-meaning dupe. He missed Ethel terribly, Judith perceived, and 'imagined Dora was very like her (!) and Dora traded on this supposed resemblance'. To Judith she was not just manipulative, she was unimpressive: 'the poor woman was so pitifully inefficient that pity was the only kind response'. Judith responded by turning away from the family, emotionally and geographically: 'I went to boarding school soon after they were married and kept out of their way as much as I could after school finished'.[216]

According to Pollyanne Hill, now in her eighties, the ill feeling came entirely from her half-sister. Others in the family say that Judith was not the only one who had difficulty getting along with Dora.[217] Referring to Judith as she was known in the family, Hill insists that Dora 'admired Doo'. She recalls that Dora preserved 'every little scrap of paper' on which Judith wrote poetry; 'whereas Doo was inclined to just throw them out, Mum saved every little bit'.

> She wanted us all to read her work, absorb her, appreciate the fact that she was our sister. She was proud that Judith was a part of the family. Any tension at all was purely on Doo's part. [It] was only in Doo's imagination; all in her mind. It was just in Doo's general attitude that she felt this business of Mum usurping her place, producing two children.[218]

Though Judith was never close to her half-sister, she was always kind to her. Hill remembers that Judith gave her a subscription to *Walkabout* in her teenage years. The magazine, published from 1934 until 1974, and with an interest in both culture and science, was designed to promote travel within Australia. Hill stayed with Judith and Jack McKinney at their home in Mount Tamborine in the 1950s. In 1968 Judith told a friend: 'I love my half-sister Annette very dearly, though I don't see much of her'. It was somewhat of a surprise, then, when Judith did not mention either Hill or her brother in *Half a Lifetime*: 'perhaps a mention would have been understandable, but we weren't mentioned at all...well, we accepted it'. Veronica Brady's biography maintained the silence.[219]

Silence was a common response to difficulty in the Wright family. Judith, her brothers and her father responded to the trauma of Ethel's death by not speaking about it. Looking back, Judith said: 'the reasons nobody spoke of her [Ethel] after she died were mainly because my Dad mourned her terribly and couldn't mention her without crying'.[220] Judith seems to have suffered in a similar way. She dealt with her mother's death by trying to forget the years she had spent with her. In her interviews for the National Library of Australia, when Judith was in her seventies, she confessed to having problems with her memory. Extraordinarily, she said that until that time she had not thought about her childhood.

I've only just got around to remembering those things. I think my memory's not all that good. Seventy-two this year and although my childhood comes back in fits and starts, I have a problem with it, the reason being that my mother was very ill during most of my childhood and died when I was ten. So that a lot of that area there is more or less blacked out for me.

Old age may explain why Judith incorrectly remembered being ten years old, rather than twelve, when her mother died. On the other hand, it was a significant mistake from someone who could recall events which took place when she was two. The mistake was not a one off. In *Half* Judith said that she was eleven years old when her mother died. She also said that Phillip remarried just two months after Ethel's death when in fact it was in the following November of 1928, fourteen months later.[221]

Judith's memories of her mother were tainted by her death, so that it was painful to remember her at all. Because memory is only maintained by the act of remembering, Judith forgot. In 'Wedding Photograph 1913', she wrote:

> And she, pointing out birds or pansies' eyebrows,
> gentle, fighting increasing pain – I know her
> better from this averted girlish face
> than in those memories death cut so short.

In his memoir, Phillip recalled his wife with minimal detail. Of Ethel, in over 100 pages, he wrote: 'we had known each other since childhood, though apart from short social visits to Swallowfield at long intervals, we had seen very little of each other'. After another sixty pages he mentioned her for the second and final time: 'On 3 September 1927 my wife Ethel died'.[222]

The final poems in Judith's scrapbook of juvenilia are written in a well-controlled, mature hand. They speak of the dead and of travelling to where the dead are now. They still speak of escape, but far less joyfully. One poem, 'I Will Come Back', expresses a desire to return to the past.

I will come back to ye, all my dear mothers,
Mothers of wind and of water,
I that was once your daughter,
...
I will come back to ye, merry my brothers;
Brothers of creeks all a-glister,
I that was once your sister,
...
Ye that have given me all of my laughter
Ye that have wept with my weeping,
Ye that have slept with my sleeping,
I will come to ye again.
When I was young, 'twas ye taught me,
When I was lost, then ye sought me;
I will come to ye again.

Judith said that she went to boarding school in 1929 to escape Dora. But she may have gone to the New England Girls' School (NEGS) anyway, for it was where her mother and aunt had gone at the same age of fourteen. Situated just outside of Armidale, it had a reputation as the place where wealthy rural families of New South Wales and Queensland sent their daughters. With an annual fee of £106 in 1931, NEGS was the fifth most expensive girls' school in the country. But money was not the only barrier to entering NEGS. Parents had to provide two references for their daughter and a statement of their health with the application form. The school boasted grounds covering 150 acres, including a horse paddock for girls who chose to bring their ponies from home. The NEGS uniform could be purchased exclusively at David Jones. Highly controlled social events were arranged with boys from The Armidale School, mostly sons of graziers.[223]

Judith felt that NEGS was a kind of preparatory school, albeit modelled on a British boys' grammar school with its espousal of masculine values: 'there were no references to exemplary females', wrote Judith, 'though Mrs Beeton and Coco Chanel at least might have been held up as encouragement'. Indeed, NEGS catered to those parents who wished only that their daughter would get married 'well'; a separate stream titled Domestic Science tutored girls in 'home-making' skills alone. Judith was not part of this stream but the school had a particular notion of how all girls should behave and think. Hygiene, singing and divinity were compulsory subjects for girls in the mainstream, who were prepared for confirmation by the chaplain. A fundamental objective of the school was instilling proper, though not overly zealous, Anglican values. A NEGS contemporary described headmistress Miss Nona Dumolo as the 'hub from which radiated a balanced religious fervour'. It was in keeping with Phillip's approach to religion. Hill recalls that her father 'did not talk to the children about God but wanted them to have a religious background'. At NEGS, a deeply reverential attitude towards the English monarchy was also encouraged. When describing NEGS's values, Hill, who went there herself, uses one word: 'conservative'.[224]

The values of honesty and integrity which Miss Dumolo was said to embody did not always filter down into the student populace, according to Judith. In an undated, unpublished short story titled 'Save the First Dance', Judith describes the experience of going to a private boarding school. 'What I felt most', the unnamed protagonist begins, 'when I first left home for that boarding-school was above all how thin, how limited is human character'. She was disappointed to find that her companions 'seemed bent only on reflecting their parents' bored commercialism, and finally serving the equally limited men they would marry to their best advantage'. The girls were obsessed with fashion, with looks, with knowing what was vulgar and what was tasteful, with gossip and with becoming powerful by these means.[225]

In a draft speech about Judith, probably delivered at NEGS in the 1980s, New England historian Geoffrey Blomfield asserted that 'it would be foolish to claim much for the school' in Judith's success, and acknowledged that she did not enjoy her time there. His words may not have stirred loyalty in the current crop, nor self-belief: 'few, if any, old girls will ever climb as high up the mountain as Judith. The pity is that so few even attempt the foot-hills'. Blomfield, who was familiar with the school, identified aspects of its culture which prevented their rise, and which were similar to those Judith identified when describing it decades earlier: 'to-day NEGS is trying harder than ever to train mountaineers – people who will leave behind and below bias, bigotry and snobbery'.[226]

And yet, while the values of the student population did not accord with Judith's, and perhaps never would, an undated NEGS prospectus, seemingly from the 1930s, shows that it was much more than a preparatory school, and that it provided unrivalled opportunities for girls to develop a vast range of interests outside marriage. Compulsory subjects included English, Literature, Arithmetic, French, Latin, and several science subjects including Geology, Biology and Zoology. This allowed girls the option of sitting for public exams and attending university. At a time when few rural women attended university, especially by undertaking science courses, NEGS provided unusual academic opportunity: the options at NEGS were seemingly endless. When girls were tired of pony riding, they could practise their instruments in one of the ten soundproofed music rooms, browse the library or sit in the reading room. They could retreat to the art studio or photographic darkroom. Another way in which NEGS was more than a preparatory school was its emphasis on sport and outdoor activities, pursuits not strictly necessary to forming a good marriage. Team sports were compulsory. Daily drill lessons were taken. Horseriding, the NEGS prospectus stated, was an 'important part of the school'. In summer girls were taken to the nearby swimming pool. On first arriving at NEGS all girls had to have a tennis racquet.

The compulsory nature of these activities, and the school's related emphasis on good health, while in some regards suggestive of a progressive attitude to femininity, enforced a uniformity onto the lives of students and allowed NEGS to closely survey the girls' bodies. This extended to being weighed twice annually. On entering NEGS every girl was examined by a physical education mistress. As stated in the prospectus: 'defective postures receive special attention'. This mimicked, though less dramatically, the practice of taking nude posture photos of new students, rife amongst elite American universities in the 1930s.[227]

Judith, who felt physically defective in many ways, resented the compulsory sport and must have hated the detailed monitoring of her body. By the time she arrived at NEGS, at fourteen, she was intensely self-conscious. Puberty had been difficult. Her periods were heavy and it took a stranger to tell her that she needed to wear a bra. Her sense of shame extended to more public manifestations of her physicality as well.

> ...I knew, painfully as many girls know it, that at the ugly age of fourteen I was not only condemned to wearing glasses – and males seldom make passes at such girls – but was tongue-tied and spotty and beginning to bulge awkwardly and unable to play games with conviction in a world where games and boys were evidently to be of the first importance.

Although describing herself as 'asocial', Judith believed that her appearance and lack of sporting prowess made it difficult to make friends anyway. And while this bothered her at times, it seems she had a powerful disdain for most of the girls in any case, as expressed in 'Save the First Dance': 'I looked at them, despaired, and became sullen and ugly to protect what was in my own heart. Spinning my cocoon of camouflaged dislike, I learned to live in it.'[228]

Judith felt ugly and alone as a teenager, but she had her consolations. In the same year at NEGS was her cousin Tina, whom she had spent many happy days horseriding alongside. Tina was tall, attractive and outgoing; everything Judith was not. Hill recalls that Tina was 'full of joy'. Tina was also loyal to Judith, taking her to friends' houses, for example, and providing her with a gown for their first dance. Judith and Tina remained friends all their lives. Apart from Tina, Judith's other consolation was literature. She loved having access to so many books at NEGS, and frequently read them under the table in classes she disliked, such as Arithmetic. Her English teacher, Miss Young, also made her life more interesting. She dared to suggest that George Eliot was as good as Dickens and Thackeray.

But Judith still felt intensely alone at NEGS. When May Wright died, during her first year there, she remembered resolving: 'I was now entirely on my own: nobody was going to love me or look after me'. Judith, not uncommonly for a teenager, especially perhaps for one who has lost their mother and, in a sense, their father, longed to be loved in an absolute sense. In love's absence she built a defensive wall around herself that did not admit any pretenders. Arguably this wall remained in place until her late twenties, when she met Jack

McKinney. Then, she wrote to him: 'I was never happy 'til I met you…
you made me'.[229]

Judith's understanding of herself as different from her peers,
in ways both good and bad, was heightened by two horseriding
accidents. The first broke her elbow, which healed badly and had to
be broken again by a doctor. Afterwards her arm would not straighten,
preventing her from partaking in sports at NEGS. 'As a concession to
conformity' she would play golf by herself, with the ultimate aim of
finding a spot to read and 'spend happy hours alone'.[230] Enforced rest,
while recovering from the accident, had mixed effects on her learning.
It meant that her mathematical skills, already dismal, suffered. But by
then she had determined to be a writer and school, as she told it later,
actually constrained her ability to engage with literature.

As an adult Judith reflected on the difference educational styles
made to her development as a writer. While undertaking correspondence school she often finished her lessons in the morning and was
encouraged to pursue her own reading in the afternoon. Boarding
school brought an abrupt end to this freedom: 'there seemed always to
be a bell ringing to signal a move to another lesson in another class-
room, or to a meal or to organised sport which took up much of the
supposed free time in the afternoon'. But it was more than this. School,
believed Judith, prevented her from taking her 'own way through the
text'. Educational institutions had a profoundly homogenising effect on
people's minds and it was only the freedom of correspondence school
which made her 'desire to be a writer into a reality', to enable and
strengthen her unconventional thinking. Perhaps it was a characteristic
bequeathed on all graduates of that system, she ventured.[231]

In a second serious horseriding accident, when she was fifteen,
Judith 'really damaged' herself. Riding with Tina, far from the house
at Wallamumbi, her horse fell suddenly and Judith landed heavily on
the ground. She lay there, next to the dead horse, for a long time,
coming in and out of consciousness while Tina fetched help. Adults
spooned brandy into her mouth and placed her in the shade. An
ambulance eventually came from Armidale and gave her morphine.
When Judith was examined in hospital it was found that she had
broken her pelvis in two places. The incident was reported in *The
Armidale Express*, under the title 'Serious Accident', the first newspaper

reference to Judith in a life of many. She spent nine weeks at Scots Hospital in Sydney, with her legs and hips in plaster. At the end of her time there it was discovered that one leg was 2 centimetres shorter than the other. More astonishingly, a gynaecologist told her that she would never have children. But by then she had decided that she had no interest in boys. It was the ultimate confirmation of her failings as a female, as defined by the way that she had been brought up to understand her gender.[232]

In fact, Judith did go on to have a daughter, Meredith McKinney. McKinney said of her mother's experience growing up that it was 'one long trial'. Judith, at eighty, reminded her 'beloved cousin' Tina: 'your happy childhood wasn't mine'. Judith's ill and dying mother dominated her home life. That she felt she could not relieve Ethel of her miseries made her feel inadequate. It seemed she did not possess the necessary feminine qualities. But, amongst all this unhappiness and pain, there were glimmers of hope. May had given her granddaughter an impressive and unconventional example of what a woman could do on her own. Sybylla, though 'a little over the odds' with her stockwhip, had done it too. With these women in mind, onwards Judith went, out of her unhappy childhood, her tortured teenage years, into young adulthood and the streets of Sydney.[233]

CHAPTER 4

Becoming Modern

Much of Judith's young life reflected the strength of gender divisions within her society. She knew, from a young age, that her brothers would inherit the land she could not. She saw how her mother's illness emphasised the isolation a pastoralist's wife endured. She observed the disappointment and dismay of others who regarded her, and her unconventional grandmother, as unfeminine. Although boarding school was not an easy existence, there – in books, in the opportunities the school provided for further education – she glimpsed more of the world beyond, where being a woman was not as limiting as her familial society seemed to suggest. In 1934 she would be cast into it: to Sydney, a modern metropolis which had more in common with cities half a world away than with Wallamumbi, New South Wales. On the street, at the cinema, in her various living quarters, Judith encountered new models of living. It was at this point that her life diverted most radically from the traditions and expectations of her family.

Judith's three years at the University of Sydney are only briefly canvassed in current biographical literature, creating the impression that this was a time of little importance to her development as a poet and intellectual. It was an understanding established in Veronica Brady's *South of My Days* (1998), which addressed the period in just eleven out of a possible 500 pages. In *Half a Lifetime* (1999), Judith gave the period a similar weighting, possibly unwittingly. Compiling the book in her eighties, principally from memory – a memory that was notoriously bad – Judith could not add much to Brady's account of the period. For Fiona Capp, in *My Blood's Country* (2010), the university years did not represent a significant period in Judith's life; she mentions only in passing that Judith studied and lived in Sydney. It is in Brisbane, in the early 1940s, that Capp identifies a life-defining shift from country to city: 'desperate to escape the expectations of the conservative, rural society she had grown up in, she fled to Brisbane in the spring of 1943 and immediately felt as if she had entered a foreign country'.[234] Almost a decade earlier Judith entered a place that would have been, by most measures, even more foreign.

The effect of these biographical works, whether deliberate or not, was to suggest that Judith's university experience did not substantially change her; that what happened there mattered little to her life and career beyond. Could this have been the case? Although Judith had some metropolitan attitudes before leaving New England, Sydney, its university and the cultural norms that existed within both, altered her. This Judith's father predicted. Phillip's attempts to prevent her from leaving, detailed in this chapter, underscore how significant her move to the city was. It was not just that Phillip did not like cities in the same way as 'many country people' did not like them, as Brady put it.[235] It was much more than this. As discussed in Chapter 2, Phillip was a principal protagonist in a plan to reorient Australia towards the regions. In this chapter we see how young people and tertiary education were central to that plan. In leaving New England, Judith was indicating, at eighteen, that she did not want to be a part of it. What she sought was something altogether different.

Judith's migration to the city echoed the major transformation of Australian society during the period. As Phillip's political experience would increasingly demonstrate, the pastoral station was no longer the centre of power. The cities were. As a teenager Judith must have seen that the rural ideal Phillip and May had sought was fraying at the edges. Large numbers of people were moving to the cities, where there was more work, and where the promises of respite from working life, to pursue leisure or just be idle, seemed more plausible. The increasing density of cities such as Sydney changed its way of life, as did the phenomenon people were calling 'modernisation'. And so while in leaving New England for Sydney, Judith was diverting from a family tradition in one sense, in another she was doing what Wyndhams in Australia had always done: seek to be part of the action, to occupy the sphere of society which shaped all others. And, increasingly in Modern Australia, the influential went to university.

Once in Sydney, Judith's behaviour evolved in ways consistent with a new understanding of femininity, embodied by the so-called Modern Woman. Very little has been written about the impact of modernity on university students during this period, but new conceptions of identity had a significant impact on the way people – particularly women – thought of themselves. The Modern Woman, as discussed by the media of the day, rejected established ideas about fashion, behaviour and her body. Her defining characteristic was a tendency towards provocation. In Sydney, the Modern Woman was variously condemned and revered. Judith, a naturally confident, independent, even brazen young woman, entered this contentious territory and took her position with fortitude. She became a modern exemplar. By the standards of New England, and of still many in Sydney, Judith during these years might have been deemed shocking – *if only they knew.* But within another Sydney circle, made up of young provocateurs like herself, within the anonymity of a city, within the bosom of independence money afforded, she was just another modern woman making her own decisions. It was an anonymity and independence unthinkable in New England. Judith was changed by Sydney because it made change possible.

At NEGS Judith had known that she wanted to go to university. This is why she, unlike her cousin Tina, persevered with school. Such perseverance did not extend to Mathematics, which she withdrew from in her final years, objecting to aspects of the discipline. Equations were 'sensible [but]…things like long division used to get me completely'.[236] This would be an important decision. Without Mathematics Judith could not matriculate. Unmatriculated students could study at various universities in Australia in the 1930s, but at the University of Sydney they could not graduate. Yes, they could attend lectures and sit for exams. It was just that every time their name appeared on official, and public, university material a telltale asterisk would sit alongside, denoting their lowly status. In 1934, there were eight people enrolled in first-year Arts on this basis, from a class of 153 students. At the University that year there were 3,043 students.[237]

Without graduation, going to university could have no obvious vocational outcome. Why did Judith want to go? When asked late in life, she said that she went to become a writer and that university enabled her to attend to her most urgent requirement, to 'be let loose in a library', and not just any one. She yearned for the expanse of an internationally stocked institution. In 1932, the year that Judith finished at NEGS, New England could not provide this. In Australia at the time, there were no universities outside of the capital cities. While Armidale was beginning to pioneer rural tertiary education, with the establishment of a teachers' college in 1928, that institution's library was a small room with a couple of bookshelves. Country libraries, in general, Judith dubbed 'absolutely unhelpful', confirming Humphrey McQueen's description of them, during the period, as consisting of nothing more than a dictionary, a handful of westerns, some light romances, a few detective stories and an 'out-of-date encyclopedia'.[238]

The Fisher Library, at the University of Sydney, provided a strong contrast. It was widely considered an 'outstanding library of its time' and 'worthy of any institution in the world' when it was built twenty-five years earlier. In Australia it provided the best access to the latest thinking from around the world. A generous bequest in 1885 by shoemaker Thomas Fisher allowed the University to expand its collection from 12,000 volumes to almost 250,000 by 1920. The book fund continued to finance the purchase of books, even during the Depression when no other sources were available. The Fisher's impressive collection was matched by its building, another product of the bequest, which was so grand that it was compared to Westminster Hall in London. Spanning 50 feet, the open timbered cedar roof included intricate gothic detailing, most notably gargoyles which Assistant Librarian John Le Gay Brereton described as 'grin[ning] in stony ecstasy from every cornice'. By the early 1930s, 250 students could sit at one time in the reading room, surely grinning at their own good fortune.[239]

When asked how she had felt about the prospect of going to university but not graduating, Judith said later that she had known degrees were used by women 'for teaching and that's all'. It was another instance of the young Judith eschewing conventionality with apparent ease. But had she worried that she would not be admitted in the first place? Official University documents from the period stated that the unmatriculated could only be admitted in exceptional circumstances. Judith had not considered this a serious possibility: 'they didn't mind as long as they got paid!' How could she, a nineteen year old from New England, be so confident? Judith's actual experience may have been less straightforward than her accounts portray. She did not, for instance, mention that Phillip was angered by her failure to matriculate and told her she would live to regret it.[240]

Moreover, the idea that she would make a living from writing must have seemed unlikely. This was 1930s Australia and she was a country girl. While Miles Franklin was an inspiration, her trajectory was rare – almost unique. To embark on university with no realistic vocational plan was, of course, a privilege made possible by her family's wealth. Some of Judith's contemporaries approached university in the same manner; often they were women who planned to meet their husband at university, or understood that any vocation they undertook would only last as long as they were unmarried. In some rare instances, in Judith's, society's expectation that a woman will be financially dependent on a man enables her to pursue an improbable, financially insecure profession.

Going to university would mean living in Sydney, and this held an allure mixed up with the usual attractions for a nineteen year old. Recollecting her first dance in New England, in the year before attending university, Judith recalled that her 'views on Keats and Shelley' had to be kept 'entirely to myself'. Those sons of graziers, her prospective life partners, had no interest in literature. In turn she found them boring. Their conversation was more likely to have run, as it had down the generations since George and Margaret, to rain, prickly pear, sheep and cattle prices. Looking back on this time, and her desire to go to university, Judith said: 'I needed to know what was going on'.[241] Something was happening elsewhere, something tantalising.

But it would not, in fact, be so easy to leave in the first place. There were things which threatened her from finding her way to the University, to the Fisher Library, to the reading room there with its open timbered roof, its gargoyles, its gothic carvings and fourteenth-century patterns alluding to a universal experience of contemplation.

In her memoir Judith evoked an atmosphere of anti-intellectualism within her family and the wider New England circle. She would, after all, be the first descendant of great-grandparents Weeta and Arthur Mackenzie to attend the University of Sydney. Many Wyndham descendants, including Judith's brothers, were 'rather wary of academia', notes cousin Cedric Wyndham, being 'practical men of the land'.[242] It was a similar situation to that which Patrick White remembered facing:

> Almost all the Whites remained wedded to the land, and there was something peculiar, even shocking, about any member of the family who left it. To become any kind of artist would have been unthinkable. Like everybody else I was intended for the land, though, vaguely, I knew this was not to be.

David Marr said of these generations of Whites: 'they were not readers...the stud book was the only volume they took willingly from their shelves'.[243]

And yet Judith's family was not so unaccustomed to reading and higher learning. Female cousins in more remote branches of the Wyndham family tree attended the University of Sydney before Judith, and her aunt Weeta paid for the university education of a number of cousins who followed.[244] May's allocation of finance to her grand-daughters' education spoke powerfully of the value she placed on education. Judith's great-grandmother on her mother's side, Angela Nina Spasshatt, whom she remembered well, established a school after the death of her husband, a Scottish surgeon and Fellow of the Natural History Society of Glasgow. Spasshatt, wrote Judith, had had 'enough lady-like education' herself to teach English, French, Writing, Arithmetic and Music to daughters of the 'New England gentry'.[245] In the early decades of the twentieth century it became increasingly common, and acceptable, for such daughters to look to university.

Nonetheless, the prospect of Judith attending the University of Sydney 'terrified' Phillip. His rural politics were premised on the belief that cities were 'unnatural and immoral places for human beings to live in'. Sydney in the early thirties *was* becoming less connected to nature and, by the standards of the times, less moral. As a result of the Depression, 33,000 people were homeless in Sydney during

1933 and 400,000 people were living in homes made from iron, calico, canvas, hessian and bark, in shanty towns on the edge of the city. Violent battles between the police and Unemployed Workers' Movement, often over tenant evictions, were common. Gambling, particularly SP bookmaking, took off with the advent of horseracing broadcasts. So too did racketeering. Street violence was on the rise and police corruption was blossoming. Judith was told: Sydney would be 'dangerous...with notorious murders, rumours of white slavers, razor gangs and other dangers rife for the unprotected young woman'.[246]

For many in the country all this immorality was no accident, but linked to the Lang Labor state government, elected in 1930. In rural areas outside the mining electorates anti–Lang sentiment was strong. Some of Phillip's fellow 1917 strikebreakers regrouped in a citizens' militia to confront the Premier. Rural separatist movements galvanised this discontent and were reinvigorated. Country Party historian Ulrich Ellis notes that members of his party felt so desperate when Lang was elected that the 'creation of New States appeared to be the sole hope of escape'. In 1931, he wrote, New South Wales 'faced the prospects of civil war'.[247] Though Lang was dismissed in 1932, rural conservatives remained alarmed by the knowledge that Sydney had elected a government which dramatically expanded the public service and threatened to withhold bank savings. They worried over developing socialist movements, mainly gathering strength in cities. And though Australian universities traditionally stood as a fortress against such radicalism, developments such as the creation of a Labor club at the University of Sydney in 1925, and the public broadcasts of philosophy professor and communist sympathiser John Anderson during the early 1930s, were evidence that even they were not completely free from the metropolitan madness.[248]

The Country Party and members such as Phillip had long recognised that the lack of rural universities intensified the movement of young populations towards the city. Phillip wrote about the phenomenon in his memoir:

> There were too many inducements already for young people from the country to look for city jobs, without forcing the best brains among them to go there for education and almost certain subsequent absorption.[249]

Judith was just nine when Phillip helped form the Armidale University Establishment Committee and progress towards the establishment of a New England university was swift throughout the 1920s as influential and wealthy figures came onboard.[250] There was reason to think one might exist in time for Judith. And then came the Depression. It was not until 1935 that the New South Wales government returned to the idea and agreed to support it. By then Judith had been out of NEGS for three years.[251]

Yet, even if UNEC had been up and running by 1932 it is unlikely that Judith would have agreed to go there. A university is more than its curriculum. Founding student Keith Leopold recalled that the UNEC library was a small room and that Armidale, with a population of 7,000, was 'rustic'. Though it had, by then, two cinemas and several cafes, the culture of the place was unsophisticated by city standards and depressed by a regional drought that did not abate until 1945. In contrast, Sydney in the early 1930s was just emerging from a massive cultural transformation which did nothing short of connect it to the great metropolitan centres of the world.[252]

Judith knew something was going on in Sydney. Something had happened there in the early decades of the twentieth century that separated it markedly from the large rural towns and port cities throughout New South Wales. While many country people saw this development as a drift towards the dangerously immoral, many in the city, especially young people, viewed it as progress. An exciting forward movement was occurring; Sydney was becoming 'modern'. Historian Jill Matthews writes of this time: people 'felt themselves being drawn into the modern world and they called themselves and others modern'. Tradition, which meant British colonial culture and economic practices, was its antithesis. The 'modern' manifested itself through all kinds of cultural practices – frequently considered American, always exciting and glamorous – such as dance, radio, photography, fashion, design, advertising, architecture and urban planning. Cinema, writes Matthews, was perhaps the most profoundly affecting of all these practices, choreographing the others with the image of glamorous

Hollywood, particularly the starlet: 'moving pictures blazed like a comet in the night-life sky with the other practices and entertainments streaming away in brilliant tails, scattering the sparks of modernity into everyday life'.[253]

The city and the country were increasingly touted as opposites. If the city represented an American flamboyance, the country maintained traditional, British values. If the city was excess, the country was restraint; this was often how it was thought of by those whose livelihood was threatened by an expanding metropolis. The widespread desire for experiences of the modern (cinema, stockings and magazines) pulled Australian capital and labour towards the cities, where secondary production most easily occurred. Primary producers countered shifts towards greater manufacturing in the Australian economy by arguing that it posed a moral threat. Whereas primary production took 'the materials of nature and transform[ed] them through human skill into objects of use', secondary production was simply a 'commercial process of turning those objects into commodities, especially cheap commodities, to be sold for a profit as an end in itself'. The rural economic system encouraged restraint; the metropolitan one encouraged greed. In the 1970s, Phillip observed with disapproval that attitudes towards material goods had shifted in accordance with the geographical shift so many Australians had made: although prosperous, his family had 'small material wants compared with modern days'.[254]

If Phillip worried that his daughter would yield to the city's seductions he was not alone. Much of the discussion about new cultural practices was concerned with their effect on young women. Many believed that her 'traditional fickleness and love of bright distraction' would find 'a new outlet in the ever-changing fashions of daily life and its amusements'. Advertisers seem to have shared this view; young women were their primary target.[255] In newspapers and magazines it was explained that the city's increased movement and population made social exchanges less formal, and less governable. The young rural woman, in particular, was troubled over. In 1922 the *Truth* ran an article titled: 'The Vortex. How Country Girls are Drawn In'.

> The girl who comes from the country to the city walks in a happy dream. There are shops, and shops, and shops, with wonderful displays

of things to wear...She marvels at the cafes and the swagger hotels with the constant stream of people passing in and out of their lounges – people who seem to spend all their time eating and drinking and have no more serious business in life to claim them...

The mass of people and buildings are 'overwhelming, incredible'. The city 'stupefies her'.[256]

Phillip wanted to prevent this becoming Judith's fate. When she said that she wanted to go to university she was, after all, just seventeen. Remembering their discussions, Judith wrote: 'he and Dora kept putting alternatives to the idea of university, including a couple of years at Hopewood House'.[257] It may have been a kind of concession – for Hopewood House was in Darling Point, Sydney – but the place was a finishing school. According to a 1941 advertisement for Hopewood, it was the 'only school of its kind in Australia', instructing young women in deportment, entertainment, housekeeping, citizenship, language, music, arts 'and all accomplishments'. A 1936 edition of *The Sydney Morning Herald* reported on its third anniversary dance by describing a series of elegant dresses worn by guests. The host, a Miss Nancy Jobson, 'received her guests wearing a gown of lees-of-wine georgette. She added a spray of daphne, which was presented to her by her pupils'.[258]

The suggestion of Hopewood House could hardly have been more out of keeping with Judith's aspirations. There, education was a means to marriage. There, women were practical about the benefits of status and wealth. Judith, on the other hand, was already attached to the more abstract, idealistic values embodied by education and literature. And she had already rejected the prospect of marriage. Phillip and Dora's suggestion indicates that they discounted Judith's ambitions, or did not understand them. Or maybe it was just a negotiating strategy. For Judith recalled that the prospect of Hopewood House made staying in New England for another year, until they could agree on something, more appealing. Judith's 'dear aunt Madeleine' offered her the position of governess to her cousin Cecily which, by then, Judith gratefully accepted.[259]

But this was only a short-term solution and by the end of 1933 the same dichotomy was at work. Though Judith's recollection of being presented with only two life choices – marriage or university – seems overly neat, at the time it may have appeared this way. Leaving home, by permanent arrangement, was a priority: 'Dora and I were not compatible and I could not see how we could get on together in the same house for long'. Options for leaving home and working, in a manner considered respectable by her society, were limited. Continuing to governess was one option but Judith had dim memories of her own governesses – whom she saw as chronically unhappy and desperate to escape through marriage – and she had no interest in teaching.[260]

University, on the other hand, fast-tracked entry into adulthood. Donald Horne, a student between 1939 and 1941, wrote of the transition:

> In my first fortnight at Sydney University I knew I was now a *man*... Before Christmas we were boys and girls. In March, by beginning our first term at university, we became men and women.[261]

This would be especially true for Judith, for whom attending university would mean living away from home. At the time, most young adults, even married ones, lived with their parents and adhered to strict rules governing social outings. Though university colleges attempted to maintain such standards, in truth – as Judith's experience bore out – they did not.

Phillip must have been a tolerant man. Given his anti-metropolitan views, given the liberties that life in the city, away from home, would afford his daughter, and given that university could have no clear vocational benefit for Judith, many parents would have simply said 'no'. Judith recalled that her father was 'terrified that going to university was going to be the ruin of me'. Terrified, he let her go. Today, Judith's daughter, Meredith McKinney, believes that Phillip's 'preparedness to send Mum to university...was pretty enlightened for a pastoralist'. This open-mindedness and tolerance became part of his identity as a parent, such that when Judith continued to rebel against the family's expectations, in the years following university, 'he felt a bit slapped in the face', explains her daughter, as if his efforts had not been appreciated. Judith's response, to accuse him of being 'outraged and reactionary', when she made unconventional, life-changing decisions, 'didn't suit his own self-image at all'. But, in time, and in other ways, Phillip must have felt that Judith was an appreciative and loyal daughter. She dedicated her first book of poetry, *The Moving Image* (1946) thus: 'to my father'.[262]

Phillip's decision to let Judith go to university reflects on his daughter's personality too. At seventeen, she was wilful, patient and brave. For someone who rarely ventured into a town like Armidale, Sydney must have been intimidating. But perhaps the prospect of Sydney in 1933 – with its trams, cars, masses of people, flats, fashions, gambling scene, its sophistication and its degeneracy – was less intimidating than home, now: Dad, Dora, Bruce, Peter, three-year-old Annette and baby David.

Phillip's acquiescence might be read as a lesson in parental foresight. For though Judith was undoubtedly influenced by metropolitan culture, ultimately she would revert to many of his views on the city itself, as discussed in Chapter 2, and spend her life outside them. She came to detest their incessant consumption, pace and pollution, and her personal letters reveal a considerable irritation whenever she travelled to them. She told her brother, in 1972, that a recent trip to Sydney may have 'shortened my life by months'.[263] And yet, while Judith may have come to abhor cities, it was only in them that she had the freedom to pursue unconventional ways of thinking and behaving. Gaining entry to university would be the first, formative move in this direction.

Did Judith encounter barriers to tertiary education, other than those created by her family? Her entry was the result of opportunities that were quite unusual, though not unprecedented, for a woman of her time and place. Women had been attending the University of Sydney since the mid 1880s but it took time before they constituted a sizeable population. During the 1910s and 1920s only 12.5 per cent of students were women; by the early 1930s it had increased to 27 per cent. Chapter 5 will show that women on campus faced opposition even then. Yet, by the 1930s, being a woman was less of an obstacle to tertiary education than being poor or, worse, being poor and from the country.

Students who attended public rural schools were the least likely to attend university and, once there, this personal history affected their university experience, as demonstrated by the story of Kathleen Price, ten years older than Judith, who grew up in Young, New South Wales. At her public high school, promising students were encouraged to move to the city; a metropolitan public school was thought to offer more opportunities than a rural one. Price remembers being the only person from her coeducational school that made the move. After attending North Sydney Girls High School, she received a scholarship to the University of Sydney and another, for her living expenses, to the Women's College. Still, she hurried through an Arts degree, not completing the final year, in order to gain a basic teaching qualification. Her parents needed her to earn money. If she had had the opportunity, said Price, she would have completed a long degree, like Medicine.[264]

Similarly, Nina Christesen, whom Judith would befriend during the early 1940s at *Meanjin*, recalled the constraints created by her family's economic situation. Christesen, who was four years older than Judith, also won scholarships for fees and board. The Women's College at the University of Queensland stipulated that residents could not be in paid employment and, as it was during the Depression and her father could not find work, she was forced to decline the residential scholarship and work during the day to support her family. Evening classes offered limited choice and she, like Price, chose the practical option of a teaching degree.[265]

Price and Christesen's experiences are supported by evidence showing that university students came mostly from metropolitan private schools during the 1930s. Lloyd Edmonds said of the University of Melbourne: 'of course, the overwhelming majority were private school boys'.[266] Of the women who attended Australian universities, most came from similar backgrounds. In 1935, at the University of Sydney Women's College, where Judith would ultimately find herself, approximately two-thirds came from private schools. Of these, two-thirds were metropolitan. While this was the dominant group at the College, there was a sizeable minority who came from private rural schools. One in every four or five of Judith's colleagues shared her background, making it difficult to accept, at face value, her statement afterwards that she felt 'something of an oddity' at the University, being 'almost the only one with a pastoral background'.[267] One other student, a White family member, came from NEGS that year.

Then, as now, a lack of money was more likely to make you an oddity at the University of Sydney. Less than 10 per cent of students in 1934, the year that Judith entered the University, were on state scholarships. But, as suggested by the previous stories, even these students relied on a family to provide their living expenses or, at the minimum, forgo the potential income their adult child could contribute. Without a scholarship, university was prohibitively expensive for average families. That year, the tuition, board, compulsory union and services fees for an unmatriculated Arts student living at the Women's College were about £169. Then there were clothing, entertainment, books and living costs outside of term time to consider. That £169 was about one-and-a-half times the average annual female wage, and it could not be loaned from the government. Working was difficult, if not impossible, since most subjects ran on weekdays. Price remarked of the period: 'it wasn't the thing to do'.[268] The thing to do was to have your expenses paid for by your family.

Judith acknowledged the difference money made. It was as if her grandmother May had propelled her into independence: 'I paid my way through university...on my grandmother's legacy'. Another advantage may have been her timing. The University of Sydney was under severe financial strain after the Depression because the reduction in produce prices impacted on the income of many rural middle-class families.[269] The student population actually shrank in the late 1920s, and by 1934 was just recovering; that year there were only 355 more students than a decade earlier. The University was also affected by substantially reduced government grants. The 1934 Calendar made special mention of the University's 'present most urgent needs' and described its funding as 'totally inadequate' in an appeal to potential benefactors.[270] Judith's sense that the University did not care that she was unmatriculated, as long as she could pay, was probably spot on. If Judith had been born a decade later she may have had more trouble entering. As it was, she had no trouble.

For all this, did Judith's time in Sydney really change her? Certainly, it allowed her to behave in new ways and provided examples of other women doing this. These were women who took advantage of new freedoms, the hallmarks of which historian Stuart Macintyre sees as 'higher education, professional careers, less constrictive clothing and even the freedom of the bicycle'. Freedom was everything. Moving around the city independently, browsing in a shop, refreshing at a restaurant or cafe: these would not have been the doings of Ethel Bigg when she was eighteen. Before World War I it was not considered respectable for young, middle-class women to walk the streets unchaperoned. By the late 1920s, as the female workforce increased, women were regularly seen shopping, travelling and dining by themselves in Sydney. Judith embraced these liberties, travelling every direction in the city on trams. Just for fun.[271]

This shaped the way Judith viewed Sydney, and enabled her to witness, for the first time, sights already familiar to the majority of Australians. This, she said, provoked in her a more critical attitude towards society. While the Depression had eased by 1934, unemployment did not get below 7 per cent and hovered around 10 per cent throughout the 1930s. The effects of this were shocking, for Judith had never seen poverty before: 'whatever miseries the streets of Armidale might have held, I had not seen them'. Now she did: 'Sydney, beyond the beaches and the cleanliness of Rose Bay...was simply a dirty and sorrowful city...poverty was pretty rife'. Judith concluded that 'it was not possible not to wonder what had gone wrong'.[272]

While other writers have suggested that Judith's remarkable sense of empathy developed as a child, within the isolation of a New England pastoral station, it seems worth asking how realistic this is. If someone does not bear witness, how much are they likely to understand? What if Judith had not left New England for several more years? If she had been in her mid twenties before she saw poverty for the first time? Had not begun to *wonder*? As I suggest in the remaining parts of this chapter and the following, if indeed Judith did begin to wonder, documents from the period suggest it was a gentle form of wondering, and that her starting point was not one of obvious empathy towards the less fortunate.

Newly acquired liberties gave young women the opportunity to observe their society independently, but they also created change at the most intimate level. Popular understandings of women's bodies – the way they should look, as well as their desires and capacities – shifted significantly during these decades. No longer, at least according to advertising, popular films, song lyrics and other forms of popular culture, were young women expected to look and behave demurely, or to cover up. This change was best illustrated by its extreme realisation, the flapper, a modern woman whose hemline was short, whose hair was shorter, and who did not disguise her make-up. Certain behaviours, such as drinking and smoking, were said to follow. Although the flapper is most closely associated with the 1920s – hemlines, for instance, were lowered by 1930 amongst the fashionable, with skirts hugging the female form – her attitude and disposition remained influential into the following decades. At heart, the flapper celebrated confidence and knowingness, even around men, and shunned modesty. If she wanted to wear a swimsuit in front of men on Bondi Beach, she would. The flapper was upfront, and not easily romanced like previous models of young women in popular culture. In short, the flapper confronted established understandings of women.

Many were repelled by the example she set. In 1925 the *Truth* printed a poem, 'Recipe for a Flapper', disparaging the model. To become a flapper, it instructed, 'locks should be/ removed until the absolute acme of hideousness is reached'. A woman should denigrate tradition as 'Old-/Fogeyism' and set her heart upon the 'Promised Excitement' of new behaviours, fashions and products. Once she was removed of 'all traces of Sweetness and Innocence', she should be stuffed 'tightly with a forcemeat of Evil Wisdom and Cheap Wit'. Suggesting a sexual promiscuity, the *Truth* described the flapper as sporting 'come-and-get-me eyes and a lurid tongue'. It was a brutal, even violent, fantasy of female disfigurement which implied young women were passive, easily prejudiced subjects of popular culture. Criticism came from other quarters too. Prominent Australian feminist Rose Scott 'deplored bobbed hair and smoking', and said that young women 'who went in for surfing are the limit'. For Scott, 'the modern woman was in relentless pursuit of the attention of the other sex'. Such advocates for the advancement of women believed this model of femininity was neither freeing nor dignified.[273]

But what of Judith? Did this new, provocative model of femininity influence her behaviour? Although there is some contention amongst historians about whether the glamorisation of a more forthright and provocative female persona actually changed the lives of young

Australian women (Anne Summers, for example, notes it did 'not produce a sexual revolution'), for a woman like Judith, who lived on a healthy income and had no deeply held religious convictions, life was very different from the majority. Diaphragms, the most popular, safe and effective method of contraception, were used mainly by middle-class women as they required medical assistance to administer, and this was not provided by the State.[274] Similarly, in the event of an unwanted pregnancy, money gave women access to medical abortions, as is starkly illustrated in *Come In Spinner* (1951), Dymphna Cusack and Florence James' fictionalised account of a group of young women in early 1940s Sydney.

If canvassing Judith's intimate experiences appears nosey, one should consider Matthews' defence of discussion, within historical scholarship, of the 'apparent trivia' of 'women's bodies, beauty, pleasure and sexuality' during the 1930s. Shifting conceptions of women's bodies had a profound effect at the personal level, she argues: they altered a woman's understanding of her own 'subjectivity – of desire and self-affirmation'. A woman's licence to govern her body enabled her to more fully participate in all aspects of public life, and this changed society as a whole.[275]

Understanding the degree to which Judith embraced such attitudes helps make clear the impact of her time in Sydney, where images and examples of the Modern Woman were more available than in country New South Wales, particularly on a remote pastoral station. Given that biographical accounts of Judith have given scant attention to her time in the city, this is one way of testing whether that emphasis is appropriate. And, since many aspects of 'modernity' were bundled together, even by those experiencing them, and pitted against 'tradition', it also reflects Judith's amenability to new poetic modes and intellectual approaches. Certainly, Judith's university contemporaries tended to see all culture divided between old and new, between tradition and progress. One editorial in a University of Sydney student magazine rallied the troops to the latter cause: 'it is our duty to adapt ourselves to these new surroundings, and we cannot do that if we sanctify the customs and traditions of another century'.[276]

How a person looked and behaved, in the context of such a paradigm, carried weight. Whether a young woman chose to wear a skimpy bathing suit, or engage in rigorous outdoor activity might tell us more about her attitude to social change than statistics such as the age at which she was married, or whether she was in paid employment. Such acts signified one's support for the 'new'. Did eighteen-year-old Judith Wright, who, as she would tell Jack McKinney in later years, had come fresh from an isolated pastoral station with a 'nineteenth-century atmosphere', who wore glasses, 'was tongue-tied and spotty and beginning to bulge awkwardly', who had never had a boyfriend, who spent her spare time reading in a tree…Did she become a Modern Woman? Or did she, as the editorial put it, sanctify the customs of another century?

A photograph from 1938, two years after Judith left university, shows her striding along a Sydney street.[277] She wears a long, fitted skirt and matching cream jacket, which emphasises her waist. From her hand hang leather gloves; under her arm is tucked a matching clutch. Above her dark cropped hair a smart black hat sits pointedly askew. From underneath she looks dead ahead, making no concession to her photographer: no smile, nor any pretence of shyness. Judith walks boldly. Behind her, a man in a doorway studies her rear. Another photograph, this one a portrait, reveals a knowing but incomplete smile dressed in dark lipstick. Her frock incorporates the fashionable element of a bow tie. Judith's description of these years indicates that she did, like the *Truth* girl, walk in a 'happy dream'. In just the way that newspaper warned parents, Judith embraced the liberties the modern city afforded her. She revelled in fashion, the cinema, the beach and extensive socialisation. And just like the flapper who enjoyed these things, Judith's attitudes to sex and to her physical and mental capacities radically challenged previously dominant ideas of femininity. Behaving respectably was not a priority; having fun was. She became the quintessential Modern Woman.

Judith's account of this time reads like the enunciation of a strategy for social success. According to Judith, the motivation behind her female friendships was to a) become popular, and b) meet popular men. She was neither sweet, nor innocent.

> Fairly astute over how to get where I wanted to be, I made friends with beautiful girls. Cecily Nixon, with extraordinary depths in her green eyes and her wide white smile in a tanned face, was...for once without a male nearby. I inveigled her into my seat and clung to her thereafter... she put up with me from then on and I tagged near her picking up male crumbs from her table.

The strategy led her to become 'part of a group of undeniably beautiful women and my glasses and thick ankles seemed to cease to matter'. Judith was invited to balls. Men who were 'unlucky with the others, fell back on me, so to speak, and there were plenty of them'. Of course money aided these efforts at social leverage. May Wright had stipulated in her will that Judith should receive an income while at university. This allowed her to acquire a dressmaker who fashioned current styles, which she considered another necessary line of attack, given her comparative natural disadvantage: 'if I was not beautiful like my friends, at least I had clothes'.[278]

In second year, her efforts were rewarded when the student newspaper *Honi Soit* mentioned her in their social column. 'Quadrangles', which so often reported on the beautiful Cecily Nixon's latest doings, isolated Judith when describing a men's informal: 'Judith Wright in cigar-brown crepe contributed to the general gaiety'. She was part of the popular crowd. Nixon's weekend tennis parties were reported in the University newspaper.[279] When they weren't playing tennis or attending balls, Judith and her friends travelled by tram to Bondi Beach. Sometimes they slept there overnight. And, of course, they went to the cinema. American films were influencing the fashion houses in a way never before seen. When Greta Garbo wore her little velvet hat over one eye in the 1930s film *Romance*, it was said to influence women's hat positioning for the next decade. Judith's own placement reflected the influence of fashion and cinema in her life. She remembered: 'those were the times when Hollywood was a major influence on everybody's life'.[280] Not everybody's, but certainly Judith's.

A contrast might be made with Kathleen Price, who attended the Women's College a few years before Judith. Her story demonstrates how some others, including more 'traditional' women like Price, regarded women who went to dances and prioritised socialisation.

Price was 'shocked' by their behaviour. She described herself as shy and considered some of the more confident women to be living lives 'way out of my experience'. She found the difference 'overwhelming'.

> I had been brought up in a very strict Methodist home where you didn't dance, and didn't play cards...and only went to Church on Sundays... and to meet with people who thought nothing of those things, and had such totally different attitudes to such things...also smoking was just beginning, and a few of the girls smoked.[281]

Judith did not say whether or not she smoked, nor whether she attended church. Judging from her accounts, the former seems likely; the latter very unlikely. She certainly danced.

Phillip's reaction to his daughter's financial extravagance suggests he too found some of her behaviour shocking. Judith had not imagined that her father would see the itemised details of the expense account he had set up. When he did, she was 'pulled up sharply', but considered herself 'well ahead of the game' with a complete wardrobe for any occasion. Looking back, Judith remembers asking herself at the end of her first year: 'what, after all, was I doing at university, apart from having a ball, or a series of balls?'[282] She knew, she said, that her passion for frivolity and fun was set against deprivation widely experienced outside the University and, she said, she had felt guilty about it. The conviction with which she appeared to be carefree and confident betrayed a deeper uncertainty, inflamed by Phillip's recriminations.

One aspect of the Modern Woman which Judith found difficult to emulate was her enthusiasm for sport. Still, she tried. At NEGS, as noted in Chapter 3, Judith had been 'unable to play games with conviction', being both uninterested and immensely self-conscious. At the University of Sydney Judith became secretary of the athletics club. It seems unlikely that Judith actually participated in the sport given her lack of experience and the fact that it was an overwhelmingly male-dominated activity. Young women of the period tended to favour tennis, swimming, cricket and football; it was not until the mid 1950s that a separate athletics club for women was even formed at the University. In the mid 1930s, her participation in athletics would have been as unorthodox as a woman boxer's today. That she volunteered to help administer the athletics club is further evidence, if it were needed, of Judith's interest in spending time with men; one of her tasks was to organise the club party; another might have been watching club members exert themselves in undersized clothing.[283]

Though she did not play sport, Judith revelled in exalted physicality. She delighted in bodysurfing, which she had mastered in her youth on annual holidays at May's beachside cottage. Surfing remained, throughout her life, a 'joy'. The opening line of 'The Surfer', from *The Moving Image* (1946), expressed it similarly: 'he thrust his joy against the weight of the sea', and made clear the association Judith had between surfing and sex. As a student, she remembered, she slept on the beach. Another poem, published in 1974, and titled 'Surfer', describes surfing at sunset with one of her university boyfriends, Johnny. Perhaps they stayed there together.

> Forty years from the first to the last lover?
> Lord, what a span for wrestle and kiss to cover.

The rhythm of the waves and the enthusiasm of the surfer suggest a memory of reciprocated sexual pleasure: 'the waves come in. You breast them, over or under,/ find your feet again, wait for another'.[284]

Of her casual interactions with men Judith remarked later that they were, for her, 'quite an innovation'.[285] Sex before marriage, indeed sex without any intention towards marriage, was quite an innovation for any woman of her class and time. Literary scholar Susan Sheridan has noted that Judith was one of a number of women writers of her generation who 'mostly led lives of apparently conventional hetero-sexuality'.[286] It may be that the degree to which her sexuality and its associated behaviour broke with convention has been underestimated. In her late teens she embraced a sexual identity which defied the expectations of her upbringing, and which arguably emboldened her for a life of sexual transgression, including writing about sex from a woman's point of view; living 'in sin', albeit in a monogamous relationship with Jack McKinney; and having passionate affairs, often in secret, after his death.

Back in the 1930s, sexual freedom could only be offered by a city like Sydney, and only taken up by some women. There, young women with money were making decisions about their bodies which appeared to be unbound by the expectation of marriage and the need to preserve a weak, childlike physical form. Moreover, around the city, the emphasis on desire and choice created a frisson, argues Matthews; brimming with 'mass-produced and mass-consumed phenomena', the place itself, 'excited, created and re-created libidinal wants and longing'.[287] What made Judith's autonomy and freedom of desire all possible, of course, were her living arrangements, ones that she could have only found within the city. Virginia Woolf may have prescribed a room 'of one's own' for cerebral purposes; Judith found it could function to liberate at a variety of levels. It gave her space to pursue poetry and men without the expectations of convention. Surely this was the pivotal moment of 'escape' in her life?

For her first year, Judith stayed at a boarding house, run by a cousin of Dora's, in Military Road, Neutral Bay. Living in a boarding house was no small thing since, for many in the country, such tenements represented the worst aspects of city living. In the same property would be strangers. The 1920s saw a spectacular increase in the number of flats in Sydney, particularly in Neutral Bay, and though the real threat of flat living remained unspoken, it is clear that in the popular imagination they represented a moral danger. Opponents of flat development alluded to a sexual deviancy encouraged by close-quarter living.[288] Neutral Bay at least had the virtue of being middle class. Judith liked the fact that it offered views of the harbour but resented being 'looked after' by her step-relative. Also living at the house were the mother and sister of novelist Nina Murdoch, a connection Judith considered, for a while at least, 'glamorous'. But her stay ceased towards the end of her first year when Dora's cousin sold the house.[289]

Without informing her father, Judith secured a room-for-let in Glebe. This, she later joked, was a 'dreadful thing to do' for a middle-class woman. Inner city Glebe was home to many of Sydney's slums, and violent struggles between police and members of the Unemployed Workers' Movement often took place there. Judith knew that Phillip considered the suburb 'a very low address indeed'.[290] Moreover, little about the house, for which she was the only lodger, suggested middle-class propriety. Judith recalled that it was cheap – only fifteen shillings a week – and dirty. Her room, which sat on the upper floor of the two-storey terrace house, contained nothing but a double bed. For meals, she ate at the local workingman's cafe. Judith recalled, 'There was a sort of shower room downstairs but it had to be cleared of mops and buckets, and hot water brought in a bucket from the wood stove... the dunny in the backyard was not inviting and the landlady and her man were chary with the cleaning and the laundry.'[291]

The location and condition of the house were not Judith's only act of rebellion. Whereas in Neutral Bay she could be observed by a family member (albeit a remote one), Judith arrived at the Glebe house anonymously. This was a period in which it was unusual for young, middle-class women to live by themselves.[292] So widespread was a belief in the importance of respectability that the University stipulated acceptable student living conditions, stating that 'no student shall be allowed to attend the lectures or classes of the University unless he dwells' with a parent or guardian, a relative who has been approved by the University, in an educational establishment such as a college, or in a boarding house licensed by the University. Judith was probably risking her place at the University by staying at the Glebe house. She knew that it was not 'respectable'; all that might have made it so, she remembered, was its proximity to the evangelical Anglican church, St Barnabas, next door.[293]

But Judith was a modern woman who understood that morality could be determined by individuals, not by a religion, or by social mores disguised by terms such as 'respectable'. By the end of her 'heady' first year she had a boyfriend, 'in fact a couple'. During her second year she got a new one, John, the subject of 'The Surfer', in which she declared him her first lover. When she returned to Wallamumbi with one of these boyfriends, a medical student, he 'took one look at his psychiatry textbook and said we had a problem', referring to Dora. Judith, her miseries and her desires to escape them, were being validated in all manner of ways.[294]

For male students, Judith's independence – so rarely achieved – may have added to her allure. In Donald Horne's student memoir he describes his campaign to lose his virginity, which relied on finding a woman who would make herself and a space available. Horne may not have been the kind of man to whom Judith was attracted but, judging from his memoir, his attitude to women was shared by many male students.

> There seemed to be some subtlety in relationships with women that I could not yet understand, but I now had my eye on a woman who, though I did not love her, might settle the question for me. She did not look like a film star, and she wanted conversation to be about personal relations between people, a subject that bored me as meaningless and non-discussable. But there she was.

What is more, she had her own flat. It was not long before Horne found himself in her bed where his 'delight was reached with a puzzling suddenness'. He became 'immediately proud that I had now fulfilled one of the technical requirements of manhood, performing an act that many men in Arts II had not yet achieved'.[295] Tellingly, he knew.

Frank accounts of students' sexual lives from this period are thin on the ground. If Horne were all we had to go on, it would seem women did not stand to profit much from sex with male students. And yet Judith's account offers an alternative perspective. She was as strategic as Horne, and similarly cavalier about commitment. But for her the stakes were higher since she believed she risked her life if she became pregnant because of the damage to her pelvis caused by the horseriding accident. Judith imagined that she would never be able to have children (later, she said that she had only been able to because her father had funded medical specialists) and this gave sex a completely different meaning. She spoke cryptically, but deliberately, about the precariousness of her position. Late in life, writing to her cousin Tina, she said that at university she 'never dared to have a love affair with any but medical students...and had to keep picking them up and dropping them not to get too involved. Knife-edge stuff that was'.[296] Medical students had, presumably, a better knowledge of contraceptives. It seems that what she meant by 'not getting too involved' was not getting engaged, and therefore being expected to have children.

Judith might have risked more than most but she was shadowing the flapper in seeking casual sexual encounters; there was cultural precedent for her bravado and breeziness. In the year after university, Judith left for Europe and 'acquired a young man on the voyage'. Elsewhere she described Tony as someone whom she 'picked up'. The relationship was short, but they did spend nights together in London. They slept on the embankment, 'as everybody did, and enjoyed ourselves thoroughly'.[297] Where there was opportunity, Judith was persistent.

> On the voyage home I met a young man who attracted me. We started a flirtation – and by that time I wanted more from a flirtation than a few kisses. I got the kisses but Philip (let's call him), though unmistakably sexually attracted to me, would have nothing to do with what I regarded as 'love'. At last I discovered the reason for this remarkable self-denial – he was a Jew and did not think it fair to a non-Jewish girl to get involved on that level. He would not and could not marry me so bed was out of the question.[298]

The apparently random use of her father's name is striking. Was it a genuine slip? Or a provocation to would-be biographers? Was she simply having fun with us by spelling 'Philip' with one 'l' instead of two, as her father's name is spelt? It is hard to imagine that both Judith and her editor would overlook the name's significance. It might have been her way of saying that even in old age she could be scandalous.

The passage confirms that Judith had settled any moral concerns about sex outside marriage; she knew most men could overlook them too: she was surprised when 'Philip' did not. Back in Sydney she was reunited with John, to whom she had agreed to test her relationship by not having any contact while she was away. He was unimpressed when she told him of her 'overseas experiences'. From this she concluded that 'faithfulness', at least on the part of women, was an absolute necessity for men who wanted to pursue a 'respectable profession'.[299] These must have been the terms in which John couched it anyway. There was that word 'respectable' again, and there was Judith treating it with disdain.

Respectability eventually imposed itself on the nineteen-year-old Judith. Her reassuring, but evasive, letters to her father about her new lodgings did not work. He asked a Sydney friend of Ethel's to check on Judith in Glebe. The friend arrived from Woollahra to find Judith working on the floor, surrounded by a sea of papers; the room's only piece of furniture, a bed, an alarming reminder of Judith's moral precariousness. She was 'horrified'. Digesting the scene, 'she hauled me out by the ear and made me go to Women's College'.[300] It was there that she remained.

∞

Aspects of the University of Sydney Women's College reflected Judith's upbringing; it was a conservative establishment managed by a powerful woman. Yet the College enabled her to observe, and pursue, behaviours which would not have been possible in New England. The experience was influential.

Phillip had always wanted his daughter to attend the College. As well as providing basic protection against the city, the College secured one's attachment to the influential class. Principals during the period were from prominent, wealthy families, who had studied at Cambridge or Oxford. New South Wales families of wealth and status were connected with the College through council positions and as alumni. Windeyer girls went there, as did White girls. Though scholarships were provided, the majority of students paid fees which Judith remembered being substantial, and they were.[301] With around seventy students in residence at any one time, the College provided its students with an entrée to a highly sociable college life, dominated then by the men's colleges.

For some, this was its primary appeal. A 1934 article in *The New Nation* magazine noted that both the city and country mothers would be concerned to know that the Women's College conducted 'dances, tennis parties and hockey matches' which brought together girls who 'in after life' would meet as 'doctors, dentists, architects' and so on.[302]

And yet, in 1953, college historian W. Vere Hole defended the institution against claims it was little more than a ruling-class conduit, hosting tennis parties so that the children of rich families could meet. Rather than being prospective chemists and journalists, critics suggested that residents tended to be of limited academic ability or aspiration. Hole returned that the 'wealthy dilettante' had rarely found a place in College.[303]

Judith's admission to the College suggests that money continued to determine selection during the 1930s, despite efforts to ensure an atmosphere of 'intellectual enquiry' by Principal Susannah Williams. Until Williams' departure in 1935, she had worked to reduce the number of unmatriculated students admitted, and introduced a regulation obliging residents to pass their university subjects. Unmatriculated students who sought degrees in Massage were first in the firing line. But such reforms were not completely effective. The college's biographical register shows that, even in 1935, only fifteen out of the outgoing twenty students gained degrees. At the admissions stage there were gaps as well, as Judith's entry demonstrates. By the time she arrived at the College, she was not only unmatriculated but had failed one university subject. Why Williams admitted Judith under these circumstances is unclear. Judith was, it seems, the beneficiary of either a sympathetic and astute Principal, who saw her potential (personal interviews between the applicant and Principal formed the selection process, though no notes of these interviews have survived), or the less-selective entry due to the College's poor financial situation after the Depression. Perhaps the College wanted to retain its connection with influential families. Whatever the reason, her admission was exceptional for Hole tells us that 'it has been the policy' not to admit unmatriculated students, 'except in a few instances.'[304]

Did the College reform the wayward Judith, or give her access to other aspects of metropolitan life that took her further from her New England upbringing? Perhaps the most significant impact on Judith at the College was incoming College Principal, Camilla Wedgwood. This was a time when the Principal was expected to have a personal relationship with every student. They were a guardian and mentor. In Lent term 1935, Wedgwood assumed the position and exhibited an unconventional model of femininity. She demonstrated that women could live independent, intellectual and passionately ethical lives, whilst maintaining middle-class respectability. She was both of the new world and of the old. For Judith, she was a 'magnificent principal to say the least...wonderful!'[305]

Certainly Wedgwood had attributes which the College valued. A member of the wealthy English Wedgwood family, Hole noted approvingly that they had been 'provincial leaders for generations'.

Her father Josiah Wedgwood was a former colonial administrator and lord-in-the-waiting. Wedgwood had a confident, upper-class English accent and excellent academic qualifications. After graduating at Cambridge, she tutored in the new Anthropology department at Sydney, producing well-regarded research from overseas field trips. Some predicted that if she had returned home she would have taken 'a prominent part in British anthropology'.[306]

But Wedgwood was also a bold choice who embodied an unorthodox model of femininity. In the same issue of the college magazine in which Williams was remembered for her distinctive flower arrangements, Wedgwood was introduced by her first-hand account, 'Sorcerer Hunting in Manam Island, New Guinea', in which she relayed: 'there was a sorcerer hunt going forward, and everyone had gone to the village graveyard. I ran into my house, seized a notebook and pencil, slung my camera over my shoulder, and rushed off to the scene of action'. Wedgwood was, remembered former student Ronia Craig, 'forthright, unconventional and completely fearless...the first truly emancipated person of her sex I had encountered'.[307]

Though Wedgwood came from wealth and status, she came also from a line of social reformers. Her father modelled a progressive gender position, attesting that he had never met anyone as intelligent as his wife, with whom he attended Fabian Society lectures. Wedgwood was a committed Quaker, who performed extensive charity work, housed German refugees in 1937 and, during World War II, was a pacifist. Though Wedgwood was said to loathe feminism, she was awarded a Coronation Medal for being a 'prominent feminist leader'. She showed young women, by example, that they had opportunities outside of marriage. Judith reflected that she set off among students 'more ambition towards careers than they otherwise would have had'. Was she thinking of herself? The following chapters of this book show that Judith became a more serious student in her final two years, passing all remaining subjects, and committing to finding a new kind of poetry. Evidence in Chapter 5, however, shows that Judith was not apparently influenced by Wedgwood's approach to poverty and social change.[308]

The College itself, during Wedgwood's time, while not overtly feminist, enabled its residents to control their own lives in ways consistent with new models of gender and sexuality. Though Judith would have preferred to have lived independently, she described the College's practical arrangements as 'fairly free'. This is supported by other accounts. 'Those in authority', Hole wrote, did 'not maintain a constant surveillance' on residents. While Judith was there, the Friday evening curfew was changed from 11.30 pm to 11.50 pm, so that residents were 'able to sup comfortably after the pictures without having to fall into the 11.10 tram from town with lacerated throats'. Overnight leaves were granted, with permission from the Principal. During the 1920s there was an attempt by the College to put 'night visits' by men on the agenda of the college's committee meetings, but a student's request that 'no interest be shown in these nocturnal serenades' was adhered to. When Kathleen Price arrived at the college in 1923, she was, as mentioned, 'shocked' by the behaviour of some residents, including those who smoked. In Judith's second year at the College its shop began selling cigarettes, although smoking was still regarded by many as unfeminine.[309] The College had an open mind towards religion, being the only non-denominational college at the University.

As well as turning a blind eye, the Women's College seemed in some ways to actively encourage women in their romantic pursuits. During Judith's time, a new directive ensured that 'leaves' be written in the Letter Room, 'which will relieve...the embarrassment of male visitors'. Each year the College dance attracted around 300 people, including residents and their guests. There was also an informal dance, and a College 'hop'. In the College magazine romance was spoken about directly. One poem, titled 'Love', read: 'I have made lyrics about Love,/ and lambs in spring-time and their glee./ I have made lyrics about Love,/ but what is this has come to me?' It suggested a young woman who had passed from innocence to world weariness. It was an image that challenged notions that sexual innocence was an important part of a young woman's respectability. Moreover, imagery in the poem that suggests both love and virginity lost − buds struggling to be free, a young lamb taking its 'first free breath' − also suggests sexual desire. That the Women's College did not censor such material indicates its liberalism. Veronica Brady's suggestion that Judith wrote the poem is plausible, although the poem was not reflective of her poetic output during these years, as will be argued in Chapter 8.[310]

Being moved to the Women's College was not so bad for Judith. Both the institution and its Principal allowed Judith to continue to explore her city, her body and her mind. Former collegians remembered that Wedgwood went on hikes with residents to discuss their problems, or would refuse to retire until the last one came in from evening leave. But Judith did not remember Wedgwood for these maternal displays; it was her commitment to intellectual endeavour and independence of mind that she recalled. As long as you remembered your poetry, Judith said of Wedgwood, 'she didn't care what you did'.[311] *She* was a modern woman. And she was just one of many that Judith would encounter in Sydney. It was a world away from the nineteenth-century atmosphere of New England, aspirations towards wholesomeness and respectability, and sentimental verse about love and flowers. At night, residents such as Judith would place their ear at Wedgwood's bedroom door and listen to her recitation of T. S. Eliot. In Wedgwood, in Sydney, Judith had found a way of life for which she had been yearning.

CHAPTER 5

A Very Model Student

In Sydney, Judith sought fun, frivolity and freedom. It was a dramatic disavowal of New England respectability, but did it reflect a longstanding dissatisfaction with the values she had grown up with? Published accounts posit that Judith was a born agitator, that she was driven by a unique ability to perceive the world and a remarkable empathy for others, and that this inclination distinguished her from her family members, who were more engaged by the immediate challenges of pastoralism and maintaining social and cultural standing. Although Judith did not directly articulate this formulation, her publicly recorded recollections support it. In *Half a Lifetime* (1999), she described her dismay at discovering poverty for the first time in Sydney. As mentioned in the previous chapter, she had felt frustrated, at times, by her passivity and self-indulgence: 'what, after all, was I doing at university, apart from having a ball, or a series of balls?' She mentioned that she had, 'under the tutelage of the radical left-wing philosopher John Anderson, taken an uninviting step into criticism of society'. And she recalled that she had started a 'social comment column' in the University newspaper. Similarly, in interviews, Judith said that as a student she had felt it 'might be possible to establish a sounder basis for a more just society', and was 'certainly interested in social amelioration in some way'. She recalled her desire to join the Spanish resistance against the fascists, driving ambulances, and she remembered that she had marched with other students to Trades Hall, behind John Anderson, singing 'The Red Flag'.[312] Was she already the radical she would become known for?

Judith stressed that at university she had not been politically active. But even to have shared sympathies with those on the Left must have set her apart, radically, from her father. As Chapter 2 showed, socialism was regarded as an enemy in the political movements he was active within. Brady believes that Judith's thinking diverged notably from her family's, explaining that her trips home on university holidays 'turned many of the family into firecrackers'. In any social equation, Brady writes, Judith tended to favour those whom she saw as the victim. When Judith recalled how she had felt when the poetry she had written at university was rejected by publishers, she asserted that she came to the conclusion that 'Australia was no place for experiment'; also she had a sense of herself at university as an oddity. These sentiments seem confirmation that Judith lived, at least intellectually, outside her social context, committed to philosophical positions that held little weight within her immediate world.[313]

Almost no primary sources have been used to substantiate this picture. Judith unfortunately did not keep letters from the period. While Judith's reminiscences tell us how she thought, felt and acted as a young adult, she was inclined to skimp on the detail. This was understandably so; what might have been important at twenty was not at seventy or eighty, when Judith recorded her life. By then she had other things on her mind. And, as the opening lines of her memoir indicate, she was uncomfortable about privileging life narrative above those matters: 'autobiography is not what I was to write. It forces the writer into far too much introversion or into arrogance'.[314] That was one way of looking at it. Another would be to point out that the 1930s were a vibrant period in Australian intellectual life, especially at the University of Sydney, and that she, one of Australia's most influential writers, came to maturity within it. How the time and woman interacted warrants more than a few pages of discussion. Perhaps it is not the subject's job, or even that of the biographer who sets out to capture an entire life, to address these aspects. But for Australian intellectual history the following are apposite questions: How did Judith engage with the often controversial, sometimes groundbreaking ideas circulating at the University of Sydney? How much of her response was informed by her cultural inheritance? To what extent was she changed, intellectually, by her time at university?

The broader question of this book remains: To what extent was she born? And to what extent made?

The following four chapters seek to provide answers by drawing on new primary material. In this chapter, I look at intellectual activity outside the lecture halls, chiefly that occurring in the student news-paper, *Honi Soit*. Revealed here is a significant body of work Judith produced as a student: thirteen columns and one poem. This material allows us to hear, directly, thrillingly, the feisty voice of a young Judith Wright, and offers new insight into the development of her thinking. It shows the considerable degree to which Judith was influenced by the undergraduate culture of the University of Sydney between 1934 and 1936. And that, from this vantage point, she may have been 'out there', but she was not an oddity. She was, rather, articulating many of the dominant mores of her time and class.

What were these mores? What did campus life look and feel like? To date, there exists relatively little scholarship on undergraduate life in this period. Perhaps it has been considered an uneventful, even comparatively spiritless, moment in undergraduate history. For it has been argued that students at the University in the mid 1930s were overwhelmingly apathetic and politically conservative. As suggested in Chapter 4, most students came from comfortable backgrounds with little personal need to agitate for social change. Donald Horne, whose account of campus life in the late 1930s dominates readings of the period, put it bluntly: 'most' students were there because 'their parents had enough money to buy them careers as doctors, lawyers, dentists, or engineers'.[315]

This is not, perhaps unsurprisingly, the image portrayed by the University of Sydney's own history, which emphasises that the number of scholarships and bursaries meant that 'in both social and economic terms it was now quite a diverse group of undergraduates'. The Women's College claims, too, to have hosted a 'heterogeneous bunch' during the 1930s. Beverly Kingston has argued that a proliferation of scholarships and bursaries in the early 1920s produced 'a rather more democratic group of students than at other universities at the time – with a good proportion of Catholics', but also suggests that rising fees and falling enrolment numbers, a product of the Depression, may have shifted the balance over the decade. It is worth noting, for the purposes of this discussion of campus life, that even those students who made it to university without paying full fees were unlikely to have as great a presence on campus as those that did, reducing the impact of their 'diversity' on the student population. They were much more likely to be evening students or engaged in paid work around lectures, with little time for extracurricular activities. Many bursaries and cadetships were provided by industry or arms of government, such as the Education department, producing a 'cautious, conservative group', as Kingston terms it, who did not risk their academic results by participating in campus life and were compelled to complete extra tasks. Judith recalled that evening students were 'not much in touch with us'.[316]

Who did she mean by 'us'? Those attending campus during the day were a tight-knit bunch. Wright said: 'all of us knew people in other faculties'. A typical Arts timetable provided ample opportunity for social integration with four lectures a day, and no tutorials. A favoured meeting spot was the 'Quad', a strip of lawn within the University's main building, where the contents of lectures were dissected. The early to mid 1930s saw a surge in the number of societies to cater for this crowd of lingerers. There were cultural societies, such as the Book Club, with its lunchtime readings, a literary society, and the popular Sydney University Dramatic Society, whose crowd scenes Judith would join in, while 'quoting Prufrock to myself'.[317] There was an abundance of sporting societies. And then there were the political, philosophical and religious societies.

In terms of left-wing societies Sydney was no comparison with its Melbourne counterpart in the period. Historian Alan Barcan notes that a brief period of political activity during the late 1920s, spurred by the Depression and demonstrated by the establishment of the Freethought Society – which attracted writers Amy Witting (then, Joan Fraser), James McAuley and Harold Stewart – was followed by a resumption of political 'apathy' on campus. Indeed, membership of the campus Socialist Club fell from 150, in 1931, to just ten, in 1934. By 1937 it had ceased to exist, along with the Public Questions Society.

Barcan believes that for students of this period societies provided the 'attractions of a marriage market' and little else.[318]

Indeed, during the mid 1930s editors of *Honi Soit* berated students for not being more involved in extracurricular activities, such as their newspaper. The 1935 editor complained that 'the majority of students concentrate wholly on their academic studies' and neglect the cultivation of a 'cultured mind' or 'cultural life'. The 1936 editor diagnosed a 'tendency nowadays to take too much for granted' amongst undergraduates, and described them as lazy. He instructed new undergraduates to become involved – or else leave and join a technical college – because central to a university education was the development of a 'tolerant, sympathetic, unprejudiced outlook', an outlook fundamental to 'all culture'.[319]

And yet, even if most students were not active, many were engaged by political issues, in much the way Judith was. Major forums for discussion were hugely popular. Barcan tempers his depiction of mid 1930s conservatism by canvassing such instances, including the regular debates held in Union Hall, where various social questions were considered, such as the relationship between education and class. *Honi Soit*, though it may have been produced by a small group, was regularly read by the vast majority of students each week. Barcan also notes that it was during this period that the Joint Committee for Peace, an amalgamation of six groups, including those with a Christian or labour ethos, galvanised a large part of the University population. A peace ballot was held in 1935, in which half of the student population voted. Judith remembered: 'in 1934, '35, '36...we all knew that there was going to be another war and that Hitler was rising in strength and menace'.[320]

The University's history argues that this threat prompted more conversation than the Depression and was a 'stimulus to a new wave of student activity', including study circles and discussion groups. Certainly, the weekly issues of *Honi Soit* from 1934 to 1936 show that Europe was a frequent topic of conversation ('Is war inevitable?' asked one 1935 headline).[321] And this seemed to spur a level of interest in student organisations, with many issues dominated by discussion of changes to the management of student affairs and bodies, such as the Students' Representative Council (SRC), the Graduates' Association,

Honi Soit and *Hermes*, the University literary magazine. Reform usually aimed to increase student governance. Although it goes unnoticed in these general accounts of student activism, the most persistent, most challenging discourse which emerged from *Honi Soit* during these years, presumably reflecting discussion which took place around campus, was on the changing status of women.

An appreciation of what could only be termed a multifarious dialogue around women allows us to better understand the young Judith within her time. For we know that Judith had an ongoing involvement with the paper and was critical of its attitude towards women. A basis for this was her own appointment. In her memoir she wrote: 'I volunteered my services to the student newspaper *Honi Soit* where I was, shamingly, given the job of social reporter'. It was to their shame because it was because she was a woman. A decade earlier, she described it similarly: 'I was on the staff, the writing staff, of the University newspaper, *Honi Soit*, but as usual they shunted me on to doing the social column. That was for women'. She named the men who had more meaningful jobs: there was Hugh Gilchrist, associate editor in 1935 and editor in 1936, and Alan Crawford, editor of *Hermes* in 1935 and SRC publications director in 1936 and 1937. They were 'all very upstage', Judith recalled, whereas she was 'just a woman from the country'. Brady, typically, draws out what Judith suggests: 'she was to deal only with social reporting, the area to which women journalists were usually confined', since the male editors paid little attention to 'just a woman from the country'.[322]

Were all the women at *Honi Soit* making cups of tea and describing dresses for the social column? Was Judith patronised because she was a rural woman and effectively barred from the informal intellectual discussion which took place on campus? Certainly Gilchrist and Crawford dominated the literary scene, with the latter also winning the University prize for poetry. These students seemed to have cultivated a power amongst the student population, even according to Donald Horne, who would join their circle of influence, becoming an editor himself. At first blush he was in awe of them: 'Alan Crawford has the ability to walk into a room as if he were descending a magnificent sweep of stairs'. Horne's account of their socialisation, which occurred in small groups, shows that women were not always directly excluded but that they were not regarded as natural companions. They got together to talk about dreams, literature and psychology, in cafes or back alleys. And, amongst them, the general consensus was that whereas they were genuine intellectuals, even radicals, all women, in the end, hungered after respectability, and that this amounted to a threat. When women broke into their group, at times, seeming to display their same 'heightened consciousness' through swearing, smoking and drinking, ultimately Horne could not believe it.[323]

And yet, as dominant and homosocial as this group was, it did not have complete control over campus literary life. The situation was simply more dynamic. For women did fill positions of authority – journalistic, literary and political – on campus, despite what Judith suggested. At *Honi Soit,* in Judith's first year, women filled the positions of social editress, associate social editress, chief-of-staff and two subeditorships. By the beginning of 1935 the situation had improved, with women assuming the positions of news editor and sporting editress. In 1936 a woman was put on Features, a post which allowed its practitioner to choose their subject and complete articles 'at their leisure'. Given that women made up less than one-third of the University student population, their numerical representation on the *Honi Soit* staff – approximately half – was not altogether bad. And while the senior positions of editor and associate editor remained the domain of men, in 1936 *Hermes* came under the editorship of Margaret Walkom, who also became vice-president of the SRC that year. *Honi Soit* applauded Walkom's 'good sense and moderation'.[324]

Judith had said that appointing women to the social column was a form of 'shunting', and Brady that it was a way of 'confining' them, but Robin Curtis, who was social editor before Wright, was not so restricted. She became the Women's Arts representative for the SRC. Being 'just a woman from the country' did not prevent Economics undergraduate Marie Moyes, who hailed from Armidale, becoming secretary of the Freethought Society. A certain amount of women's participation was assured because management positions of the Sydney University Women's Union and the Women's Undergraduate Association, which formed part of the SRC, were only open to women. Yet women also held office in the SRC, where positions were open to men and women. Walkom's role as vice-president in 1936 had been filled by Margarie Booth the previous year. And while six of the top seven SRC positions were filled by men, women constituted five of the twelve overall membership positions. It was not equality, but neither was it out and out marginalisation.[325]

It is far easier, from history's standpoint, to be clinical about the bounds of possibility than it is when standing, twenty years of age, centre stage within them. Perhaps it was difficult to decipher the limits of patriarchy, especially when other aspects of campus life seemed to reassert the primacy of males. From the outside it is hard to judge a person's particular vantage point within a situation, let alone their emotional response to it. Yet both are crucial issues. Was Judith only dimly aware of the participation women had within the magazine and on campus generally? Was she distracted, angered even, by the comparative participation of men, believing that she could have done their jobs? There may have been legitimate reasons why Judith would distort the situation, perhaps even unconsciously, when she gave her accounts as an older woman. Could she have been seeking to excuse her role as a social columnist, which might have sounded superficial, certainly humble? Perhaps Judith's first concern was to represent how it *felt* to her, and that it *felt* as if she was not taken seriously as a woman.

A reading of *Honi Soit* between 1934 and 1936 shows that this may well have been the case. When women were discussed in *Honi Soit* their bodies and their attire was, often times, the central issue. The attitude of articles and issues varied, probably a result of different authors and an admirable lack of editorial control. But it was not unusual for a woman to be the butt of a joke – just because she was a woman. In one issue, the newspaper breathlessly reported on an 'important law suit' taking place between the Women's College and St John's, a men's college, which centred on a large amount of women's underwear that had been 'donated' to the men and not returned. This line of humour was much vaunted in *Honi Soit*. One issue asked: 'who are the two Arts girls who caused so much comment in the daily press by their incredibly short shorts?' And, referring to the growing participation of women in sport, it insisted that anyone who doubts this 'has only to note the ceaseless activity on the University courts, and the ever-increasing number of new and exciting shorts'.[326] Though such lines were delivered in a light-hearted tone, together they created the impression that women were inherently silly and that their value came primarily from their bodies. One typical college news column was almost entirely devoted to discussing the men's colleges – in this case, their preparations for the Easter Rowing Regatta. The final and tenth paragraph reported news from the women's colleges:

> Sancta Sophia have only a handful of freshettes, but they are said to include the best looking person yet come to the 'Varsity. The Women's College also claims to have among their freshettes the best looking person yet to come to the 'Varsity.[327]

That was it. According to *Honi Soit* the women were running their own race. For a young woman wanting to be taken seriously it must have been frustrating, even demeaning.

On the other hand, when directly addressing women's sport in a dedicated and sizeable weekly column, *Honi Soit* took it seriously. One 1936 column on women's cricket, appearing on page two, could not have been more complimentary, noting that the cricketers had 'good reason to be proud' and assessing their bowling and batting perform-ance in detail. There was no patronising, nor reference to appearances. This was in the context of Australian journalism's widespread trivialisa-tion of women's sport, and women's relatively recent enthusiasm for sport across the Australian population.[328]

The column was not an aberration, but part of a dynamic and sometimes daring dialogue on the role of women in society. There was another line of discussion in the pages of *Honi Soit* during these years which, though not progressive by today's standards, certainly reflected a discontent with the contemporary status quo, and was framed in ways that responded to contemporary feminist debates. In 1933 the results of an American survey of women undergraduates' knowledge of physical intimacy was included on the front page. Titled "Fresher' Girls – Sex Solution Comes from Scientific Study', the sub-title screamed: 'Should a Girl Tell? Dangers! Pitfalls! Temptations! All the best paths to be followed by the Freshette'. Whether young women should be 'advised' about sex, and the hormonal inclinations of men, was the article's debating point. Assumptions about men's and women's sexuality were typical for the time – *Honi Soit* did not report whether women had actually *had* sex, just if they 'knew' about it, and it was taken for granted that women were not sexually desirous – but the suggestion that women should 'know how to make a man either kiss her or not kiss her', that women should have *knowledge*, made in the article, engaged feminist problems of the time. Prominent early-twentieth century Australian feminist Rose Scott believed that women would only gain equality when the 'animalistic' tendencies of men were widely understood and society effectively curbed these drives through, for instance, the strategic design of women's attire. A younger generation of feminists questioned this strategy and embraced styles which put more of a woman's body on display, claiming that women were empowered by sexual knowledge.[329]

Honi Soit seemed to endorse this newer feminist model, although arguably from a self-serving standpoint. In the same article, it was reported that the survey asked female undergraduates what they thought of 'petting, smoking, using make-up, and falling in love', for these were considered typical behaviours of the Modern Woman, and were controversial amongst older generations. The primary editorial contribution to the discussion was to encourage young women to be sexually active. After reporting the survey's findings on women's 'knowledge' of petting, the editors added: 'any local Freshettes who also know are requested to call at the *Honi Soit* Office.' The final advice to young women, made by the survey – 'that life is just give and take' – was coupled with another editorial intervention: '(And How!)'[330] *Honi Soit*'s enthusiasm for newly developing feminist approaches was perhaps partly hormonal, but it was also daring and provocative.

Honi Soit's liberal attitude towards women and sex also accorded with majority student opinion, as it was represented at debate night, and was part of a bigger feminist issue, contraception, which many considered in need of urgent reform. In 1936 a debate was held in Union Hall asking whether or not contraceptives should be legalised, with the newspaper reporting an 'overwhelming decision' in favour of legalisation, and the widespread dispersal, and instruction, of birth control.[331]

Another frequent point of discussion in the paper was whether or not women were suitable for university study and, by extension, professions. The paper reported that 'one of the most criticised sections of the students in this University is that of the Women Undergraduates'. Amongst their most serious misdemeanours was being unattractive. Others suggested that intellectual women were mean, for it was widely understood that 'normal' women were nice. A 1934 *Honi Soit* article sought to deal with the accusation of unattractiveness. Titled 'Female Beauty', it noted that female students 'have from time to time been cut to the heart by the slurs cast on the comeliness of University women', but were told to 'take consolation in the fact that such sallies are not found in Sydney alone'. The editors reported on the results of an 'inspection' of the appearance of Californian university women, as judged by a jury of eight men. The 'findings' were not encouraging for Californian women, but the *Honi Soit* editor applauded the 'courage' of the survey authors.[332] You could almost hear the tittering.

It might have *felt* to a young woman who had set her sights on an intellectual life that she would not have been taken seriously by the men who appeared most likely to dominate public life. That they might have been assessing her appearance, something Judith was self-conscious about, before her mind, would have been a reasonable assumption, based on such articles. Judith was not the only woman of the period to feel that her appearance prevented her from advancing professionally at university.[333] Though we cannot quantify this pressure, the power of such experiences in shaping young lives, particularly those of women, is something most of us would intuitively recognise. And it points to the perspicacity of Judith's long-held conviction that emotions can be truer than facts.

Nonetheless, as a student Judith might have been buoyed by the fact that, when directly considering women's rights, and not distracted by their hormones or wit, the editors of *Honi Soit* were at least prepared to air a more progressive position and reproach those who would not. An anonymously authored article in 1935, titled 'University Women', noted that while the tone of criticism directed towards female students was 'flippant', it did not prevent its damaging quality. It cited arguments made against women – that they 'were frivolous in regard to their work', that they 'have a bad influence on the rest of the students' but were, at the same time, 'intensely anxious about their lectures and essays...that they neglect everything else, even the important matter of dressing well' – and pointed out that these were 'glaringly contradictory'. Within the University this was not universally recognised. In a letter to the editor, for instance, it was claimed that women spoke very loudly, using exaggerated vowel sounds in the Fisher Library. The correspondent's accusation, that 'they almost universally talk like immature pedants', exploited the belief that women were dumb and childlike. Some academics opposed women students, with *Honi Soit* noting that one professor had argued that higher education was wasted on women, the majority of whom became full-time mothers. He accused them of being a 'nuisance' on campus who simply came to have a good time. *Honi Soit* rejected the assertion, arguing that women had taken 'an active and intelligent part in University life', especially in proportion to their numbers. The newspaper also canvassed the opinions, quite neutrally, of high-profile 1930s feminists Bessie Rischbieth and Jessie Street, who sought to extend women's roles in the professional spheres and achieve equal pay. When the latter came to speak to the Public Question Society in 1935, *Honi Soit* reported Street's arguments on its front page: 'the right to earn wages...is a fundamental human right, and the foundation of all liberty'.[334]

Honi Soit did not have a fixed editorial position on women or their capacities during these years. Both feminist and patriarchal views were published. A young woman witnessing all this might have perceived that articles that took women seriously were overshadowed by a more pervasive, patronising attitude towards women in the newspaper. And if one's treatment by the organisation also had a patronising quality, it is understandable that this was the overall impression one gained of it. Judith, and her biographer, suggested that she was made to feel unappreciated. If details were light on, a reader might have assumed it was because the episode was not an important one in Judith's life, or perhaps that she was not prepared to indulge in self-pity. Nonetheless, the reader comes away understanding that the writer's first semi-professional involvement in publishing taught her that a woman could try for years to be respected without reward. *Why bother?* the reader might conclude. *Why did she?* she might have wondered. Further investigation of exactly how long Judith was involved, and in what form, prompts quite different questions.

First, back to this: 'I did the social column I think for two years', Judith recalled in an interview, 'under a pseudonym of course'. When asked why 'on earth' she used a pseudonym, she said it was because she was a woman and she thought that most women had to do so 'in those days'. Brady provided further clarification, with a quote from Judith's then unpublished memoir: 'she was given charge of a column – "under a pseudonym, of course; women were not regarded very highly"'. According to her own account, Judith reluctantly accepted the role of social reporter because it at least gave her some kind of profile: 'I became, if not well known, at least familiar to the mighty of more senior years and a habitué of the Quad'. This allowed her to do something which she felt was more meaningful: 'since I wasn't being taken seriously as a writer, I started a social comment column in *Honi Soit*'. She remembered working for two years, in total, at *Honi Soit*. Brady's narrative is slightly different. She explains that Judith was initially a reporter and then, in second year, became editor of the social column. In her third year, according to Brady, she was promoted to subeditor of 'social reporting'. Both accounts depict Judith working on the newspaper for most of her three years, struggling to gain respect.[335]

The archives tell a different story. In 1935 and the first half of 1936 other women were credited with the positions of social editress and associate social editress, under names which appear in official University records and other documentation; they were not pseudonyms. Further, Judith did not write for *Honi Soit* at all in 1935 (an examination of the *Honi Soit* staff lists shows that all names belonged to real people). It was in 1936, her final year, that she began working for the newspaper, under her real name. In the first issue of 1936 she was listed as a subeditor, alongside two others. Halfway through 1936, a small notice stated: 'Miss Judith Wright (Arts III, the Women's College) has been appointed Personal Editor, the position of Social Editress having been abolished'. The following year, when Judith was bound for Europe, the title 'Social Editress' returned; it must have been she who objected to it.[336]

Another fact which has not been put on the public record further challenges the image of Judith as powerless within the campus literary scene. In 1936 she became a committee member of *The Arts Journal*, an annual student publication which published poems, short stories and literary articles. Neither Judith nor Brady make mention of this journal. It was a detail forgotten, perhaps. Judith had, after all, confessed: 'there's not very much in my memory of what was going on in the literary field' at the University. But her involvement in this publication belies the image of a subdued and frustrated social columnist, which Brady constructs and which has been reinforced by other critics, such as Anouk Lang. Based on Brady's account, Lang writes: 'as interested as she might have been in such [artistic and literary] developments, Wright was barred from writing these articles herself' while at university. 'Despite her best efforts', Lang explains, Wright was 'shut off, in a way directly attributable to her gender'.[337]

Judith's actual involvement in *Honi Soit* was limited to one-and-a-half terms of subediting, and one-and-a-half terms of writing the social column, in which time she produced thirteen columns. The idea that she spent years working on the newspaper with no recognition is an overreach. The notion that she was forced to write under a male name was either an embellishment or a mistake, perhaps resulting from confusion with another period in her young adult life – for example, while writing for *The Bulletin*. No record can be found of a 'social comment' column, but it is possible that Judith wrote articles for *Honi Soit* since many were unattributed. Some of these articles, such as the ones quoted above, offered opinions on topical issues, such as war, women and the state of modern literature. Another explanation may be that Judith was thinking of the social commentary she incorporated into her social columns when she remembered starting a 'social comment column'.

Social editresses typically reported on overseas voyages, engagements and children's births amongst the staff, students and recent alumni. Those that preceded Judith were always cheery: 'quite the most exciting event that occurred during the vacation was the announcement of Gwen Stevens' engagement on the same day that the Duke of Gloucester announced his'. Theatrical performances, balls and society events were always of interest. There was an emphasis on fashion: 'bright colours and floral materials were popular at the Arts ball'. Individuals who stood out were mentioned by name; Judith's friend Cecily Nixon was often recalled for her on-stage performances and ball attire. Sometimes the tone was cheeky, sometimes it was subtly so: 'Cecily Nixon [wore] a chiffon with broad stripes arranged in an intriguing fashion'. Occasionally men were the subject of this subtle mockery: some of the 'important males were...'[338] Awards were given for fashion sense and, on one occasion, humorously, a man was the recipient.

The column, entitled 'Quadrangles', like much of *Honi Soit*, specialised in enacting a tone of ambiguity. Sarcasm was its mainstay. Describing some new landscaping feature on University grounds, the 1935 social editress wrote:

> None of the paths lead anywhere in particular, it must be admitted, but they look so orderly and well-planned...that we think paths must be like women students who cannot be expected to look decorative and be useful at the same time.

Whether the writer endorsed the sentiment was, typically, unclear. 'Quadrangles' was not so much provocative as naughty.

And while the column could be mocking and sarcastic, in the fourteenth issue of 1936, when Judith became editor, its tone changed markedly. This new voice was equally, if not more, sure-footed, but wittier and clearer in its disparagement of the patronising attitude of men towards women. 'Quadrangles' began:

> One of the science lads was hanging over the bar explaining to the barmaid with excited fervour the intricacies of the functions of a complex variable. When he had finished, the barmaid nodded her approval and said: 'I used to do arithmetic, too, when I was at school.' (True story).

The column went on to characterise as low the level of discussion taking place in the Joint Committee for Peace, not a topic generally aired in the social column. The columnist considered the accusation that students were 'indifferent' to politics, based on their lack of involvement in extracurricular activities, and countered: 'there are as many people who take an interest in affairs outside the societies as inside'.[339] It was as if the author were countering accusations of apathy that would be made in history books of the future. 'Quadrangles' was going somewhere it had not been in the previous few years; it was reaching beyond subject matter of strictly 'social' significance.

What do we learn from these thirteen 'Quadrangles' columns? Firstly, even in her early twenties, Judith was an accomplished writer. Confidence, originality and ability were on full display. That the social column was used to nullify talented women is not supported by her boisterous tone. Secondly, Judith blended in to her environment – or at least, did a good job of pretending to. Her voice was that of the typical *Honi Soit* lad. She could be lackadaisical and sarcastic with the best of them. This puts some important aspects of her history in a new light. For, as was fashionable and funny in *Honi Soit*, she demeaned the lives of the underprivileged, as well as overt forms of political action. Whether or not this was a form of performance, designed to gain much-needed credibility amongst her maligning peers, or, conversely, an attempt to parody her peers and their attitudes, is a question worth bearing in mind. So, too, is the possibility that Judith was more a product of her background than current accounts posit.

But as the above column demonstrates, Judith was also, at times, critical of the attitudes of university men towards women, which supports fundamental aspects of her account. She satirised the paper by highlighting its sexism. She spoke about men the way they spoke about women. And she overdid the cheery tone of 'Quadrangles' when discussing engagements and ball gowns to such an extent that it was clear she did not take them seriously. When, as a woman, Judith complained that university students were too boring, she challenged previously dominant beliefs that women were naturally demure. Her confident bravado, the same one that saw her drawn to the outside as a child, that helped her ride horses, that made her sure from the age of sixteen that she would become a writer, that allowed her to leave New England for Sydney, and then move to a run-down boarding house in Glebe, was fully evident in her 'Quadrangles' columns. Here was the Modern Woman in full-flight: provocative, careless and flirty.

∞

Honi Soit writers liked to make fun of someone and, as we have seen, this was often women. The goal was to be cute and witty in one's disparagement. The trick was to appear unbothered either way. Earnestness was a no–no. Judith found a new subject to mock. Her first column included an original poem describing 'the perfect student'. 'Quadrangles' was not usually written in verse; not only did Judith change the columnist's job title and the column's subject matter, she changed the form in which it appeared.

> University Specimens
> No. 1: The Perfect Student
>
> A lousy frowsy dastard
> With a self-contented kink:
> Whose head is stuffed with paper
> And whose humour smells of ink.
> He works and sports and frivols
> In an ostentatious way.
> He's aware of current happenings
> And discusses them all day.
> He's a very model student,
> But whatever he may think,
> He's a lousy frowsy dastard
> With a self-contented kink.[340]

Poetic parodies of 'types' were in favour in 1936. Judith's could have been modelled on 'Recipe for a Flapper', published in the *Truth*, and introduced in Chapter 4. Like that poem, 'University Specimens' was critical of the superficiality and self-centredness which some characterised as 'modern'. By way of emphasis, the phrase 'self-contented' is repeated; it seems Judith had some sympathy with those, like the New States movement and the Country Party, that believed metropolitan life encouraged selfishness and arrogance; that in the city there was a lot of talk and not much action. In her memoir Judith explained that she had not felt completely comfortable with the apparently frivolous life she was leading as a student. As noted, she remembered asking herself: 'what, after all, was I doing at university, apart from having a ball...?'[341] It was the understandable response of a young woman who had grown up being told that value – economic, as well as moral – came from hard work and primary production. But, as she also suggests in her memoir, other aspects of these columns indicate that feelings of disquiet, of guilt even, were an undertow; that, like many a student, she also loved having fun, and that talking, writing and partying were central to her life. At the surface level, at least, Judith was, according to her own definition, 'a very model student', whatever she may have thought. In the succeeding twelve columns Judith exhibited, ostentatiously, many of her model–student characteristics.

In one important way, the columns suggest more continuity with her background and fellow students than Judith's own accounts allowed. They rested on the assumption that one's economic status was an expression of one's worth; that, as according to the Wyndham mythology, economic success and social power were the products of skill and ingenuity. By the same reasoning, a lack of these must suggest some essential human failing. In her columns, Judith repeatedly made fun of the less fortunate; it was, in fact, her trademark object of fun. And she must have calculated that her fellow 'self-contented' students would find the topic funny, not tragic.

Her target, in three consecutive issues, was the University Settlement. Known simply as the Settlement, it was a charitable organisation founded in 1908 which followed the example of the nineteenth-century English Settlement movement. Today it claims its original inspiration was the radical belief that:

> ...the conditions of the poor would not improve until educated people were prepared to live and work among them; to befriend them, assist them and learn from them; to abandon the security and comfort of their leafy neighbourhoods and risk disease, crime and the disdain of their peers.[342]

Women's College Principal Camilla Wedgwood was vice-president of the Settlement council. A 'staunch supporter', she believed that the

College should not be 'an ivory tower' and that those living within it should interact with the public, especially on charitable terms.[343]

Although Judith told us that she had deeply admired Wedgwood, she was clearly not so influenced that she could be moved on this point. She did not, as Wedgwood implored of her students, risk the 'disdain of her peers' by 'befriending' or 'learning' from the poor. In fact, she made fun of them to ensure the esteem of her peers. Judith described the people who received charity there as 'Settlement Scavengers'. They were, humorously, so hungry they got excited by a hat in the shape of pie.

> Public opinion has at last prevailed and John Neil's hat has again resumed normal proportions – or is he afraid that a 'pork pie' might prove irresistible to the Settlement Scavengers?[344]

In the next issue the Settlement people were merely graceless.

> ...any misunderstanding about the Settlement's quest for bottles has been avoided. It did at first seem possible that some people might resent the implication that they were possessed of bottles of one particular kind. It seems, however, that any kind will do and further that a surprising amount of money can be made from these things.[345]

Judith's apparent naivety regarding fundraising and bottle collection suggested a woman comfortable in her ivory tower; alarmed more by the possible infringement of her fellows' reputations, even if just in jest, than the deprivation which such fundraising efforts sought to address.

It was as if poor and working-class men were sluggish, mechanical and insensitive to social mores, in contrast to university men who were strapping, vigorous and competitive; if these natural disparities existed then their relative positions within society were simply an accurate reflection of this. Describing a sporting event that was intended to bring undergraduates into contact with the poor, Judith wrote: 'we hear that one prominent football player overwhelmed the Settlement scavengers the other day by handing over three trunkfuls of cast-offs'. It was funny that people were so desperate, so lacking in pride, that they were willing to lose a football match to retrieve used clothes. The victory was a cause for celebration, an affirmation of student athleticism in the face of excessive drinking: 'so Beer does Build Bonny Babies!' In the same issue she joked that a solution to the 'unemployment problem' could be found in the University erecting gates that impeded the progress of the 'free-born College man' getting to and from class. He would 'naturally' knock over the gate and, 'like a patient ant', a University employee would put it back.[346]

It might be argued that Judith was being sarcastic, or just facetious in these columns; that her too earnest celebration of student self-centredness was meant to draw attention to this tendency amongst the student population. It has to be acknowledged that sarcasm is conveyed by tone, and that tone is difficult for the non-contemporary reader to properly decipher. Indeed, Judith's thirteen columns could be interpreted as an ironic illustration of the 'very model student' she described, for they seem designed to be as insensitive, profligate and snobby as possible. Were they parody? Was she merely performing the 'university specimen' who spends his days discussing 'current happenings'; whose 'humour smells of ink'?

If it was parody, there was little to indicate it. Judith expertly mocked those who were too unsophisticated or too poor to behave as she did. She snickered at students who ate their lunch out of brown paper bags. She swaggered in her privilege:

> And while we are feeling in such a good mood, isn't it nearly time somebody died and left the University enough money to build a bridge and tidy up the University Park generally? We dislike these heaps of oddments lying about the lake: in fact we consider the whole thing a blot on the fair face of the University.[347]

Yes it was performance that bordered on caricature, but unlike genuine satire nothing in the columns acknowledged the darker reality; that, for others, such attitudes had a real life force. For they helped maintain the class structure of Australian society, which in turn justified a disparity in wages and other inequalities, such as the inaccessibility of tertiary education for most of the Australian population. Student frivolity and self-centredness was often mocked in *Honi Soit*, but as with Judith's columns, the privilege which underscored such arrogance – the social and economic structures which gave these young people the freedom from labour to joke about their own self-absorption and silliness – was never itself questioned or even brought into light. It was fun to make fun of the fact you could exist purely by having fun. It was a circular joke which admitted no outside perspectives, nor mounted any systemic criticisms. And it was private-school humour of the most common variety. Judith was a NEGS girl, after all; or at least knew how to wield her humour for popular acclaim.

Judith's columns do, however, reveal an unmistakable dissidence, not regarding privilege per se, but the conventions that go with it. She would not go along with the niceties. While canvassing the comings and goings of campus life, such as overseas trips and job appointments, Judith's 'Quadrangles' were decidedly more colourful than earlier ones: 'Una Fitzhardinge sailed last Friday for New Zealand, and from there she may go on via Cape Horn, which we hope will behave itself nicely for her.' Whereas the tone of previous 'Quadrangles' had been all good table manners, Judith elbowed her fellow diners. And she seemed to be the life of the party. It is easy to imagine that she was becoming 'if not well known, at least familiar to the mighty of more senior years and a habitué of the Quad' through her columns.[348]

Of some columns it is difficult to tell whether Judith was being playful or making a serious point, and what that point may have been. Depicting an SRC party as a kindergarten get-together, she described the hostess, Robin Curtis, who had edited 'Quadrangles' only a few weeks earlier, as a 'little Miss' who looked 'younger than ever in a charming spring ensemble, featuring the new hip-length skirt, white socks and wide sash'. Judith painted a silly scene of grown-ups 'handing round the bread and butter and all-day suckers'. Men were dressed in rompers, bow ties and straw hats. Was she being derogatory or just revelling in *Honi Soit* humour? It was not uncommon, during the period, for university and college students in the United Kingdom and the United States of America to dress up in infant's clothing for fun, or because they had been bullied into it. Judith jested: 'being unaccompanied by their nurses it was found somewhat difficult to keep the party in order, but the absence of smacks made things much more enjoyable'.[349]

One thing was certain: this was a woman who wanted the world to know she was confident and full of fun. Her brazenness extended to reporting that one 'highly respectable personage, with his hat over his eyes and his coat collar turned up' was seen entering the University Hotel, a notorious drinking venue, with 'a gleam in his eye and sixpence clutched in his hot little hand'. Typically mischievous, she wrote: 'we are not sure, however, that we believe this story, so we had better leave him in anonymity'. In one short column Judith referred to daytime drinking and smacks; she had used the word 'orgy', the phrases 'living dangerously' and 'profane horseplay'; and she had paused to reflect on the 'hot blood stirring' within all who were touched by spring. In Chapter 4 Judith's strategy for attracting men was described: make friends with the beautiful women; pick up their 'male crumbs'.[350] Here, in a 1936 issue of *Honi Soit*, we may have found another.

As Chapter 4 made clear, Judith's behaviour mirrored that of the provocative Modern Woman. These columns reveal she thought like one too, urging others to dispense with traditional manners, such as respecting one's superiors and working hard. Fed up with good behaviour, a frequent refrain of her columns was that lectures were not worth attending, and that students should study less. One story was introduced with the clause: just as we 'were beginning to think it was worth coming to Law lectures after all...' Like her allusions to sex, these columns were not the output of a 'respectable' woman. They were an attempt to define oneself as rebellious.

> There must be someone, somewhere, under some obscure bushel, who doesn't merely creep about this bright, young University, blinking like an earthworm dragged from its hole and carrying Aristotle's *Ethics* under its paralytic arm.

Judith might be remembered for her earnestness, but it was not always so. She lamented that no student had made 'a little printable whoopee'; that they seemed all so frustratingly serious.[351]

> It would be a great thing not only for the Personal Editor but for the University as a whole, if someone threw a beer party in Fisher instead of hibernating there, or heckled a lecturer instead of taking all his

words for gospel truth and writing them neatly in a black folder, or did anything instead of talking about doing it.

'Deeds, not words, are wanted', Judith wrote, in a challenge to her mostly male prankster colleagues. Parties, and their inevitable heavy drinking, she reported with relish. Of the *Honi Soit* annual dinner, Judith testified that 'four editors added dignity to the crowd – well, three did, anyway. The fourth compensated, however, by knowing three verses of "Grads and Undergrads"'. After this, Judith noted, there took place 'a large number of confused speeches and toasts' before the party reconvened elsewhere.[352]

Behaving well – listening at lectures, getting married – was boring. Judith described the marriage of one medical student as a 'loss'; the engagement of two others as 'casualties'. As stated in Chapter 4, late in life Judith revealed that she had favoured medical students as romantic partners – perhaps she was thinking of herself when reporting the news. The engagement of one medical student was to a woman who, Judith explained, 'once did Arts – two terms of them', and who 'once turned up in time for a lecture', but with 'good sense gave up the practice'. In an appeal to campus humour, Judith reinforced the stereotype of women who studied Arts as principally motivated by their desire to find doctor husbands, and concurred that Arts students lacked common sense. Mocking social custom, she added: 'their married life should be very happy, because they have the best wishes of *Honi Soit*'. Marriages were treated with as much dread as flings were celebrated. Judith reported that one male student, away in Austria, was receiving 'lessons in German by a very pretty Austrian girl, who speaks nothing but French', before being seen dancing with another woman in Cambridge.[353]

It was not just niceties that Judith wanted done away with; these columns show that she was, at times, discontent with the treatment of women on campus too. Redirecting the ritual interest in women's clothing in 'Quadrangles', she discussed men's: 'this new urge for colour in male attire is all very well...but what did we meet the other morning, but a purple shirt! This seems to us to be going too far'. Employing the plural pronouns 'we' and 'us', Judith trialled a new perspective: now the group, the anonymous but authoritative 'Quadrangles', was viewing, and assessing, each man. He was put on notice. Some issues later she reported: 'one of the University's best known leaders of masculine fashion has lately taken to wearing a lipstick handkerchief'.[354] The use of the term 'masculine' must have been ironic for Australian masculinity did not usually extend to ornamentation of this kind. The purple shirt and the lipstick handkerchief reflected a more feminine, dandyish aesthetic than was conventional, but she drew attention to them in an environment where men's attire was not usually discussed; where the frequent discussion of women's attire trivialised and, at times, humiliated them.

In another column, Judith alleged that women were treated like objects – all in good jest, of course. Describing a 'meat-fight' in a medical class, presumably some form of dissection which had got out of hand, she wrote that it caused 'the usual amount of damage to the windows, the women and other negligible furniture'. In a clear example of sarcasm, she highlighted the absurdity of their destruction, cheering: 'let's all go down and wreck The Great Hall!' It was significant that she chose to criticise this prank, for mostly Judith was positively electrified by such humour. She reported approvingly of the chemistry students who painted epithets on each other's laboratory coats. One read 'Little Audrey', another 'The Great Lover'. She rejoiced in the wit of SRC office bearers who discovered they could clean their office *and* have fun with water pistols. These were 'found to brighten the housework up amazingly'.[355]

The most direct criticism of the representation of women came when Judith referred to a long-standing advertisement in *Honi Soit* which featured an attractive woman smiling. These words were printed above her head: 'I'm so glad I bought a Remington Portable'.

> Have you noticed the way *Honi Soit* has been brightening up its advertisements lately? These beautiful women who are all so glad that they bought a Remington Portable, for instance – a different one every week, at that.

In previous 'Quadrangles', and in advertising lingo at the time, the word 'brightening' tended to be used in connection with tennis parties, laundry detergents and ladies' hats. In Judith's hands it became syrupy and sarcastic. The personal editor strategically distanced her boss from any criticism, writing: 'one would almost think the last Editor was in charge again', referring to W. P. Ash.[356] Perhaps he had a reputation concerning beautiful women. But even if this were just another instance of Judith indulging in *Honi Soit*'s nudge-nudge wink-wink humour, on this occasion she was also making a serious point. She ridiculed the increasingly prevalent practice of using young, beautiful women to sell products. She drew attention to a fundamental deceit: that women were so stupid that they got euphoric about typewriters.

In her second last 'Quadrangles', Judith showed that her interest in improving the position of women was limited. Her most keen desire, at this stage of her life, was to be witty and well regarded by her fellow students. She concluded the column with a statement from her 'Special Correspondent from the Medical School':

> Something has to be done about women students knitting during lectures. One professor I know of in the Faculty of Medicine put a stop to it by producing halfway through a lecture, his own work, and paced up and down the rostrum knitting defiantly at the women students.

Over the preceding years there had been complaints that women students knitted in lectures so vigorously, and so loudly, that the lecture could not be heard. The accusation suggested that women were not engaged by the subject matter of university courses, but attended simply to fill in their time while looking for a husband. Judith's correspondent explained the situation with mock disquiet.

> Previously I had approached one of these female offenders and asked her did she get very much out of her lectures. She replied that in second term she had produced three jumpers, two scarves, and a pullover during Physiology alone, and was now starting a pair of bed socks for her fiancé, as she found his feet got so very cold at night.[357]

It was witty for sure. But Judith was not quite the victim of sexism — that country woman who was 'shunted on the social column' — that she had told us about. In fact these columns are more suggestive of a woman comfortable amongst the literary crowd rather than of one who was 'upstaged' by it. She was clearly trying to fit in, and in doing so adopted a recklessness towards society. It was not apathy, altogether, but an attitude which indicated that she had little to fear, personally, from changes or problems within society.

Later, Judith remembered that, as a student, 'poverty was something new to me', and that witnessing it in Sydney allowed her to see something 'had gone wrong' with society. But her description of 'most people' as 'half-starved and subdued' was, these columns suggest, reflective of a latter-day sympathy, not one she harboured as a young adult.[358] The columns make it difficult to believe that Judith arrived at university already truly committed to philosophical positions unpopular within her social and familial circles. Equally, they cast doubt on Brady's claim that, even before she arrived in Sydney, Judith believed some people were victimised by society and that, in turn, the poverty she witnessed there 'troubled her'. Brady reported that Judith returned to her family on holidays full of views that shocked and disturbed. Perhaps it was a case of Judith slowly changing her views while at university; of being influenced, more than has been allowed, by some of the more controversial ideas circulating there, rather than of her arriving at university unencumbered by her family's views.

The columns remind us of the limitations of oral history. And they suggest, as this book has more generally, the importance of environment in shaping a person's thinking. At the age of twenty-one, having had little meaningful contact with underprivileged people, Judith had a very different approach to that which she later developed. Previous biographical readings have not adequately reflected, or explored, this development; of how Judith went from thinking of privilege as a reflection of human worth, to believing that it was shaped by structural forces.

And finally, the columns animate the young Judith Wright in ways that have not been visible before. They show her exhibiting a knowingness, a complete sacrifice of the traditional qualities of femininity. The public staging of this persona – clearly identifiable not only as female, but as 'Miss Judith Wright' – was indeed a form of 'social comment' given that it occurred in an environment where many still believed a woman's role was in the private realm, and in which debate raged about whether or not women should even 'know' about sex, let alone write suggestive jokes about it. Judith bore striking resemblance to that controversial modern woman caricatured by *Truth* who exhibited no 'traces of Sweetness and Innocence'. Her position, on everything, may as well have been 'complete conceit'.[359] Judith – sharp, good with language, knowledgeable of contemporary culture, and with a life-experience that made her unsentimental – was pitch perfect.

CHAPTER 6

The Shaping of an Intellect

The thrust of the Judith Wright life narrative, told with small variation by the subject herself and Veronica Brady, is so strong that aberrant details, counter winds and inconsistencies have had a way of being left out. The formal component of Judith's time at university was not a point of interest for Judith or her biographer, and so very little of it has been put on the public record. And yet, what an interesting education she had. Normally a biographer of a poet might suppose such an education would make its way into their subject's early work. As it stands, consensus has it that Judith's groundbreaking first collection, *The Moving Image* (1946), was shaped almost entirely by World War II and her relationship with Jack McKinney. In this chapter I show how that collection also reflected, strongly, the preoccupations and frameworks of her lecturers about a decade before the war came to an end. These men were articulators of new ways of thinking, who guided their students away from existing orthodoxies. Just how Judith, on her own mission of provocation, responded to such intellectual provocations is fascinating to examine. Did they shape the young poet?

Judith ushered her reader and would-be biographer away from this question, assuring us there was nothing to see here; no influences to explore. She maintained that the courses she took, the lecturers she studied under, did not change her outlook significantly, if at all. What she encountered at university almost entirely confirmed her thinking; it did not shape it. When prompted by interviewers, Judith recalled details of her lecturers and curriculum, but she was neither expansive nor rigorous about the accuracy of these recollections. Similarly, Brady discussed Judith's academic studies over the course of three pages, and inaccuracies abound.

Judith did acknowledge that aspects of her formal education had some influence. Anthropology, arguably the least well accepted, least prestigious discipline at the time, was thought provoking. Her 'main mentor' was something more amorphous.

> When I think of the university I remember the smell of Fisher library... that has been an influence on my writing...But also of course the work I was allowed to listen to in anthropology, which seemed to me very far ahead of anything...and the philosophical stuff, up to a point.[360]

Could it be that, at age nineteen, twenty and twenty-one, Judith was not stimulated by any but two of her lecturers? As shown in Chapter 5, in her column for *Honi Soit* Judith did mock those who studied hard at exam time as dreary and conformist, and suggested lectures were a waste of time. It is very possible that Judith arrived at university with some antipathy towards her university lecturers and curriculum, despite having strived so hard to get there. Little in her childhood would have made her reverential towards these men from the city, whose knowledge and authority were gained from books and who were unlikely to have much respect for Country Party thinking. Figures of authority within her society, people such as Phillip and May, had built their success without the aid of tertiary education. Though they respected formal education they had little time for reading. Practical self-sufficiency was their mark of success. Even the term 'intellectual' was, within the Wright family, a cause for suspicion. Judith's half-sister, Pollyanne Hill, insists Judith would have never identified with it – and for good reasons.[361]

After leaving university there were other reasons for Judith to feel antipathetic about her tertiary education. The rejection of intellectual authority within Judith's childhood married well with Jack McKinney's philosophy, which she embraced in the decade after leaving university. For Jack, dominant Western intellectual approaches relied too heavily on reason, and overlooked emotional perception. All knowledge offered by university departments was constrained by this limitation. Over the course of Judith's life this was borne out by her experience of Humanities departments, which inevitably operated within the intellectual frameworks she, for the most part, found abhorrent. In 1968 she explained that Philosophy departments 'indoctrinated' students such that graduates were unable to appreciate Jack's work. This meant he only ever received limited institutional recognition. She was not always happy about the way her poetry was taught either. In fact English departments, she told a friend in 1977, made her want to 'throw up'. There were some redeeming features of universities – mainly Science departments – for Judith did accrue many academic friends from them. But by the time Judith came to give her account of studying at university, in the 1980s, she probably had less respect for universities than she had begun with.[362]

It is, therefore, hardly surprising that her accounts tend to portray the intellectual content of university as underwhelming; a sideshow to what was in the Fisher. Psychology lecturers were not 'particularly outstanding'; the English curriculum was 'scarcely what I had in mind'; and History was 'terrible at Sydney University'. 'Frankly', she said in 1987, it 'still is'.[363] These were courses run by men who did much to shape the Humanities and Social Sciences in mid-century Australia. Their work formed theoretical touchstones for Judith, but rarely in a positive sense; most of her lecturers became, for Judith, examples of what was wrong with academia.

Brady, personally sympathetic to Judith's perspective in the 1990s, was not engaged by the question of how her subject was influenced by other intellectuals, instead emphasising how Judith came to her thinking through perception and intuition, in part in accordance with Judith and Jack's philosophy. In her chapter on Judith's time at university, Brady emphasised Judith's apparently innate abilities in critiquing conservative aspects of her university curriculum: 'even as a child she had questioned the status quo'; 'even as a child she had questioned the right of Empire'; and 'she questioned...this world' of the University.[364]

In fact, there is scant evidence that Judith did question it. As Chapter 5 showed, Judith could be critical of others but not on philosophical grounds. Her politics, as expressed through these columns, were typical of that world too. The trajectory which Brady presents – of Judith as intellectually and politically more 'progressive' than her lecturers – of intuitively approaching the Humanities in a way which would only become familiar decades later – is not supported by an examination of the university courses Judith was taking or by a close reading of her early poetry.

In addition to the philosophical reservations Judith and Brady had about the importance of Judith's tertiary education, there were practical reasons for their brevity on the subject. By the time she came to give her account, fifty years had passed since Judith had been an undergraduate. Understandably, she could not remember her lectures in much detail. She also believed, as already noted, that her energies should be directed towards social change rather than researching her own biography. And Brady's depiction of Judith's lecturers relies almost completely on Judith's unchecked recollections.

In this chapter I examine the content of the subjects Judith studied between 1934 and 1936 and the approach of her lecturers in all areas apart from English, the subject of Chapter 7. This content will be compared with published accounts of Judith's thinking, including that expressed in her early poetry. To what extent, if any, did the formal education of Judith transform her intellectually? Is a more historically attuned understanding of these formative intellectual encounters possible? And what might that reveal?

Silences, as any student of history knows, can be telling. Sometimes the matters to which Judith gave least attention in her personal accounts are the ones which prove the most complex and intriguing. This was the case with her study of History. For first year, Judith chose the subject, together with English, Philosophy and Psychology. It was a slightly unorthodox selection, which would not have been possible if she were studying for a degree. It bothered someone – who, she did not say – for she recalled, 'caring nothing for the suggestions of others' and choosing subjects which would help her become a poet.[365] Given that the most acclaimed poems of her early publishing career – 'Bullocky', 'Nigger's Leap, New England' and 'South of My Days', amongst them – turned their gaze to the past, Judith was wise to choose History and extend her schoolgirl knowledge. Indeed, over the course of her life Judith became more than a poet with an interest in history; she wrote two book-length historical works and incorporated historical research into many of her published lectures and essays, in effect claiming the status of a historian. Her time as a student in the discipline is worth considering, and especially so when we consider that *The Moving Image* was largely concerned with the colonial period in pastoral Australia, an area of study pioneered by the then Challis Chair, Stephen Roberts.

Judith revealed nothing more about the subject than the one word she used to describe it: 'terrible'. Except perhaps to Veronica Brady who explained that Judith:

> ...soon parted company with history, or with the way it was taught – Britain and the Empire, with Australia figuring only as a part of the Empire. This was the way she had been brought up to see things, but even as a child she had questioned the right of Empire. She disliked the approach of the Professor, Stephen Roberts, who had little time for things Australian, and she later called his pioneering *History of Australia* 'that bloody book. Not a word about anything but trouble with the natives...and not a word about our justification or otherwise for taking the land'.[366]

The statement: 'parted company with history', though you would not know it from Brady's book, or any other existing biographical account, in fact meant failing the subject. Judith's enrolment card, a copy of which is kept in the University archives, reveals that she did not 'enter' the exam. It is an important detail to overlook in the biography of a historian. This leads us to wonder why Judith did not 'enter' the exam, and the remainder of Brady's statement seems to provide an answer: Judith, in 1934, did not respect the approach of her lecturer because he took an uncritical view of the British Empire. Judith, even as a child, and certainly as a nineteen-year-old, understood what historians of the period failed to: their history of Australia was premised on the fiction of terra nullius. Brady's is a large claim, which deserves thorough assessment.

But before making such an assessment, it is worth examining some other details. The inclusion of quotation marks in Brady's account indicates that Judith related part of it. This we cannot know for sure since Brady's reference directs us to Judith's interviews for the National Library of Australia (NLA) – and a thorough examination of that source reveals it did not come from there. The source for this statement is especially important because of the inaccurate assertions it makes about Roberts, the most straightforward being that he did not write a book entitled *History of Australia*.[367]

Though Brady suggests Judith was surprised by the content of History, the University Calendar would have informed her that first-year British History consisted of sixty lectures in the 'General history of Great Britain, 1485–1688', followed by thirty lectures on 'Australian history'. The reading list was entirely focused on Britain, indicating that at this level Australian history was indeed considered primarily through the lens of Empire. A further thirty lectures on the economics of European imperialism were offered for those seeking a distinction. Second-year British History, taught by Roberts and Wood, was based on a similar model (sixty lectures on Britain, thirty on Australia) but the reading list included more texts on Australia (including two by Roberts) than on Britain. If Judith had wanted to study more Aus-tralian history, she needed to persist beyond first year.

But what of the more substantial claims Brady makes for Judith about Roberts? Judith, later in her life, was highly critical of Roberts' approach. In a 1977 letter to Barbara Blackman, she referred to Roberts as that 'awful old man' who wrote 'a most inaccurate book' in *History of Australian Land Settlement 1788–1920* (1924) which became a 'standard authority'. *Cry for the Dead* (1981), for which she was conducting research, was going to challenge that authority. Roberts' 1924 book was amongst the hundreds of books Judith took notes on in preparation for *Cry*. In 1987 she used Roberts to demonstrate the racism of influential historians in an article for *Aboriginal History*. There she claimed that Roberts ignored early forms of Aboriginal resistance in *The Squatting Age in Australia* (1935) until page eighty-seven, by which point in his narrative the area he was discussing had 'long been occupied'.[368]

But was this the basis for Judith's rejection of the subject in 1934? Strangely, Judith was not asked to explain why History was 'terrible' in her interviews for the NLA. In her memoir she did not discuss the subject. Our only source, then, is Brady's incorrectly sourced account, in which she asserts that the reason Judith did not approve of the subject was that it had 'little time for things Australian'. Yet Brady's own statement exposes the very flaw of that assertion; Roberts did indeed write a 'pioneering' history of Australia, even if not by that title. His master's thesis, which formed the basis for his *History of Australian Land Settlement* (1924) and *The Squatting Age in Australia* (1935), was undertaken at a time when little detailed scholarship on the first fifty years of the British colonisation of Australia existed. Ernest Scott believed that Roberts' research got to 'the core of Australian history'. A 1925 review by Keith Hancock considered that, being the 'fruit of very extensive and careful research', Roberts' book would be 'invaluable to all students of Australian history'.[369]

A more recent estimation of Roberts' project to understand the grounds – legal, political, economic – on which settlement took place, described it as a 'massive task'.[370] Roberts' research continues to illuminate our understanding of Australian history, such that lawyers and judges have referred to his work in native-title cases. Justice Kirby, in the Wik judgment, drew on Roberts' findings to argue that squatters occupied land without any right under British law; and a native-title claimant has done similarly to contend that the British government intended pastoral leases to coexist with native title.[371] In short, to say that Roberts had little time for things Australian is akin to characterising Henry Reynolds as having little time for things Australian; both men have been pioneering exponents of Australian history, within their respective periods, but from different perspectives.

Maybe Brady – and certainly it seems Judith – meant that Roberts had 'little time for things Australian' in a more fundamental sense; that his sympathies were with the Europeans who arrived in Australia, and not with the original Australians, the Aboriginal people. This, it is reasonable to assume, was the real substance of Judith's objection to the teaching of history at the University of Sydney in 1987, when she claimed it was still 'terrible'. By using that same word to describe both periods she implied that what was wrong with it in 1987 was also what was wrong with it in 1934. It seems safe to guess that Brady's account of Judith objecting to an imperialist version of history was based on conversations with her subject.

Could this be possible? To understand the likelihood of Judith objecting to Roberts' approach on the same grounds as she would decades later, we need a fuller understanding of the intellectual context in which Roberts' work appeared. And, of course, we should be clear about what Roberts said about Aboriginal people and their dispossession.

Roberts' accounts of Australian history were original because they dealt, in detail, methodically, and with reference to a wide variety of primary sources, with the early years of Australian colonisation. Roberts began his research believing that the story which would emerge would be a 'romantic' one of hardship against the odds. This was the dominant narrative which had emerged from previous histories, of which there were few. Wrote Roberts in 1924: the 'number of people publishing books on Australian history could easily be counted on part of one hand'. He was shocked, then, to discover that primary documentation relating to the period was 'so complete'.[372] These accounts led him to tell a very different story. In Roberts' two books, particularly the second, he tells of colonisation by way of capitalism.

While Roberts uses the term 'settlement' in the title of his first book, the process of colonisation he describes is not at all passive; it occurred because of aggressive, economically driven, even manic land occupation by the English ruling class; by folk such as the Wyndhams. Instead of soldiers they used sheep and cattle to 'invade' the land. Constantly pushing against government decreed boundaries, the settlers/squatters (Roberts considered both terms problematic since their meaning constantly changed) forced the official colonisation of land over a series of stages. Their sole motivation was money. And, in the 1820s, profits came from wool. The game was finding land to put sheep on. In Roberts' account, these settlers/squatters of the 1820s and 1830s were driven by desire, not rationality or idealism; moving beyond the frontier became a 'thirst', a 'pine', 'an irresistible urge' – even an 'orgy'. The 'mania' continued, and was enabled by an undemocratic, shoddy administrative structure.[373]

Roberts' primary contribution to existing scholarship was his documentation of inequality within early colonial society. He explains that the wealthy 'pure merinos' who benefited from this highly unbalanced structure sought to retain it. And he was deeply critical of them. Having 'all the arrogance of living in a community organised on a slave-basis', they were 'dull beyond conception, proud with inordinate pride that rests on no basis, and resentful of the land which gave them their living'. He could hardly have referred to the Wyndhams more specifically – but he did. These 'pure merinos', Roberts clarified, were those 'younger sons sent out to swell the family fortunes or to work off their energies in a new and distant land'. They arrived before 1830 (Margaret and George arrived in 1827) and set up around the Hunter River (as the Wyndhams did). Wealth accrued, in this context, was the result of existing English class privilege. Roberts commends governors such as Bourke whom he viewed as attempting to democratise society by constraining wealthy elites.[374]

This was not a favourable portrait of Judith's ancestors. And, as shown in Chapter 1, it was not a version commensurate with Judith's 1959 history *The Generations of Men*. For her, in this period, the squatters were a mixed bunch. Her own great-grandparents were driven in their land occupation by George's ideas of equality, by his interest in viticulture and by a boyish sense of adventure. For Roberts, such a depiction would have been fantastical; an affirmation of the continuing influence of settler/squatter thinking in Australia. Roberts and Judith were certainly not on the same page, ideologically, but perhaps not for the reasons which Brady asserts.

What of Roberts' treatment of Aboriginal people? Of Judith's or Brady's accusation that in that 'bloody book' there was 'not a word about anything but trouble with the natives…not a word about our justification or otherwise for taking the land'? What did Roberts have to say about dispossession? It is right to say that Roberts only wrote about Aboriginal people when referring to frontier violence. His subject was the European society in Australia, and since the dominant form through which encounters took place between this and Indigenous groups was confrontational, in the 1820s and 1830s in the Hunter Valley, this is what he described. Certainly, his accounts did not encompass the multi-faceted nature of their exchanges – depicted more recently – and he did not discuss the societies that existed in Australia before Europeans arrived. Reading Roberts today the gap in his work is glaringly clear. How could he not consider the fundamental issue of dispossession? Though this is a failing of that period of Australian history that most White historians and students of history would now recognise, it is hard to believe that this was so in the 1930s.

Contemporary readings of Roberts have given different verdicts of his treatment of Aboriginal people within the context in which he wrote. Henry Reynolds, whom Judith regarded highly, wrote in 1993 that Roberts performed a 'conjuring trick', erasing Aboriginal presence in his histories to imply that, prior to invasion, Australia was 'practically unsettled'.[375] Judith's account of Roberts, apparently given to Brady in the mid 1990s, echoes that of Reynolds: 'the traditional owners were scarcely mentioned at all. Their legal interest in the land was disregarded. They had disappeared from the story of land settlement'. Indeed, Roberts' 1924 book only referred to Aboriginal people on a few occasions (there was no listing for them in the index) and only as perpetrators of violence towards Europeans. He does not enter into their motivations, or suffering, but – on the other hand – he does not completely erase them from the landscape, writing that it was 'not uncommon to see' Aboriginal smoke signals. These signals, he explains, enabled tribes to gather and organise their resistance.[376] Certainly, such a depiction is inadequate, but it does admit two things: the land was already occupied, and its occupants did not accede to the invasion of their lands.

Roberts' 1935 book gave more prominence to frontier conflict and sought to provide a moral assessment of it. Judith's criticism – that the book's 'first indexed mention of Aborigines' was on page eighty-seven – was factually based but misleading. Although not indexed, Roberts mentioned Aboriginal people throughout the book, albeit often in passing, including on page nineteen, when he described convicts joining forces with 'the blacks' to terrorise the 'prosperous Hunter River'. Because *The Squatting Age* took 1835 as its starting date, it is hardly surprising that his discussion of the Myall Creek massacre, which took place in 1838, was not contextualised by 'previous Aboriginal resistance to occupation by whites', as Judith accused. This absence, she argued, gave Roberts 'carte blanche' in dealing with Myall Creek.[377] But Roberts did not present the massacre as an isolated case.

Murder, by both 'parties', was depicted sporadically throughout the book. On page eighty-seven Roberts described squatting parties committing 'atrocities' with 'disturbing frequency', including the 'loathsome crime' of killing thirty Aboriginal people at Myall Creek. He also wrote of 'native-outrages', 'massacres' and 'ravages' regularly perpetrated by

Aboriginal people. Later, Roberts dedicated several pages to discussing Myall Creek and, while he did describe the Aboriginal people as 'completely amoral' and 'unbearably impudent', as Judith relayed in *Born of the Conquerors* (1991), he also described the massacre at Myall Creek as 'horrid', and as occurring 'under particularly revolting circumstances'. Whites killed Aboriginal people on 'the slightest pretext'. Myall Creek and Port Fairy were not rare events. In the first few years of Port Phillip, he wrote, 'it was no unusual sight to come across heaps of the bones of murdered natives'. The recorded figure of 130 native deaths in the colony, Roberts continued, was far from accurate; 'the actual number must have been huge'. Elsewhere in the book, describing the disappearance of Europeans, Roberts wrote: 'whatever the circumstances and the provocation, such episodes were no remote contingences in this period, but something to be counted on in the daily course of existence'.[378]

Neither Aboriginal people nor Europeans came away looking good in Roberts' 1935 account. The impression he gave of frontier violence was that a lot of it occurred, but that it was not regularly witnessed, let alone documented. This may have been the justification of a historian aware of the gaps created by his work, but at least Roberts was not asserting the myth of terra nullius, as Reynolds claimed. Nor could it be justifiably said of Roberts' 1935 work that it ignored Aboriginal resistance to White occupation.

Richard Selleck, in his chronicle of Australian historians, argues that Roberts depicted the 'European takeover as desirable and inevitable'. Roberts' narrative does suggest inevitability (the initial colonisation of Australia was prompted, Roberts argues, by the 'logic of a few facts'; namely, that it cost more to house Britain's prison population in Britain than in newly 'discovered' land), but he does not endorse it. Instead, Roberts presents the European takeover as messy, violent, difficult and, fundamentally, the result of less-becoming human attributes: expedience and greed. According to another historian Deryck Schreuder, Roberts' 'writings on Aboriginal Australia, in particular, are often read outside their era held up for special criticism in an Australia (of today, itself) deeply burdened by that history of conquest, invasion and expropriation'. Schreuder asserts: 'he was no racist, and much of his scholarship in the 1930s expressly exposed the ideology of European racial theory'.[379]

We cannot know why Judith decided not to sit the exam for first-year history. Perhaps she found the subject too dry and disliked Roberts' insistence on painstaking research – an insistence which Wood would have had to maintain. Apparently other students felt this way.[380] Perhaps she had insufficient interest in the Stuarts, the Puritan revolution, the political thought of Bacon, or Halifax – the stuff which made up the bulk of British History I. On the other hand, perhaps Judith found the department's approach to Australian colonial history, which made up one-third of first-year history, did not accord with her own version of that history, or with that of her family. With his emphasis on the undemocratic, self-interested impulses of men such as George Wyndham, it seems very possible Judith felt offended by, or simply doubted, Roberts' version of history. Given the state of Australian history at the time, if her objections related solely to his failure to address Aboriginal dispossession she was exceptional. It seems much more likely that she developed this critique later, when she was researching *The Generations of Men* (1959) or, more likely still, when researching *Cry for the Dead* (1981).

Judith's views on Australian colonial history in 1934 may have to remain unknown, but we do have a good indication of her perspective on it throughout the following decade. Poems written between 1940 and 1944 make up the greater part of *The Moving Image* (1946), though, as argued in Chapter 8, she may have begun writing poems for that collection while still at university. *The Moving Image* reveals an interest in the dark side of colonialism, principally that experienced by Europeans in Australia. Can we say, based on a reading of Australian history in these poems, that Judith would have been critical of Roberts during the 1930s on the grounds she and Brady point towards?

Three poems of that first collection were concerned with Aboriginal people and, in particular, the loss of their populations and culture. In 'Bora Ring', Judith lamented that 'the song is gone'; that no dance, ritual or tribal story remains of a nameless tribe: 'only the grass stands up/ to mark the dancing-ring'. Perhaps most famously Judith asked: 'did we not know their blood channelled our rivers' in 'Nigger's Leap,

New England', and described the violence which gave the landmark its name.

> ...be dark, O lonely air.
> Make a cold quilt across the bone and skull
> that screamed falling in flesh from the lipped cliff
> and then were silent, waiting for the flies.

Although this image has been recounted as evidence that, even in the 1940s, Judith had a good understanding of Aboriginal colonial experience, her understanding was very different from that within the postcolonial scholarship that praised it. Inevitably, her intellectual framework was shaped by the context in which she wrote. In the poem, the 'bone and skull' which falls from the cliff is not only not named, or given any particularity at all, but there is no explanation of why 'it' fell. Instead, the image is abstracted and a–historicised (except by the title, which provides some particularity); it floats within the poem without any authorial explanation.[381]

When considered in the context of Judith's juvenilia and university poetry, the imagery of 'Nigger's Leap' reads more like an attempt to maintain generic convention than a comment on Australian history. As discussed in Chapter 3, Judith's juvenilia regularly incorporated ghosts and fairies. Her university poetry (focused on in Chapter 8) was also engaged by supernatural mysteries and ghouls. Such figures became intensely meaningful for the postcolonial critiques of the 1980s and 1990s, but when Judith employed them in the 1940s, 1930s, and even the 1920s, they reflected the influence of Ethel's enthusiasm for Victorian Gothicism, popular within women's magazines at the time. This aesthetic, the first poetic model Judith encountered, utilised strong images which often incorporated death, flight and the menacing force of nature.

Gothicism permeates *The Moving Image*, even poems not about Australian history. In 'Brothers and Sisters', three children lay awake, their 'fluttering' thoughts and fears meeting 'tentative as moths'. The ominous final line of that poem – 'there is nothing to be afraid of. Nothing at all' – relishes being afraid. Although darker, and more sophisticated in form, 'Brothers and Sisters' is reminiscent of Judith's childhood poem 'The Flickering Candlelight'. Then she asked: 'Isn't it fun to go to bed/ In the flickering candlelight?... For who knows what horrible beasties might stop/ in the flickering candlelight!'[382]

The invocation of child ghosts was another gothic convention which Judith employed in *The Moving Image*. 'Half-Caste Girl', the third poem about Aboriginal people from that collection, depicts a ghost girl who wonders at, and is 'restless' between, 'the noise of the living' and the 'pain of the dying'. (Notably, throughout *The Moving Image*, Aboriginal people are either dead or extinct; in 'Nigger's Leap' for example: 'never from earth again the coolamon/ or thin black children dancing'.) The girl of mixed-race's dilemma is typical of non-Indigenous depictions of Aboriginality in the period. Like the 1950s character Jedda, from the film of the same name, this girl of mixed-race is mournfully and passively pulled in two opposing directions.[383] Will she sever her ties with a dying race, and join 'the living'?

Judith criticised Roberts for his focus on the hardships experienced by Europeans in Australia, but the European struggle to survive in a hostile landscape was a principal concern of *The Moving Image*. Even in 'Nigger's Leap' the death of an Aboriginal person symbolises nature's power to overcome – not Aboriginal people, but Europeans. When she wrote 'O all men are one man at last', it was not an assertion, primarily, that violence inflicted on Aboriginal people by Europeans diminished Europeans morally, but a kind of warning that the Aboriginal people's fate – extinction – may be that of the Europeans who now occupy the same gothic landscape. Nature's destructive force reduces all human beings to the same mortality.

Judith's driving vision was universalist and humanist. To include Aboriginal people in this schema, in the 1940s, was politically progressive, but not in the same way as later forms of political progressivism. During the 1980s and 1990s, when the poem was read through a postcolonial lens, it was more politically progressive to assert racial difference, a position which many sympathetic readers ascribed to the poem. But 'Nigger's Leap' does not assert racial difference, or even the importance of race in determining the events of history – such as this massacre. The poem does not contend that 'we should have known' of the colonial violence in the way that Henry Reynolds does during the 1990s, but instead that 'we' should have learnt the lesson of 'their' fate so it does not afflict 'us' too.

> ...We should have known
> the night that tided up the cliffs and hid them
> had the same question on its tongue for us.
> And there they lie that were ourselves writ strange.

The image of dead black bodies does not invite us to consider the forces which led to this massacre, or even the consequences of such massacres. Instead, non-Indigenous readers are meant to consider their own future in this apparently doomed landscape. Critically, the menacing, threatening force depicted in the poem is not people, or social processes, but nature − in the form of night. It was much the same in Judith's juvenilia. Other formal aspects of the poem, such as the sense of scale and timelessness it creates, diminish human agency and present the deaths as part of an inevitable, almost natural process of human conquest: 'night floods us suddenly as history/ that has sunk many islands in its good time'. Philip Mead regards the line as 'an attempted sublation of frontier violence into a grander economy of "man" and "time"'.[384] The poem does not, of course, deny frontier violence. But it seems to position its cause as beyond human control.

Why should Judith have sought such an effect in her 1940s poetry? Does it undermine her position of later years, based on an understanding of history through reference to the social world? Though the vast bulk of literature on Judith's poetry lauds her depiction of Aboriginal people as ahead of its time, Andrew McCann's observations of 'At Cooloolah', a poem published in *Two Fires* (1955), provide a more nuanced reading of her early poetry. He argues that while the poem describes, mournfully, the passing of an Aboriginal presence, it also 'imagines that coloniser and colonised are both part of a vast natural schema in which colonial conflict is subsumed'; that the 'much larger temporal dimension' or 'timeless natural horizon' of the poem creates the illusion that the events within it are not real, or relevant to today. They even provide a 'melancholic pleasure' for the poet and reader, a pleasure which contains and helps to resolve anxiety regarding the nation's past. McCann's opinion is that the poet was not entirely in control of such effects. Her use of the Romantic form, with its inevitable evocation of a metaphysical reality, worked to undermine the story she told: 'Wright is probably as progressive as one can be within the framework of Romanticism'.[385]

Such a conclusion has pertinent corollaries for this study: the poet's meaning is, McCann says, constrained by her schooling in a poetic language – more than we might imagine; more, certainly, than has been imagined of Judith. It is not a criticism of Judith to say that her views were informed by the society in which she lived, even if they were informed to a lesser extent, after university, than they are for most of us. Later, when she sought out different perspectives on Australian history, and these were increasingly available, Judith came to the conclusion that the difficulties Europeans faced in Australia were dwarfed by those of Indigenous people. She did this well ahead of most Australians, even those working within the Humanities, and together with other visionaries, such as Nugget Coombs, actually led Australians towards a deeper understanding of their history. Her efforts at educating Australians, made in countless speeches, letters, and in her roles on various boards, may have been strengthened by a knowledge, whether conscious or not, that her views had changed the more she learnt. Within the field of Australian literary studies, Judith's intellectual trajectory is sometimes forgotten in the race to contextualise her work within contemporary philosophical schemas. McCann's caution in treating her early work, as it so often is, as 'indicative of a progressive postcolonial poetics', is helpful: she could not produce such a poetics within the constraints of a Romantic framework or, this chapter argues, at that moment in history, and her history.[386]

Brady was not the only one to be less than scrupulous in attributing contemporary motivations to the past. Judith was also prone to this. In fact, Brady's misrepresentations sometimes derive from being too 'sympathetic and inclusive to its subject', as Philip Mead termed it, and not challenging Judith's reading of the past with alternative accounts.[387] Despite reminding her reader in *Collected Poems* (1994) that the poems were 'written out of the events, the thinking and feeling, the whole emotional climate and my own involvements of that time', the controversy around 'Bullocky' reveals an anxiety about the extent to which she was swayed by history. During the 1980s Judith became frustrated that 'Bullocky', her most famous poem from *The Moving Image*, was interpreted by some as a 'hymn to the pioneers' and withdrew it from further publication in anthologies.[388] The controversy became well known, though a minor scandal in a national literary history busy with hoaxes. Recently published letters cast new light on the affair, and suggest that Judith's reading of that poem, and her explanation of the motivations behind writing it, changed over the course of several decades.

In 1963 Judith told friend Dorothy Green that she had 'never thought of the Bullocky as a religious maniac'. The disclosure is significant given that many have, more recently, read his state of mind as a reflection of the colonial project. If he was mad, perhaps the poem was saying the whole exercise were so. But, Judith continued, given that Green had raised the subject, it was worth noting that the historical figure on whom she based the bullock driver was 'probably a kind of religious maniac'. Phillip remembered the man, on whom his daughter based the poem, as a member of 'a Brethren cult' whose most notable characteristic was that he did not swear.[389]

But it seems that, during the 1960s, whether or not he was mad was not significant. 'Let me emphasise', Judith continued in her letter to Green, that 'this hasn't anything to do with the poem'. The poem was meant to 'justify old men like him, and in fact to justify the human race, I suppose, or certain of its actions and pursuits'. When she wrote the poem, she remembered in the 1960s, she thought principally in terms of a human race, from which all actions and pursuits emerged. Judith added: 'I more or less accidentally said something that a lot of people felt needed saying at the time about *Australia*'.[390] She gave the final word emphasis. Looking back, almost two decades later, Judith did think the poem was a comment on Australian history, and that it showed the difficulties faced by European pioneers.

Then, in 1986, when her thinking on Australian history had developed, she explained to Stephen Murray-Smith that she objected to the way critics had read the poem 'shorn of context', and that it was 'being taught as an uncritical praise of the pioneers'. What was the context which Judith believed needed to be applied to a reading of 'Bullocky'?

The fact is, the old man in question…was mad insofar as he was a religious maniac, though of a gentle order as I personally knew him. Yes, the pioneers were mad all right, and often wicked too.[391]

Now his madness was relevant. The poem went from being, over a course of two decades, the 'justification' of a universal character, to the condemnation of certain actions and pursuits, represented by the bullock-driver's deranged and morally suspect state of mind.

As this episode suggests, and should be emphasised in any discussion of Judith's early poetry, a consideration of the difficulties faced by Europeans in Australia would not, in the 1930s and 1940s, have the same political implications that it would in the last decades of the twentieth century. In the later period there was an association between sympathetic portrayals of colonial Australians and unsympathetic responses to Aboriginal people — an association which Judith affirmed with her criticism of Roberts. But, she might have remembered, this association was not as well defined in the 1930s. Then, stories of colonial hardship were connected more readily with radical nationalism and the originating legends of labour politics. With that in mind, poems such as Judith's 'Country Town' were challenging when they were published in the 1940s, especially for a daughter of Country Party politics. In it, descendants of Irish convicts are chased by doubts which insist 'this is not ours, nor ours the flowering tree'. Whose tree it is does not preoccupy that poem. The doubts are about losing that which 'we have lost and left behind'. So great is the sense of displacement that, despite the century of settlement, the subjects feel 'the chains are stronger' now.

This sense of displacement, experienced by Europeans, is, in the end, the central lamentation of 'Nigger's Leap'; of how coming to a foreign (alienating and gothic) land has changed all understanding of the world, that gained through both rational knowledge and emotional perception.

> …Now we must measure
> our days by nights, our tropics by their poles,
> love by its end and all our speech by silence.
> See in these gulfs, how small the light of home.

It is a theme explored in other poems, including those based on Judith's family members: 'Remittance Man', 'Hawthorn Hedge' and 'For New England'. Such poems tell stories of struggle and hardship. They seem to be the 'old stories that still go walking in my sleep', as she writes in 'South of My Days'; they are the stories of her upbringing. In 'For New England' she asks: 'Where's home, Ulysses?' The bind was that of being, like her grandmother May, at home and not at home in Australia: 'I find in me the double tree', she wrote. The final poem in *The Moving Image*, 'Dust', potently restates the theme of hardship and suggests its continuance.

The Moving Image shows that, in the early 1940s, Judith's main historical interest was the difficulty experienced by Europeans in Australia. One could make the same accusation towards the collection that Judith made against Roberts: Why is the original fact of dispossession not treated critically, rather than just its aftermath? Certainly, as with Roberts' work, violence is depicted, but there is no moral guide for understanding it. And though Aboriginal people are presented in *The Moving Image*, they no longer exist, alive, in the present. They have effectively vanished from the landscape of the present. In McCann's terms, they operate primarily as subjects in a European style 'elegiac literature', with its fetishisation of nature as wilful and human beings as passive. The effect, he suggests, is a 'literature of extinction'.[392]

Certainly, as McCann notes, Judith did not celebrate such notions, but her mournful, passive, even accepting tone was consistent with that of those who advocated a 'smooth the dying pillow' approach, a position Judith would later condemn. When her 'half-caste' girl looked to the hills, they were the 'hills that belong to no people'. Her 'mixed' racial status undid her claims to ownership. Moreover, by presenting the land as her own – 'my blood's country', 'my land...my pastures' – it could be argued, in the terms of contemporary post-colonial scholarship, that *The Moving Image* undermined the unique relationship of Aboriginal people to their land.[393]

Too often Judith's personal narrative has been recounted with the same lack of historical context – of the possibilities, intellectually and culturally, that existed in a period – that has afflicted critical readings of her 1940s poetry. Why could Judith not accept that she was a product of her time, as we all are? It is enough to say that Judith wanted to know about colonial violence during the 1940s. This is impressive, given the state of political discourse at the time. But it is too much to say that Judith, during the 1930s, objected to the teaching of Australian history on the grounds that it did not address dispossession.

History was the only subject which Judith failed at university. It was clearly important to her that she passed ten subjects (the bachelor's requirement) because she enrolled in eleven to compensate for her fail mark. Since, for most courses, the University published a list of students in order of merit, it is possible to see that, in her first year, Judith came twenty-second out of thirty students in philosophy. This was to be no indication of the importance she would later store in the discipline. In 1991 Shirley Walker put it directly: 'Judith Wright is a philosopher', and she claimed the extent to which Judith was influenced by the discipline 'has not generally been recognised'. Most critics have acceded to Judith's claim that her experience of philosophy was mediated through the work of her husband, Jack McKinney. In 1975, she reflected that there was 'so much of the influence of Jack's work' in her poetry. The poem, 'The Moving Image', she told her daughter, was in fact an expression of Jack's philosophy.[394] There, she responded confidently to central questions in Western philosophy: 'all that is real is to live, to desire, to be', and announced her concerns with the title, which came from Plato's statement: 'time is a moving image of eternity'. But did Judith's engagement with philosophy begin only when she met Jack, in the early 1940s?

Evidence suggests Judith had more than a passing familiarity with philosophy before she met Jack. Although she remembered studying philosophy for just one year, her enrolment card shows she studied it for two. In second year she received a better mark; although she also scored a 'pass'. It put her fourteenth in a class of twenty-three students. Walker said that Judith's tutor, John Passmore, remembered her as a 'keen and proficient student', although he only taught her in second year.[395] Her results indicate that hindsight may have aided this impression. Still, Judith's description of first encountering Jack, in the early 1940s, reveals that she had a good understanding of the fundamentals of Western philosophy before then. When she read his work, she remembered, she was struck by its 'gentle naivety and a lack of knowledge of what was going on in philosophy'. *She* had a greater knowledge of the contemporary field. When she raised objections to his work, she 'was always brought up sharply against the incontrovertible fact that my criticisms were based on the very world' that he was questioning. To Jack, she had been schooled in a philosophy, and a way of arguing, which made it difficult to understand his work. It was a position he, and Judith, retained throughout their lives; even today, their daughter Meredith McKinney advises against seeking to appreciate her father's work via the study of Philosophy within a university department.[396] And so Judith set about 'undoing' her conceptual framework gained at university.

But exactly what kind of conceptual framework had university Philosophy given her? Was it simply an introduction to Western thought? In 1934 first-year Philosophy focused on the use of logic in language and argument. Second-year Philosophy considered Greek philosophy, with an emphasis on Socrates. While these subjects looked, on paper, to be an uncontroversial exploration of the basis of Western philosophy, and indeed an introduction to the ideas that Jack would critique, there was another factor at work which made the department's teaching far from conventional; it was headed by Professor John Anderson.

Academic Kathleen Fitzpatrick said of Australian Humanities departments during the period that they were so understaffed that the best lecturers could do was 'pass on the tradition of knowledge'.[397] Teaching the 'basics', what today would be called the canon, was essential in all subjects. Yet because departments were so small, and the hierarchy within them so delineated, if the Chair had the time, he had scope to pursue his own interests within lectures. By all accounts, this was the case in the Philosophy department where Anderson explored, most notoriously, his difficult relationship with communism.

Judith's enrolment in Philosophy must have caused her father some unease. By the mid 1930s Anderson had become well known outside the University. The newly established Australian Broadcasting Commission broadcast his lectures, and newspapers published his articles on social issues. But it was his address to the Freethought

Society, in 1931, in which he questioned the value of war memorials as part of a critique of patriotism, which brought him real prominence. His ideas were attacked in the upper and lower chambers of the New South Wales parliament. The Country Party asked for his resignation. Anderson escaped with 'a strong parliamentary censure', followed by another from the University Senate. While he denied allegiance to any political party, the University history notes that 'many parents and members of the general public viewed his talks as preaching a gospel of communism'. He was, to many, a 'threat to their children'. Phillip, who was a senior member of the party which had sought Anderson's resignation and who would become president of a party, in the 1950s, which would declare Australia in 'dire peril' from the 'southward thrust of Communist world conquerors', must have been concerned.[398]

That Judith continued with Philosophy for two years suggests that she was interested at least in some of Anderson's thinking. It has been claimed that he influenced a generation of Australian philosophers, poets, public intellectuals, public servants and legal professionals (although some remember this group of intellectuals as singularly male) so why not Judith? The University history claims that his classes were 'for many students the high points of their undergraduate years'. Donald Horne concurred: 'Anderson seemed the most important person at the university'.[399]

But Judith was less enthusiastic in her memoir. Describing Anderson she wrote only that he was a 'radical left-wing philosopher' under whose tutelage she took a somewhat enigmatically expressed 'uninviting step into criticism of society'. Further in, she recalled her experience of academic philosophy when describing how she first felt when encountering Jack. To her, Anderson was useful in 'pointing out the faulty thinking, the non sequiturs and false assumptions of the political philosophers, of communism as well as capitalism'. But, she continued, 'to clear away the false was not going to lead to discovery of the true'. Here is where 'what Jack was arguing made sense'; he was finding the truth. In this light, Anderson's significance to her life became, primarily, his scepticism. Certainly this was a memorable trait; James McAuley said Anderson had an answer to every philosophy, and that was 'no'.[400]

Judith's account of Anderson has to be treated carefully. As was the case with Australian history, after university Judith's approach to philosophy was guided by a belief that academic scholarship in the discipline was seriously flawed. 'Knowing what I did of the department', in the early 1940s, she guessed that Jack's book manuscript, sent there for refereeing, would not be treated favourably. Indeed it was not. Anderson was not the reader but he probably would not have supported it either, being a strong proponent of Greek philosophy on the basis that it formed 'an important corrective to the attitudes and forms of inquiry dominating modern philosophy'. Anderson thought the modern obsession with the 'problem of knowledge' was wrong. Though Jack differed from most modern academic philosophers, a concern with epistemology shaped his philosophy, as indicated by the title of his book *The Structure of Modern Thought* (1971). In fact, Jack believed that a commitment to Socratic thinking had led Philosophy departments to become obsessed with language, and that this represented an endpoint in Western knowledge.[401] Given these philosophical differences, Judith was unlikely to have given a flattering portrayal of Anderson's introduction to Western philosophy.

But had Anderson influenced Judith politically, as her brief description of him helping her take an 'uninviting step into criticism of society' suggests? In her interviews for the NLA, Judith was more forthcoming on this question. She described being led by Anderson on a march to Trades Hall singing 'The Red Flag'. It must have been the stuff of nightmares for Phillip. But, she insisted, she was not the only one led; 'everybody was, not just me!' For her, this act – and her subsequent reading of Marx – came out of a writerly need to 'know what was going on, that was all'. When Judith recalled 'the Depression made you think', she spoke about this challenge as one which afflicted her generation at large, not her in any particular way. The 'feeling that there had to be a change was immense...I think there were few of us who weren't influenced in some way or another by Marx'. For her part, she repeated, although 'interested in social amelioration in some way or another', she 'wasn't ever a political person'.[402] As Chapter 5 has shown, if she was challenged by Anderson's discussion of social inequality, she did not portray it in her public persona.

Rather than making Judith sympathetic to left-wing politics, Anderson had the effect of making her more critical of them. At least this is how Judith remembered it. In her NLA interview she stressed that he 'offered a very good critique of socialism and communism', and elsewhere, also in the late 1980s, claimed that Anderson's influence prevented her from becoming involved in the Communist Party of Australia (CPA): 'I was lucky enough not to become one of the fish who perished entangled in the [Communist] Party Line – John Anderson's astringent critiques of their facts and arguments in my university days put me off, apart from the infighting'.[403]

Yet Anderson offered a lot more by way of 'criticising society' than criticising Soviet-sanctioned communism. To take only this lesson from his teachings suggests Judith was very selective in what she learnt; that, perhaps, her father's abhorrence of communism primed her for any critique of it. Anderson might not have been a member of the CPA but, during the mid 1930s, he accepted many fundamental Marxist principles, such as the purported relationship between base and superstructure, the class theory of society, and the idea of the State as the organ of the ruling class. The University history describes him as a follower of Trotsky during these years. Anderson's vehement denunciation of the Australian ruling class for propagating 'ideologies such as individualism, utilitarianism and liberalism to justify the continuing dominance of the State' must have amazed the young woman who had grown up regarding her father, the obvious head of their society, as benevolent and good. Anderson scholar Mark Weblin believes that during 1935, when Anderson taught Judith, economics became a focus and Anderson continued to believe that revolution was necessary in order to abolish the 'special function of the entrepreneur'.[404]

Judith's letters from the early 1950s, during the Cold War, show how far she was from becoming 'entangled' in communist politics; that she had no sympathy for claims that the capitalist state employed ideological coercion. For mid-century Australian writers, a divisive question became whether politics could, or should, be separated from literature. As John McLaren has detailed, the conservative Australian government devised various strategies for separating 'literary from political issues', such as withholding funding from organisations, projects or individuals who were regarded as left wing. It was a scheme, McLaren writes, driven by 'a paranoic fear of communism and anything that could be associated with it'.[405]

During the 1940s and 1950s Judith was repelled by one of the most basic of Marxist concepts: that ideology is pervasive. To her, it was possible to separate ideology from literature; in 1952 she affirmed 'politics and writing don't mix'. Two years later, her position was put to the test. Judith's former publisher and *Meanjin* editor Clem Christesen wrote asking if she would support his petition against attempts by the Australian committee of the Congress for Cultural Freedom (CCF; funded by the American Central Intelligence Agency, or CIA, though this was not known at the time), to undermine his magazine on the grounds that it was sympathetic to communism. The original alliance between Judith and Christesen, which saw Judith move to Brisbane in 1944 to volunteer for *Meanjin*, was forged on the understanding that 'politics and writing don't mix'. A 1944 letter, from Judith to Christesen, shows her praising his approach: 'I think your policy of keeping clear of political bias is the only possible policy for a magazine such as *Meanjin*...and [I] would be wholeheartedly with you there'. Personal and professional disagreements in the 1940s saw their relationship degenerate into rare pieces of tense and confrontational correspondence.[406]

During the 1950s Christesen claimed his politics were unchanged. He was still a liberal and declared no connection with the CPA. Nonetheless the Australian Security Intelligence Organisation (ASIO) classified him as a 'communist sympathiser'. The claim threatened his tenuous funding arrangement with the Commonwealth Literary Fund and his position at the University of Melbourne. In response to Christesen's request, Judith replied: 'I do not regard the modern techniques of "charge and counter-charge" and complicated political manoeuvring by whatever "side" as likely to reach any solution to the world's problems'.[407] It must have been a frustration for Christesen, who also identified the need to go beyond charge and counter-charge.

Judith declined Christesen's invitation to sign or amend his letter of petition and pointed out that he could hardly have picked 'anyone less suitable' than her for assistance. In his original letter he had provided Judith with a list of members, presumably of the CCF, in order to gain her knowledge of them. Judith replied that she knew none of them, except Spender. Stephen Spender was a well-known writer and editor of the anti-communist British magazine *Encounter*, also, it was to be revealed, funded by the CIA. She told Christesen that he was brought to her, 'at a day's notice', in Mount Tamborine, in southern Queensland where she lived, 'by some of the Brisbane members, or at least I suppose they were members, though I don't know them and cannot even remember most of their names'. In fact, she recalled elsewhere, these 'members' constituted 'a flanking bodyguard of sinister black-suited guides or guards', which must have signalled that the visit represented more than literary camaraderie. To Christesen she said only that Spender 'seems reasonably interested in Australian flora and fauna', and suggested that 'a solution' to the broader problem of political conflict should be found on different terms,

> ...terms which make a demand upon self-discipline, inner sincerity and capacity for feeling which it seems impossible for most people to compass, and less and less possible the more such 'charge and counter-charges' are indulged in.

She suggested Christesen read McKinney's work.[408]

Perhaps ironically, Anderson's greatest influence on Judith was to heighten her suspicion of communism and communist sympathisers. His criticisms of the State for maintaining its authority through ideological coercion made less of an impression, evidently, than his criticisms of party alignment. She would not be the only one. A group of students, loosely known as 'Andersonians', and which included James McAuley, Joan Fraser (who later wrote as Amy Witting), Harold Stewart and A. D. Hope, were said to have developed a position which mixed Anderson's thinking with anarchism. It has been claimed that Anderson had the effect of 'immunising' his 'leftist disciples' of the 1930s against the CPA. McAuley, of course, was so well immunised that in the 1950s he went on to edit the CCF-funded *Quadrant* magazine, and work closely with Latham, in an effort to counter the influence of communism in Australian intellectual life.[409]

In a further irony, and in another indication that Judith's enthusiasm for Anderson had its definite limits, she did not continue with third-year Philosophy which, in 1936, was a course on modern philosophy. In it, 'theories of knowledge, and of space and time' were addressed, subjects which would preoccupy Judith and Jack in the early

1940s, and help form *The Moving Image*. It seems that Anderson's main influence on Judith was to confirm any suspicions of communism that her father may have encouraged; to in fact treat any promise of social solution with doubt. Jack's philosophy, which was critical of almost all academic philosophers, and the broader intellectual approaches endorsed by the University, might have been characterised by its scepticism, but he and Judith maintained that ultimately it would 'lead to discovery of the true'.[410]

At university, Judith remembered, she was most excited by the prospect of studying Psychology, Oriental Studies and Anthropology. Being new subjects, they 'seemed to hold more hope for the thinking I thought the future would demand'. Though her results for these subjects were similarly unremarkable, she was more expansive in her written and verbal accounts of them than of other subjects, implying that they affected her more deeply. They were certainly cutting edge. The Psychology department at the University of Sydney was the first in the world, with Henry Lovell appointed as the first Chair only a few years before Judith arrived, in 1929. According to Kathleen Price, who attended the University ten years earlier, 'a lot of women said they would not marry a man who hadn't been to Dr Lovell's course', so original and convincing was his analysis of personality as dynamic and reactive, and so admired his opinions on the best ways to treat women. Her mother, a strict Methodist, was horrified by the concepts Price brought home. She remembered that when 100 of her peers sat down to Lovell's lectures all were excited to be there – and other sources concur.[411]

For Judith, although Psychology was 'quite interesting', the subject was conceived 'well before the revolution in psychology and most of what we got was behaviourism, which rather bored me'. Her hopes in the subject's capacity to think about the future were confounded. The University Calendar suggests the subject was more behaviourism than marital relations, but Lovell may have strayed from course prescriptions, as Anderson did. The fact that Psychology was a prerequisite for studies in Education and Anthropology indicates that it aimed to understand external behaviour and group dynamics, as opposed to pursuing rigorous internal exploration, later made famous by Freud. In the exam, as well as responding to questions on 'scientific method', students could choose from a list of 'special branches' that ranged from psychology of mental tests and abnormal psychology, to comparative and animal psychology.[412] Judith yearned for an understanding of culture more than science.

To this end, in her final two years she took Oriental Studies and Anthropology, the former of which was focused entirely on Japanese culture in its pre-modern form. As a child Judith had written a poem titled 'The Lady of Japan', in which she observed of the woman in a picture: 'Oh, little lady of Japan, in your long kimono/ How many things you seem to see, how many things to know'. The young Judith, typically, proclaimed a greater desire for adventure than for fragile feminine beauty, concluding that she did not envy the lady for she had never 'climbed the rugged pines'. Ostensibly concerned with 'European Intercourse and Foundation of the Tokugawa Shogunate, 1530–1650', Judith remembered Oriental History for its exploration of 'all kinds of aesthetic concepts, and different views'. It was 'quite the most civilising course' she did at university, and 'very important to me.' An unconventional subject, it gave her insight into a culture which was 'tremendously different from ours'. Run by Arthur Lindsay Sadler, the subject introduced Japanese culture not as words on a page but as a whole aesthetic and sensibility. Sadler and his Japanese wife invited the small class to have lunch in their garden. Judith recalled the experience 'fascinated' her.[413]

Oriental studies presented culture in its purest form. When asked whether the subject caused any disquiet amongst her compatriots, Judith remembered that it did not acknowledge the Japanese present. There was such little discussion of contemporary Japan that she was 'scarcely conscious of Japan as a presence, except as a possible trading partner, until Pearl Harbor'. Then, everything changed. Yet Judith's grounding in Japanese culture seems to have instilled in her sympathy for the country that many Australian survivors of World War II did not share. Later, in the early 1970s, when Judith's daughter Meredith McKinney studied Japanese language before pursuing further study in Kyoto (what was to be the beginning of a life-long career in Japanese studies), Judith was an enthusiastic backer.[414]

Anthropology, however, was Judith's favourite university subject. The department was headed by Australia's most influential anthropologist, Adolphus Peter Elkin. His junior, Bill Stanner, who spent most of his time gathering data in the field, would become a dear friend and political ally for Judith. In 1935 first-year Anthropology examined 'primitive sociology' and provided an introduction to the study of culture with reference to the oceanic societies, Australia, New Guinea, Melanesia, Polynesia, Micronesia and Indonesia. Selected groups from other parts of Asia, Africa and America were also considered. A vast sweep of societies, they were linked only by their Western categorisation, 'primitive'.[415] As that word suggests, anthropologists considered such societies an earlier version of their own. In 1930s Australia this was both soothing (the extinction of Aboriginal people, seemed, in these terms, an inevitable, preferable step in human advancement) and disturbing (Aboriginal people formed societies of human beings, as complex as any).

Anthropology was not a widely respected discipline in Australia at the time. Possibly related to this was the fact that women were overrepresented in enrolments and awards for Anthropology, distinguishing it from the vast majority of other disciplines.[416] At the University of Sydney a department was formed in 1925, but it remained the only one in the country until 1949. Judith remembers the course being 'looked down upon by the university' because Elkin did not have a degree and his research findings on the 'mechanics of Aboriginal societies', including kinship and marriage laws, were regarded as unseemly by some. Such findings brought him 'up against officialdom'. Despite this, powerful figures supported the discipline. When it was threatened with closure in the 1930s the interventions of former prime ministers Stanley Bruce and Joseph Lyons saved it, ensuring Anthropology continued to receive direct government funding. In turn, the school operated special training that allowed unmatriculated public servants from the Department of Home and Territories, as well as missionaries, to study after receiving preliminary training in New Guinea.[417]

The close association with government extended to Elkin contributing to public policy. In 1939 he produced a draft paper titled 'New Deal for Aborigines', which has been credited with shifting public policy towards assimilation, most dramatically by removing

Aboriginal children from their parents. Looking back in 1973, Elkin understood that his work had presented assimilation as inevitable – he had seen it as a way of 'helping Aborigines to adjust themselves to the changes which had come upon them' – but he also thought it had inspired pride in traditional Indigenous cultures. Stuart Macintyre encapsulates this apparent contradiction: 'while expounding the rich complexity of Aboriginal culture, he believed that it was fragile and unlikely to withstand exposure to European culture'. When Judith sat in the Anthropology lecture hall she was enthralled, being 'interested in Aborigines, something that almost nobody I knew' was.[418]

What formed Judith's original interest in the discipline would become a preoccupying subject in her life narrative. She considered it in her memoir, at length in her NLA interviews, and throughout several published essays. Such considerations were made towards the end of her life, a period dominated by her activism in Aboriginal affairs. Judith's unease with her privilege, a product of Australian colonialism, was somewhat mitigated by the approach her friend Henry Reynolds forged with his question: 'Why weren't we told?' It implied a conspiracy of silence by the previous generation, and genuine innocence and goodwill on the part of his generation. It provided a framework for understanding racism – in short, 'ignorance' – and a way out of it: education. In light of this, Judith's juvenile understanding of Aboriginal people and her attempts at self-education became a matter of public relevance.

According to her interviews for the NLA, and her memoir, Judith developed a curiosity about Aboriginal people in response to the awkward presence they occupied in her childhood. She saw Aboriginal people working on her grandmother's station, Wongwibinda, the women in the kitchen and the men out mustering. They did not constitute a large presence; those involved in musters were mostly away from the station and Judith remembered only a couple of Aboriginal women working in the kitchen, 'for a while'. Yet they made an impression. Judith recalled the Cohen and Brown families, and referred to them on several occasions in her writing. The children of these workers were even more interesting to the young Judith. There was Bill Cohen, who was always riding a horse, and Gracie, a potential playmate whom Judith and her cousin 'were not encouraged to have much to do with'. Perhaps Judith understood, without being told, the magnitude of their difference for, she said, 'something kept us apart'.[419]

Unlike most of Judith's Anthropology classmates, from the city, she had had direct contact with Aboriginal people, but such contact had not brought about any meaningful exchange. Beyond the station, Aboriginal people were little more than a visual presence in her young life. There were always, she remembered, a 'few dark shadows' who lived in 'scattered enclaves'. Elsewhere, she described these remote figures as 'seldom visible on the fringes of our lives', so much so that they 'might as well not have been there at all for all the mention they got' in her household. Yet the workers, their children, even the shadows, made her think. Throughout the years, she 'wondered about them'.[420] This was why she enrolled in Anthropology.

In such accounts, studying Anthropology was the first adult act in a life of striving to uncover; the end of childhood wonderment, the beginning of adult knowledge. In the introduction to her collection of essays *Born of the Conquerors* (1991), Judith explained that enrolling in Anthropology formed part of her journey from being 'born of the conquerors' to participating in the Aboriginal Treaty Committee, 'at last to do something to redress the old wrongs', and on to writing that very book, the fulfilment of a promise to see 'some kind of justice'. Beginning, 'I spent a couple of years at Sydney University in the then new anthropology course', Judith explained that she had been alerted to Australia's violent history by two incidents, both of which became the subject of her poetry. The first was her father's story 'of the driving of an Aboriginal group suspected of killing cattle' over a cliff, and the second was being told about an Aboriginal bora ring, which existed on her grandmother's property.[421]

The implication was that Judith's interest in anthropology was, in part, a product of such stories. It is a confused chronology for, as Judith also notes, she was told the cliff story just 'a few years' before writing 'Nigger's Leap, New England'. This is supported by her memoir, which depicts her father telling her the story in 1943. That was several years *after* she studied Anthropology. The bora ring story may have been a part of her childhood, for she remembers reference to 'bora paddock'. Yet it was most likely just a name, for in her childhood it was never acknowledged that 'only three or four generations earlier'

Aboriginal people had been in sole possession of the land. And her father, she remembers, although affected by the cliff story, generally understood that the past was justified. Anything else would have been a betrayal of his kin, she said, who tended to feel 'scorn and contempt for Aborigines'.[422]

Other accounts were more straightforward in linking Judith's upbringing with her interest in anthropology, and compounded Judith's dubious chronology with further inaccuracies. A biographical note, which prefaced *Born of the Conquerors*, explained:

> Keenly aware of her background as a member of the 'pastoral aristocracy', Judith Wright strove to uncover the real history of the land, the dispossession of Aboriginal people and the destruction of the environment. She studied anthropology under Professor A. P. Elkin at the University of Sydney in the 1930s, but found the academic discipline was arid.

Brady saw it similarly, but emphasised the importance of Judith's family in forming this interest:

> [Anthropology at university] was of great interest to a young woman from a pastoral family whose father had a feeling for the Aboriginal past and whose paternal grandfather (as she later discovered) had been unusually interested in the Aboriginal people...[423]

Phillip's memoir does not reveal such an interest, and his daughter's accounts indicate he discussed the history of Aboriginal people with Judith on only a few occasions, although these occasions became significant for Judith in retrospect. The idea that she wanted to study Anthropology in the 1930s because she had been influenced by a grandfather whom she had never met, and whose interest in Aboriginal people she only discovered by reading his diaries in the late 1940s, is similarly confusing.[424]

As has been emphasised throughout this book, there exists a failure to adhere to proper chronology in accounts of Judith Wright's life. Part of this came about through Brady's lack of interest in historical timelines. Part of it may have been due to the changing positions

Judith assumed in the latter decades of her life. As well as those already discussed in this chapter, Judith's treatment of Elkin serves as an example of these changing positions. In 1991 she was critical of him, noting that after a couple of years studying Anthropology at the University of Sydney she concluded that 'for anthropologists... Aborigines seemed little more than objects of study'. Similarly, in 1999, she described being disappointed to find that Anthropology at university was 'dominated by thoroughly British or American attitudes towards the "primitives" it studied'.[425]

Earlier, though, Judith had been much more respectful of Elkin. In the 1960s she sought, and accepted, Elkin's advice when she was approached to edit a book of Aboriginal legends. He suggested that to do so 'would be an act of appropriation'. When researching *Cry for the Dead* (1981), she asked friend Len Webb to recommend an anthropologist who could advise her. Webb suggested Elkin, but Judith said she wanted to know more before making contact, as she was 'feeling rather inferior...and I don't want to get things wrong'. In 1977, she contacted Elkin and he provided 'much useful information'. In the book's acknowledgements, she noted that she had studied under Elkin. As late as 1987 Judith said she admired the way Elkin's most famous book, *The Australian Aborigines* (1938), 'got so many people interested' in Aboriginal people, and that 'he was very much involved in trying to get recognition for them of their own needs, wants and rights'. Judith's assessments of Elkin are difficult to comprehend without a fuller understanding of her life at the times she made them.[426]

But, it is possible to see some fundamental continuities between his work and hers, in various periods. Elkin's approach to Aboriginal people in the 1930s, innovative for the times, was similar to the one which Judith took in her early poetry, written in the decade following her time at university. His reverence for the traditional lives of Aboriginal people made him particularly sad about the 'full bloods' who had 'lost' their culture. Afterwards, this approach was criticised for submitting to simplistic, ultimately patronising conceptions of the 'savage' as 'noble'. As discussed earlier in this chapter, similar critiques could be made of Judith's early poetry. By focusing on pre-contact Aboriginal culture, as Judith did in 'Bora Ring', and representing all Aboriginal people as dead, Judith arguably affirmed this same mythology. But, as also argued in this chapter, such assessments overlook the political and historical conditions of the era in which these works were produced. Drawing people's attention to the issues had a significant political impact. Elkin said of his book that its purpose was 'to enlighten white Australians and to make them think'.[427] Similar commendations were made of Judith's early poetry about Aboriginal people.

Almost half a century later, in *Cry for the Dead* (1981), Judith used an anthropological approach to fill the gaps created by a colonialist history. With little formal training in the discipline, yet conscious that she was working within it, Judith felt as she said 'rather inferior' in showing Elkin her drafts. She was determined to create an authoritative and accurate account of pre-invasion societies, including the Wadja, and positioned herself as an objective, omnipresent reporter.

> Their social system was complex, and complexly regulated; they were among the matrilineal, four-section tribes with an intricate totemic system handed down the generations in the father's line. Each knew his kin among the animals, trees, plants, stars, and his duties toward them; and acted out their parts at dances and ceremonies with a vividness of imitation that amazed the whites with its precision.[428]

It was a fluid work which discussed nature as confidently as culture, classifying and generalising, moving from the small to the large scale, throughout history, to suggest a natural order – harmony even – amongst traditional Aboriginal societies and the landscape. It was the work of an anthropologist. When she wrote such passages Judith must have been remembering her days in the Anthropology lecture hall, or passages from Elkin's most famous work, in which he too seemed to cover all variables, within a vast range of Aboriginal societies, from the significance of stars to the smallest creatures, to finally report to his largely non-Indigenous audience: 'nature is to the Aborigines a system in which natural species and phenomena are related, or associated, in space and time'.[429] Like Judith, his aim had been to transparently convey that universe to engender greater respect for it.

Cry for the Dead, published when Judith was sixty-six, indicates that she valued the anthropological approach deep into her life. In the following years she gave voice to strong reservations about the history of anthropology, but she continued to be proud of *Cry for the Dead*, and wished she could have undertaken more research along similar lines.[430] There was something about the methodology she pursued there, with its wide-ranging scope and straightforward presentation of facts, which appealed. This was the woman, after all, who famously ceased writing poetry at seventy because she believed that directly communicating information was a more urgent, political task. Although, as recounted in the introduction to this book, Judith believed that emotions were often truer than facts, she also seemed to conclude in the final decades of her life that 'facts' were more useful in changing people's minds.

Throughout this chapter we have seen how Judith's recollections of university were strongly informed by her developing mindset. It is hardly surprising that her thinking shifted, but it does not mean that Judith was not shaped by her experiences in the lecture halls, or that the frameworks presented there did not make their way into her work. What is surprising is the extent to which Judith's life narrative has remained un-contextualised, perhaps even unchallenged, by literary critics, cultural historians and biographers with recourse to ancillary material. Such analysis helps us better understand the extent to which Judith was shaped by Sydney and, in a corollary, continued to be informed by her upbringing. The following chapter will consider Judith's three years of English at the University of Sydney and ask what effect, stimulus, mould, this had on poetry which would become some of Australia's most distinctive and well known.

CHAPTER 7

Campus Literary Discussion

History, Philosophy, Psychology, Oriental Studies and Anthropology helped develop Judith intellectually. The subject matter of her lectures mirrored the major thematic concerns, though not necessarily the positions, of *The Moving Image* (1946). Australia's colonial period, tyrannical ideologies, and the loss of an 'authentic' Aboriginality were intellectual concerns of the 1930s Australian Arts faculty, and so they were for Judith Wright. What enabled these concerns to infuse her poetry was a new literary aesthetic, made famous by T. S. Eliot and Ezra Pound. Within their complex poetic prescription was the advice to younger poets to capture 'the mind of his own country', rather than their own mind.[431] Suddenly there existed an opening for a kind of poetry that was both cosmopolitan and Australian. In 1946 *The Moving Image* would fill it.

How Judith came to employ this aesthetic, and with such success, has not always been well explained. Judith's early work has been described as 'modernist', and some have rightly pointed to the influence of Eliot.[432] Other critics have viewed it as a reaction against modernist culture.[433] Her early work shows the influence of different, often contrasting, literary periods. How can, or should, this be understood?

Another vexed issue surrounding her early work has been understanding its relationship with her latter-day historiography and activism. As discussed in Chapter 6, critics have argued that 'Bullocky' was, variously, a critique of invasion and a paean to European settlement. Philip Mead has surmised that her work, collectively, has been both, and that it might represent the 'bi-polar politics of Australian white identity'.[434] How Judith's work should be read continues to be a challenge for critics and teachers of Australian literature. Yet, as this book has argued, a way forward emerges from examining more closely the intellectual and cultural contexts in which her different collections were produced.

For instance, what remains under-acknowledged in current readings of *The Moving Image* is the extent to which its unique blend of traditional and modernist diction, as Chris Wallace-Crabbe has termed it, and its assertion of Australian themes in a European aesthetic, were influenced by the literary discourse which existed at the University of Sydney in the mid 1930s.[435] For, as Chapter 8 will show, it was at that time that Judith began to pioneer this new kind of poetry. This literary discourse, different to that which took place outside the University, provides new ways of reading Judith's early work. Although it has been argued of the period that universities, and those that frequented them, were unsympathetic towards developing either an Australian tradition or literary experimentalism, original sources reveal a more lively, multi-sided debate. This chapter asks to what extent might this discussion have aided a young woman intent on formulating a new kind of Australian poetry?

The positions, sometimes shifting, often firmly expressed, of key figures within the University scene, help us understand the range of intellectual possibilities Judith was exposed to during her formative years. A greater understanding of this literary milieu also illuminates the practical difficulties Judith faced in wanting to become a writer. While her depiction of the role gender played at university has been complicated by the positive experiences of some women students, as described in Chapter 5, other anecdotes provided in the present chapter underline the nuanced but powerful barriers women faced.

To understand how this literary culture worked, this chapter draws heavily on primary documentation from the period, as well as second- and first-hand accounts by former students. For, while Judith did not remember much of the discussions which took place either inside or outside the lecture hall ('there's not very much in my memory of what was going on in the literary field'), these surely influenced her, an enthusiastic player within them.[436]

How much of this university literary discourse was shaped by the formal curriculum? What did it focus on? English Language and Literature was a large subject at the University of Sydney in 1934, with almost 200 students taking the first-year course alone. Judith was awarded a distinction that year, placing her ninth within that large class. It was her most outstanding result at university by a considerable way. To gain this mark Judith had to attend an extra sixty lectures on English 'before Shakespeare'. These lectures, it turned out, were exclusively devoted to part one of *Beowulf*. Judith read ahead, 'interested in all of what was going on', but was disappointed to learn that second-year English honours was on part two of *Beowulf*. Whereas a more ambitious student might have used it to their advantage, Judith recoiled. An extensive knowledge of *Beowulf* was 'scarcely what I had in mind', when embarking on university studies.[437] She would not do second- or third-year honours, gaining a pass in both years.

Judith's description of the department's singular focus on older, English writers is supported by official documentation. As the University Calendar shows, the curriculum did not extend to even American writers, though the Fisher Library stored their works. In fact, students had to wait until third-year English honours before developing their knowledge of 'comparative' literatures. In the meantime they studied a sweep of British (mainly English) writers including Shakespeare, Chaucer, Dryden, Pope, Swift, Fielding, Goldsmith and Boswell.

English courses within Australian universities were, at the time, not just literary; they were linguistic too. At Sydney, first-year students were given classes on 'English Pronunciation and other Study of Speech', and exercises in composition were a feature at every year level. While instruction in the 'British voice' (a particular kind of British voice) had always been important to the Australian middle class, the project was given greater urgency in the 1930s as fears grew that Australians would adopt the new sound of American 'talkies'. During the period, writes historian Joy Damousi, 'a sense of linguistic moral panic' arose at the popularity of talking cinema. Politicians and censors, newspapers and public bodies avowed that 'British morality, manners, and ethics were all combined in the nature of speech'. Challenging this orthodoxy was Alex Mitchell, who would teach in the English department during Judith's final year. His *The Pronunciation of English in Australia* (1940) stated: 'every man has the undeniable right to speak as he pleases'. Unconventionally, he wrote: 'it is false to regard Australian popular speech as a debased form of educated speech'. Yet the terms he used to describe the two Australian dialects – 'popular' and 'cultivated' – confirmed the significance of class to accent.[438]

To most 1930s university students popular did not mean good. Donald Horne recalled that, after deliberately changing his accent, because 'it seemed a negation of education to speak "like an Australian"', he immediately 'began to defend the view that there was nothing wrong with the Australian accent; it was just that some of us did not happen to use it'. Horne's posturing, no doubt influenced by Mitchell, was so cutting edge that even he could not support it. For most on campus, proper speech, like proper culture, was British. Judith recalled: 'everybody looked to England' and 'English poetry was the only influence on people'.[439] When key figures in the department are considered, it is easy to see why.

The English department appeared to run, as it always had, like a colonial outpost. Between 1887 and 1920 foundation Professor and British enthusiast Mungo MacCallum chaired Modern Language and Literature. In her study of English professors in Australia, Leigh Dale describes MacCallum as a humanist, but 'the foundation of this humanism was faith in the cultural and political pre-eminence of the British'. It was essential to him that students were inculcated with 'a sense of that pre-eminence'. Judith remembered MacCallum giving the occasional lecture during her first year. Indeed, even in 1936, his name appeared first on the English curriculum, confirming his enduring influence. During this period, writes Dale, the department was run by his 'disciples'. When being replaced, MacCallum intervened to ensure former pupil Ernest Rudolph Holme got the job, threatening to resign from the university senate if he did not.[440]

Holme ran with the party line. Horne explained Holme's lectures as 'a series of sermons on the virtues of Empire'. Judith also gave the impression of a small-minded authoritarian, depicting Holme 'thundering around a very small room'. More respectfully, Mitchell testified that 'many were imbued by Professor Holme with a life-long feeling for *Beowulf*, for Chaucer, for Dryden and certain eighteenth-century writers'. John Le Gay Brereton, who chaired the department with Holme, was more interested in Australian literature. Judith, however, did not have the chance to find that out; in 1933 Brereton died suddenly and was replaced by Arthur Waldock, another former pupil of MacCallum's whom Dale described as 'a devotee of English culture' and a 'Christian idealist'.[441]

Waldock, whom Judith recalled in greater detail than any other English lecturer, maintained the English cultural orthodoxy but did so differently. He was less stiff than Holme, and he was younger – in fact still in his thirties when he lectured to Judith. She remembered him fondly and said his work on Shakespeare was 'still very valid'. Yet it was his emotional response to literature that most impressed the young Judith; Waldock was 'a very romantic man who used to swing his gown around his shoulders as he started his lectures. He looked like Hamlet and everybody adored him'. After a pause, she added: 'he used to intone his Shakespeare'. In her memoir, Judith gave an even greater sense of Waldock as spectacle, capturing the attention of his mainly female class. He inspired, fifty years on, a linguistic grandiosity in the poet:

> ...it was Professor Waldock on whom we fixed our eyes. Tall, youngish (or so he seemed) and pale, he made gestures that raised the wings of his academic gown in angelic flight. Shakespeare for him was more a passion than a subject...Sitting with other women in Arts I, I sometimes heard small, collective sighs rising at his more moving declamations.[442]

Though these women adored him, Judith's esteem must have been especially keen. Until then she had not known a man for whom literature was 'more a passion than a subject'. Entering her finely drafted poems into a black exercise book as a child, fleeing NEGS sports classes to read under a tree, shunning the official recognition that would come with matriculating and a bachelor's degree: this is how literature had felt to Judith for all those years. At university, she recalled, she did not meet anyone who wanted to be a poet – anyone like her.[443] Nobody she had known, or now knew personally, exhibited the same commitment to literature as that which took place before her. Sitting in a crowd of 200, Waldock's angelic gestures must have lifted Judith out of her society – of wealthy pastoralists, of doctor's daughters, of the expectations of a conventional marriage and life – into one where the reverberation of words, and their spirals of meaning, were all that mattered.

And yet Waldock, for all his drama and passion, was not completely satisfying. Judith, already, had her eye on a literature not mentioned in these lectures. Produced by her compatriots, it was the literature she had glimpsed as a child reading, over and over again, Miles Franklin's *My Brilliant Career* (1901). She wondered that the Australian novelist Nina Murdoch, whose mother and sister Judith lived with in Neutral Bay, was not mentioned in these lectures. She privately considered the connection 'glamorous'. Though not a central figure in Australian literature, Murdoch did have two poems in the well-regarded anthology of Australian verse *The Wide Brown Land* (1934). Her writing, like Judith's juvenilia, was influenced by the swooning, gothic style made famous by the Victorians and popular in Australia at the time. Impending death was a fascination, symbolised by the passing of the seasons, the moon and the sea. A surge of *joie de vivre*, patently sexual, was a cause for celebration in one poem ('...while I lie at cushioned leisure/ aswoon with life and drowsed with pleasure...'), but death swiftly followed.[444]

Learning why Murdoch was not discussed in her lectures, under-standing that in fact the connection was worthless, took place via an episode which Judith only half recalled. Under the tutelage of an unnamed English lecturer, who 'appeared never to have heard of her', Judith learned to be embarrassed by the literary connection. Perhaps the episode took place in his office, after a lecture, or even *in* a lecture; it cannot have been relayed in the more informal space of a tutorial, since they did not exist. It must have been excruciating, so excruciat-ing that it could not be coherently related fifty years later: 'when I dared to mention to one of my English lecturers the fact that I lived in what might have been called proximity to her fame, I gained no kudos, in fact the contrary'.[445]

What was 'the contrary'? Shame, probably. It was to Judith's credit that the episode, awkward and understandable, but revealing, was included in her memoir. Perhaps she perceived it to be an important moment in her education; that it taught her something profound about the cultural terrain which she would go on to change. This was the place of Australian literature in this country. Judith emphasised its broader significance, explaining her lecturer's response with a characteristic desire to establish her own dignity: 'the English department had no truck with Australian writing'. It was a point she must have known her reader could nod in sympathy with, given the intellectual reach of A. A. Phillips' essay, 'The Cultural Cringe' (1958). Famously, he argued that a 'disease' plagued the Australian cultural landscape, including its English departments, which drove sufferers to denigrate works of art produced by Australians. Two pages later Judith casually remarked of Waldock: 'one could not imagine him so much as knowing the name of Nina Murdoch, nor any other Australian writer'.[446] Probably Judith did not have to imagine.

The focus within the English department on English culture was in fact tied to the authority and power of the University, and its graduates, within Australian society at the time. Ties to the middle and ruling English class – their forms of knowledge, or ways of speaking – signified status in Australia. Academics, usually British graduates, believed that any diversion towards local knowledge or culture would lower the standard of an already suspect university education. The University of Sydney, MacCallum affirmed during his time as Chancellor, single-mindedly aimed to be like an English university – preferably Oxford or Cambridge; if the suggestion was not impertinent, he might have added. Dale believes that, for MacCallum, 'local culture' would have meant English culture anyway, since university students were in a class of Australian society that believed they were still English.[447]

The same dynamic was at work in the University of Melbourne English department. In 1935 Professor G. H. Cowling responded to the idea of an Australian literary tradition with flabbergasted derision. 'Australian life is too lacking in tradition, and too confused, to make many first-class novels', he divined. 'What hope is there for Australian biography?' he asked rhetorically. And answered, predictably: 'Little, I think'. Publisher and advocate of Australian culture, P. R. Stephensen, saw Cowling's remarks as an example of academia's failure. He noted that Cowling's intellectual limitations had a pervasive effect; such statements were 'a wet blanket applied to the fire of Australian literary creativeness'. Dale's account of university professors during the period – that they had an 'utterly imperialising vision of the world' – supports Judith's conclusion that 'the English department had no truck with Australian writing'.[448]

That Australian writing was not well-regarded by most professors at Australian universities during the 1930s is clear. However, although rarely acknowledged, there was an emerging discussion of its place which demonstrates that an aspiring student writer might have considered it possible that she could one day produce *literature*. Evidence suggests that there was some interest in, and even support for, the idea of a uniquely Australian literature at the University of Sydney. Jennifer Strauss notes that in 1928 Professor Brereton became the inaugural President of The Fellowship of Australian Writers (FAW). The fact of Brereton's involvement, wrote Strauss in 1998, 'challenges the notion that Australian universities were, until very recently, consistently indifferent, even hostile, to Australian literature'.[449]

Other facts challenge it further. It seems that, by the mid 1930s, the English department was beginning to shift. Despite Dale's portrayal of MacCallum as uninterested in Australian literature, he supported the FAW in its 1930s campaign to revive the Commonwealth Literary Fund (CLF). When this was successful he became a CLF board member. The CLF sought the development of a distinct national literary tradition. Works which subsequently received CLF funding, such as Judith's *The Generations of Men* (1959), helped build this. Dale makes the useful point that, during the early decades of the century, 'nationalist and imperial sentiment were not necessarily regarded as being incompatible'.[450] Encouraging writers in Australia simply supported English literature. This may be so, but it should be noted that the English department's 'imperial' vision was of a kind which accommodated support for local creative activity.

Still other facts indicate this. By 1934, the year that Judith began university, Robert Guy (R. G.) Howarth had become a member of staff. *The Oxford Literary History of Australia* (1994) describes him as an 'enthusiastic advocate of Australian literature', and he became founding editor of Australia's first literary magazine, *Southerly*, in 1939. The magazine was published by the Australian English Association, presided over by Mungo MacCallum. In his first editorial Howarth avowed that all contributors would be Australian, or residents of Australia. Therefore, readers of the magazine would be 'stimulating the development of their literature and infusing more self-confidence into writers'.[451]

But not all his views were what we might have expected of an 'enthusiastic advocate' of Australian literature. For Howarth, Australian literature simply showed promise; there were 'possibilities of development', if not 'actual achievement'. He was clear in distancing his publication from the 'valiant nationalism' which drove 'popular' magazines, by which he meant *The Bulletin*. What he sought was the development of 'literature', but he did not seek to cultivate a unique tradition. Instead, Australian literature would fit within the tradition of English literature – if it were good enough. *Southerly* was motivated by a desire to 'maintain' the English language in Australia, 'and encourage its right use'.[452] By this he meant the English language in its completeness: its sound, style and cultural allusions; not just its grammar and vocabulary. As will be discussed further in this chapter, Howarth's reputation as an early 'advocate' of Australian literature overlooks this fine yet important distinction. Being an advocate of Australian literature would mean something different in 1939 to what it would in 1994. Yet Howarth, at least, was looking for ways to encourage the publication of Australian writers.

What is more, someone at the University of Sydney clearly believed Australian writers should be taught. L. C. Rodd, Kylie Tennant's husband, recalled attending lectures there on Australian literature in 1930. Delivered by the University librarian Henry Green, these lectures were said to be part of the English course. The official curriculum makes no mention of them, but Dorothy Green confirmed their existence and maintained that her husband delivered such lectures in the 1920s too. A 1935 edition of *Honi Soit* provides further evidence of their occurrence, and demonstrates a widespread interest in the subject. It reported: 'at the request of a number of teachers and others interested in Australian literature, a short course of six lectures on "Australian Fiction up to the eighties" will be given at the University'. Over a two-month period, Green, who had by then written *An Outline of Australian Literature* (1930), gave evening lectures on ten writers. *Honi Soit* noted that the lectures would appeal to 'those interested in the development of Australian literature; and to those who are not acquainted with our own writers'.[453] Not to be, it implied, was a deficiency.

During the 1930s Green encouraged the development of a broad yet distinct literary tradition: 'Australian literature is literature which springs out of Australia, which reflects some aspect of Australian life, though the style alone may be affected and the subject need not be Australian'. Though Green had been published dozens of times in the *Bulletin* over the preceding decades, it was under the pseudonym Harry Sullivan. If his was a version of literary nationalism, it was of a palatable kind which did not threaten the Anglo-centricity of the University. He encouraged Australian writers to learn 'from overseas without forgetting their own country'. He was convinced that 'literature is a growth of the soil', yet, acknowledging the low regard some had for *this* soil, noted that literature 'may rise above it'.[454]

In these 1935 lectures, of which Judith makes no mention, and which we do not know if she attended, students witnessed the very beginnings of Australian literary scholarship. Green asked whether Australian literature had 'developed any special characteristics'. He answered tentatively: 'I think it has, but to set them out in so many words is not easy'. Over the coming years he would try. When the Commonwealth Literary Fund began funding an annual course on Australian literature in 1940, it was Green who delivered it. Soon enough, the department proper was teaching Australian literature and Green was employed as a full-time lecturer. In 1945 Howarth began giving lectures on Australian writers.[455]

When it is said that Australian universities were slow to accept the idea of Australian literature, what is meant is that they were slow *compared* to those outside the university. Much, of course, was happening there, particularly in fiction. Strauss has identified many figures and movements from the inter-war years who had begun to form an 'Australian writing community'.[456] The same year that Judith started at university, Angus & Robertson published that substantial volume of Australian verse already referred to, *The Wide Brown Land* (1934), in which poets such as John Shaw Neilson asked 'have you ever been down to my countree?'[457] In 1924, Nettie Palmer had produced *Modern Australian Literature*, a critical study of the field. But this was not the milieu in which Judith operated as a student. Her colleagues had greater reason to distance themselves from local developments. Being at a remove from the rest of society was what defined university life, culturally, in Australia during the period, as discussed in Chapter 4. And yet this was not the whole story, and Judith must have noticed there were those amongst her colleagues, as well on the library staff, who might have been impressed by her proximity to Miss Murdoch after all.

For many students there was an inevitable connection between distinctly Australian culture and the politics of the Australian 'common' people, a politics which attracted little active student support, as shown in Chapter 5. In the year after Judith left university, *Hermes* editor and poet James McAuley made this clear. Aiming his attack at the most well-known advocate of an Australian literary tradition, Stephensen, McAuley observed: 'literary nationalism, the theory that the artist should sit and write on his own dunghill, is being hawked around Sydney once more'. The article, titled 'Less of it', was variously lighthearted (literary nationalism was 'the least charming of bourgeois theories of art') and deadly serious:

> [Literary nationalism] is expected to aid in the rousing of that patriotic fervour, that ecstatic consciousness of whatever racial characteristics our public speakers tell us we have, which is an essential ingredient in the fascist stew.

In referring to 'our public speakers', McAuley knew his readers would be reminded of those politicians and activists on the left, including communists, who were the main employers of public oratory. That they whipped-up hysteria, induced an 'ecstatic consciousness', which gave their irrational, self-interested political statements a receptive ear, had long been an attack levelled against progressive public speakers in Australia. Horne later recalled that amongst his friends, of whom McAuley was one, Australia was regarded as 'a literary dungheap in which a few featherless cocks crowed with literary nationalism or puffed themselves up with the second-rate'.[458]

McAuley's article, however, also betrayed a complex set of aspirations, pointing to different concerns within the student body. He wanted, as editor, to assert the superior quality of his magazine. Given the smallness of the global university population, and in a period which adhered to supposedly universal standards, this entailed asserting an Australian pre-eminence: 'Hermes has maintained a higher standard of excellence than any similar magazine in England or America'. It might have been a contrarian move to isolate Hermes' writing as singularly Australian – or at least not English or American. For if there was something better about this writing than that of other countries, did it not follow that it was different? McAuley explained:

> This [superiority] is so because those who have contributed [to Hermes] have cared for fine literature, and tried to produce it without being unduly disturbed by the confused quacking noises that issue from the local barnyard.[459]

Quality Australian writers, McAuley said, were united by their disdain for cultural unity.

McAuley's position, sometimes inconsistent, certainly fraying at the edges, is of a kind Dale recalls when describing university attitudes to Australian literature in the period. In her depiction, McAuley's views were typical of academics and, we must assume, students. In this light, Judith's use of recognisably Australian 'commoner' figures such as a bullock-driver and convicts in The Moving Image seems remarkable, especially given that she was the daughter of Country Party politics. This politics, as shown in Chapter 2, was defined by its advocates against any form of politics overtly based on class. Moreover, as argued in Chapter 8, there is strong evidence to suggest that Judith was using such imagery even while she was a student. Was Judith really one out of the box? Was she a lone voice amongst McAuleyan antipathy towards Australian subject matter within the University?

Just as a shift was taking place in staff attitudes towards Australian literature, so it was within the 1930s student body. Even within McAuley's editorial we glean some of this. Although he had cautioned the writer against sitting, and writing, 'on his own dunghill', McAuley conceded that one 'cannot helping feeling pleased' when the subject of successful poetry 'is a native one'. He isolated one such specimen, and beamed: 'every now and then Hermes finds someone who has thoroughly realised his subject'. The poem, attributed to 'Ian' and titled 'The Lubra', was an unflattering realisation of an Aboriginal

woman, much in the vein of Ian's 'The Corroboree', published in the
following issue.

> Her bosom is flapped with monotonous beat,
> As she droningly mumbled a croak,
> She stirred with a bone in the bowl at her feet,
> 'Mid a horrible compote of soak.

Successive stanzas provide no relief. The only attempt to cast beyond
the woman's physical depravity reveals, more alarmingly, that she
sees 'her hideous sire in his prime'.[460] McAuley's celebration of 'The
Lubra', as hateful a portrait of an Aboriginal person as any, deserves
further consideration, given his prominence as an arbiter of Australian
literature in the years following his university career.

But what is particularly relevant here is McAuley's enthusiasm for
a poetry which addressed Australian social issues, despite his commitment to a notion of universal standards, and to a measurable quality
he described as 'fine literature'.[461] One of the characteristics of such
literature was, for McAuley, description of abstract concepts. Widely
recognisable events or phenomena were referred to in 'fine literature'
but generally only as a means of demonstrating something theoretical
which had emerged from Western literary discourse, philosophy or
religion. Australian history generally lacked the gravitas which 'fine
literature' sought – it lacked gravitas because it had not, itself, been
the subject of extensive European theorising. Yet, if all else was even,
McAuley wanted it to be elevated to that category.

McAuley's position, although multifarious, certainly refrained
from endorsing anything like a national literary tradition. Yet this did
not reflect student discussion in its entirety; it simply sat at one end
of the spectrum. In the middle were students who had not made up
their mind. In 1935 the student Book Club invited Denzil Batchelor
to give an address on 'The Australian Novel, Present and Future', to
help them. Batchelor, a journalist, novelist and film critic, was an
Englishman born in India who spent several years in Australia during
the 1930s. He ventured a position on literary nationalism which must
have appealed to those who shared McAuley's disdain for the only
recognisably Australian literary tradition, bush writing. He argued that

in 'self-consciously striving' to be Australian, Australian writing had suffered.[462] Bush writing attracted scorn in another University forum that year. Writing for *Hermes*, Greek and Latin lecturer Carl Kaeppel applauded Randolph Hughes for stating that Australian literature was 'hopelessly wrong, *childishly anti-intellectual*, and seldom gets beyond the cult of the stock-rider, the wattle and the bell-bird'.[463]

Such criticisms could only be made in the elite setting of a university. As Strauss has shown, Australian authors understood on what basis critics and academics disparaged their work but continued to situate their novels in the bush because such novels sold. Strauss claims that there existed a widespread nostalgia for bush life, even though most of the population no longer lived there. Batchelor was championing a new kind of Australian literature, one which was, principally, not based on popular subject matter; one that could attract 'artistic readers'. We were still waiting, he said, for literature that was real, good and 'typically Australian'. How might writers pursue such a thing? By pursuing the 'psychological interest'.[464]

Amongst the student literati there were those who, at the other end of the spectrum from McAuley, advocated a distinctly Australian tradition. According to A. C. Beattie, who edited *Hermes* in 1934 and half of 1935, the reason the magazine existed was to allow for the development of an important literary voice; for a new Australian tradition to emerge. When he argued this, Judith was in her second year. Beattie's statement was provoked by the Students' Representative Council's withdrawal of funding for the magazine on the grounds that it was producing, in Beattie's words, 'a lot of bovril'. In an article titled 'Is *Hermes* worth fourpence a copy?', Beattie countered that whereas university sporting clubs were aimed at building muscle and team spirit, and political societies encouraged future leaders, 'we exist for no other purpose than to encourage the boys to write'. (It was a telling employment of gender specificity, as I will reflect on later in this chapter.) Boys who could write might develop, said Beattie, 'that babe-in-arms, the Australian literary tradition'.[465]

Like Batchelor, Beattie argued that, at present, there was 'no book you could pick up and say, "this must be an Australian book"'. But he was convinced that 'personality will develop'. Of course, Beattie made sure to distinguish this 'personality' from that which had come before. This new tradition, he said, might be constructed by university types: 'and why should not it be some of the boys who make those graphic phrases [in *Hermes*] which become part of the national literary tradition?'[466] The boys might come around to the idea of a national literature after all. It was a rousing call. Did any of the girls hear it, and think they might play a part in such a venture? As Chapter 8 will argue, Judith, whose pseudonymous poetry was published under Beattie's editorship, was experimenting with some graphic phrases of her own. Some were only given sense by their Australian context.

Discussion about Australian literature within the University, although more lively than has sometimes been suggested, was nonetheless over-shadowed by another discussion which dominated the literary pages of University magazines and, increasingly, its lecture halls. Judith must have been affected by it. This discussion was about the form which literature should take, and whether contemporary, experimental writers, referred to as 'modernist', were any good.

Looking back, Judith expressed dismay that English seemed to consist of Shakespeare and *Beowulf*, and that she had to go to the library for virtually anything else. Similarly, in Dale's account, the 1930s English department at Sydney was engaged in a battle against the present century. MacCallum, Holme and Waldock were 'standard bearers' of Christian, mainly pre-eighteenth-century, English culture. MacCallum's influence on Waldock, writes Dale, was discernible in Waldock's criticism, which sought to '"rescue" the creative text from modern theory'.[467]

Consensus has it that Australian writers were slow to take up what would later be termed 'literary modernism', although the term dis-guises a variety of approaches. Judith, whose poetry became celebrated in the late 1940s, is sometimes regarded as one of its earliest, albeit modest, exponents. Julian Croft argues that while some poets in the 1920s and 1930s were highly experimental, they were not widely read. More well-known poets, such as Kenneth Slessor and R. D. FitzGerald, might have been responding to the 'modernist themes' of 'relativity, time, despair, hopelessness', but were not doing so in 'modernist styles…

the forms and language they used were derived from the traditions of the previous age'. More striking, he argues, was the strength of contempt for modernism, given voice by literary figures Norman and Lionel Lindsay, as well as Stephensen, by politicians such as Robert Menzies, State libraries and 'a horde of newspaper columnists and editors [who] all attacked modern art and literature on the grounds of ugliness or obscenity'.[468]

At the University, many were suspicious of modern literary techniques but this did not stop talk of them. Where did this talk take place? During her time in the English department, Judith's curriculum did not include any contemporary writers. Nonetheless, it seems they made their way into the lecture halls. In her memoir Judith explained that Howarth 'introduced us to daringly modern authors, such as Eliot', and she referred to the 'modernity of his courses'. Thelma Herring, a contemporary who won several University prizes for English and became the first woman staff member of the department, remembered that as well as lecturing on Elizabethan and Jacobean drama, seventeenth-century poetry and Restoration comedy, Howarth lectured on 'modern poets'. These, she notes, 'were less to my taste... but fascinating nonetheless'.[469]

Discussion of such writers, Judith observed, changed the dynamic between student and lecturer, for their works challenged the notion that there could be one objective reading of literature.

> There was no arguing with Waldock and Shakespeare but Eliot's verse – with its patient etherised upon a table as an image for a sunset, its smells of steak in passageways – introduced new notions of poetry.[470]

Just how did Howarth incorporate modernist writers into his classes? Perhaps Howarth discussed them informally, as an aside when lecturing on older English writers. Or perhaps Herring and Judith were remembering a series of extension lectures, given in 1935.

Entitled 'Some Recent Developments in English Literature', these three lectures were written by staff members of the English department and published by the extension board as a pamphlet. Howarth spoke on Edith Sitwell; tutor E. J. Dobson on T. S. Eliot; and Waldock on James Joyce. The pamphlet is an especially valuable source because, during the period, detailed course outlines and transcripts of lectures were not generally kept. In 1936 this pamphlet was put on the first-year reading list. The lectures themselves, their publication and place in the official curriculum all suggest the department was becoming more sympathetic to contemporary developments at the very time Judith studied within it.

Change was about. Did the contents of these lectures show it too? Howarth, Dobson and Waldock's lectures reveal much about the style of English academia in the period. Holme, who prefaced the collection, claimed that the lectures did not advance a literary position; they were neither for nor against 'recent developments'. This echoed Dale's description of the department's methodology. Employing an 'Arnoldian discourse', lecturers, she said, disclaimed any ideological or stylistic footing; they allegedly occupied a 'place free from critical bias'. In this pamphlet we see that lectures were long and thorough. Close readings were favoured; lines from poems and excerpts from novels littered the paragraphs with secondary critics referred to sparingly. Students must have felt as if they were watching the protracted thoughts of a highly attuned and learned mind navigating its way through a writer's oeuvre, weighing and judging for 'skill', 'expressiveness', 'complexity', all apparently objective qualities. Waldock sought to bring 'the work of James Joyce into perspective, so that we may see at the outset where he stands in relation to his predecessors'.[471]

From these lectures, a recurring persona appears. This is the literary critic as detective, searching for clues to meaning, fresh to any new lead. He is experienced, insouciant and has more or less seen it all before. He knows quality and originality when he sees them. But he rarely sees them. Waldock, perhaps surprisingly, given his reputation for absolute devotion to Shakespeare, approved of Joyce, on the grounds that he extends the great tradition of the English novel (no mention is made of Joyce not being English), but Dobson and Howarth are much more downbeat about 'recent developments'.

Howarth takes his literary microscope to the infamously opaque Sitwell poem 'Aubade', stating from the start that if a poem does not express something which most people can perceive then it has failed. It seems a doomed endeavour. Quoting from Sitwell's own analysis of the poem, he delights in the connotations she ascribes to particular words, noting: 'one would have to be Edith Sitwell to realise it as she does'. The critic, though patient and thorough, eventually appears aghast at Sitwell's amateurism: 'again the poetess is mingling sense impressions and mental associations'. Endlessly open-minded, Howarth acknowledges that Sitwell has her own approach, a new and innovative one, and so 'it can be judged only by results'.[472]

In the end, though, Howarth cannot accept that poetry has different meanings for different readers. Expressionism and symbolism get an exhaustive beating in his and Dobson's lectures; specimens of these schools are considered with apparent objectivity and then discarded for failing to meet the standards set by Shakespeare or Milton. Howarth even becomes defensive of the canon, upset that Sitwell and others could associate themselves with these great masters. It seems she needs spelt out some basic principles of human perception:

> The inner private life, the mental constitution, of Miss Sitwell was unknown to Milton when he composed 'Paradise Lost', to Hopkins during his extensive activity as a poet. It was not even remotely guessed at or anticipated. They wrote sense, and used sound to aid the communication of meaning.[473]

In his conclusion, Howarth gives Sitwell the strap, metaphorically, culminating his lecture with a bit of schoolmasterly discipline, perhaps meant as a deterrent to any would-be expressionists in the audience, especially female ones. Only then do we discover why he has spent fourteen pages hunting sense in her work when it appears such a difficult task. Why dignify her work with this attention?

> Miss Sitwell has no right to take liberties – impertinent in both ways – with [greater writers'] matter and their thought. It may not seem necessary to view her seriously, but she is very earnest about it, and has imposed on many.

The audience, by this time, might have considered themselves to be amongst those on whom she had imposed. Howarth's final words conjure a literary doomsday where 'chaos is come again' if Sitwell's nonsensical, selfish and amateurish poetry is let go scot-free.[474]

Howarth's lecture on Sitwell had impact, more than he probably imagined when he called her 'impertinent'. After the extension lectures were reviewed in the *Times Literary Supplement*, Sitwell requested a copy and then wrote in gratitude to Howarth. Describing his essay as 'brilliant and penetrating and helpful', she said it gave her 'the greatest possible pleasure' and 'must have done more to help towards an understanding of my poetry than almost any essay that has been written'. She begged that they might meet one day but hoped it would not 'weary you' to discuss her work further. It was not, apparently, imperial mockery on the part of the baronet-poet, now aged forty-eight, who in London sat, 'queen of a court of admirers and aspiring writers', towards the twenty-nine-year-old junior lecturer from Tamworth. Sitwell, often described as an eccentric, was serious. Later, Howarth attended Sitwell's court, sitting alongside Somerset Maugham. In the intervening years Howarth and Sitwell corresponded and her letters reveal respect for him as a critic.[475] This strange turn of events echoed Howarth's changing attitude towards experimental writing of the 1930s, Sitwell's in particular, and indeed may have had something to do with it.

But in 1935, at least, Howarth was frustrated by obscurity, and so was Dobson. In his lecture on Eliot, Dobson said in exasperation that some of Eliot's work is mere 'incoherent raving...neither comprehensible nor even explicable by association'. Appearing at his most gentlemanly, Dobson defended Eliot against accusations that his work was 'passionless. It is merely that the *range* of passion is limited'. And more diplomatic about 'recent developments' than Howarth, Dobson concluded that although writers such as Eliot might be 'confused and confusing', this was the nature of experimentation, and that perhaps something better, milder, 'less violent' would emerge, and justify the whole strange project.[476]

Although most student discussion revealed a similar level of suspicion towards modernist writing, one poem, published in the 1936 issue of *The Arts Journal*, appeared to criticise the lecture series, and suggested that its author's response was shared by the department at large: 'English lecturers/ Frequently wax eloquent/ On the subject of/ Poetry./ The beauties of rhyming verse,/ Or blank verse (meaning, of course,/ SHAKESPEARE)/ Are explained and catalogued,/ While the poems themselves/ Are paraphrased and dissected/ With such merciless energy'. Modernist writing, with its free verse, is 'disregarded by the learned/ Osbert Sitwell, for instance, was/ Surely never an ARTS man'.[477] Not all students were swayed by the rhetorical force, the pretence of objectivity or the performance of erudition on display in *Recent Developments*.

Robert Guy Howarth's role in Judith's life requires further explanation. Certainly, as other biographers have concluded, they shared no special connection and Howarth did not encourage Judith. Yet this fact shaped Judith's career more than we might imagine. What is more, from this vantage point it seems likely that Howarth's disregard of Judith was based on his expectations of women. Just as Beattie had casually remarked of *Hermes*' role in 'encouraging the boys to write', Howarth also worked under the assumption that any professional writers to emerge from the University would be men. Howarth, then a powerful figure in a developing literary scene, exemplifies, through his attitudes and behaviours, the way gender ushered out women from public life. How effortlessly Judith might have submitted. Conversely, it is worth dwelling on what might have been if Judith had been a man. In this story, Howarth might have been a larger figure, accelerating the poet's success by a decade. After all, glowing testimonies divulge that he was an early advocate of Australian writers, open to literary experimentation, a passionate support to student writers. Why his role in her life is merely marginal reveals the more complicated, and compromising, reality of Howarth, the academic literary scene in 1930s Sydney, and Judith's early experience of it.

Also from New England, and only nine years older than Judith, Howarth's trajectory from child poet (he began when he was seven) to Oxford graduate and English lecturer was much more straightforward than was Judith's literary career. By twenty-seven he was a significant player in the Australian literary scene. At the same age Judith was a secretary. Posthumously, their importance is considered quite differently. Howarth's largely unwritten life may be the result of his departure from Australia in the mid 1950s. For during the 1930s and

1940s he was something of an 'Australian man of letters', in the fashion of a nineteenth-century intellectual.[478] Not only was he a member of the University of Sydney English department, a literary reviewer and a published poet, he was also president of the Australian English Association, which hosted talks by famous writers, and, as mentioned, was the first editor of *Southerly*. In the 1940s he anthologised Australian poetry. While the longevity of his influence might be contested, within the small world of 1930s literary Sydney, Howarth was a giant.

Howarth used his authority to encourage the writerly careers of promising students. When it worked, the bond between mentor and apprentice was profound. Pupil Alan McLeod became Howarth's life-long correspondent, appreciative poetry critic and biographer. Howarth remained his 'model'. Assessing the recollections of numerous former students, McLeod concluded that Howarth was 'fondly remembered by most of those who benefitted from his encouragement, counsel, and special considerations'. 'Most' seems a stretch, according to the available accounts.[479] Yet whether or not students appreciated Howarth's 'special considerations', they must, initially, have been boosted by them. Judith, who was struggling to see her poems into student publications, would have been changed by the kind of interest South African writer J. M. Coetzee, now derisively, remembers receiving from Howarth as a student. Though this was years later, after Howarth moved to Cape Town, his manner towards Coetzee was experienced by others in Australia. In his memoir, *Youth*, Coetzee, referring to himself in the third person, recollects:

> Howarth, who is an Australian, seems to have taken a liking to him, he cannot see why. For his part, though he cannot say he likes Howarth, he does feel protective of him for his gaucherie, for his delusion that South African students care in the least what he thinks about Gascoigne or Lyly or for that matter Shakespeare.[480]

Even without the complications of nationality, Howarth could sometimes fall short, as former Australian pupil David Rowbotham relates. Howarth attempted to mould Rowbotham's poetry without success. McLeod allows that this was a 'common phenomenon'.[481] Howarth's own poetry followed the style of seventeenth-century love poets, not popular amongst Australian writers of the 1930s and 1940s, or of any time since. His many published poems, and even his collections, received little critical attention.

Yet Howarth's interventions made a difference, if not to the writing itself then to the careers and confidence of young writers. Rowbotham, later a poet and journalist, detailed the extraordinary mentorship Howarth and Kenneth Slessor provided. While still in Brisbane, Howarth 'invited' Rowbotham to study in postwar Sydney. Once there, Rowbotham recalled feeling as if he had entered an echelon of poets, 'a company of metal'; the list of names he provided, as evidence of this poetic club, ironically begins with Judith. By then she was established. Describing Howarth and Slessor as elders, he said their support was generous. They drove him to Camden Town to meet Hugh McCrae and to Ingleburn to meet Harley Matthews. Slessor often had Rowbotham to stay at his house and they dined together. Later, Slessor offered him newspaper work.[482]

Rowbotham recalls the significance of this company of writers: 'such occurrences, when one is young and writing, count as a part of the spirit of literature; of the now probably scorned republic of letters'. Rowbotham's defence of this republic overlooks the central problem: his inclusion into that company came at the expense of others, maybe not Judith by then, but other women poets. Howarth's son, Geoff Howarth, concluded from his survey of Howarth's archive that he was a prolific letter writer who used the form to 'encourage, advise, refer and publish; to enrol support for his causes and to befriend'. In her study of early *Southerly* editors, Susan Sheridan contends, based on the evidence available, that Howarth 'offered no significant mentoring to women writers'. When it came to supporting young writers, she writes, 'it was enough that they were men, and talented'. Rowbotham's assertion that Howarth showed 'courteous attention towards all the renaissance young' is somewhat undermined by the absence of testimonies by women to this effect.[483]

Howarth's support for men became a pattern and, as Sheridan argues, this made a difference to literary careers. Sheridan's examination of Howarth's letters and published works demonstrates that those to whom he did professional favours, often reciprocated, were also his friends, and all were men. Howarth's literary circle, she said, 'was based on male homo-sociality'. In his roles as *Southerly* editor, anthologist and university lecturer he championed the poetry of friends Slessor and A. D. Hope. In a 1949 publication, drawn from his lecture notes, Howarth claimed that only eleven 'modernists in Australia' could be said to 'rank with the English and American poets'. All eleven were men, and the list included Slessor and Hope, as well as Judith's fellow student, McAuley. These decades, in which Howarth strongly supported Hope's and Slessor's work, were those in which they established positions at the top of the Australian literary scene, gaining lectureships, influential board positions and greater publishing opportunities.[484]

The tendency towards socialising with male writers is confirmed by Howarth's archive. There, his correspondents form a list of 'names' which, McLeod proudly notes, 'reads like a roster of the principal con-tributors to modern Australian and British literary culture: Christopher Brennan, Robert D. FitzGerald, Randolph Hughes, Walter Murdoch, John Shaw Neilson, Kenneth Slessor, Douglas Stewart, R. G. Menzies...' The list goes on but the only woman writer to appear on it is Edith Sitwell.[485]

Howarth's poor record in supporting women poets confirms the negative effect of this homo-sociality, a dynamic of which Judith was surely aware in her determination to become a writer. To be published in *Southerly* in the early 1940s would mean a lot; then, few other publishing options existed and no other magazine had as solid a literary reputation. Sheridan argues that Howarth's treatment of Gwen Harwood, in her early publishing years, throws into question *Southerly's* 'performance on both publishing women and publishing innovative writing'. She suggests that the fact that Harwood 'wrote allusive, highly wrought poems' was not as important as the fact that she was 'an unknown woman, who lived in Hobart'. Harwood's letters reveal a frustration with *Southerly*; they would lose her submissions, forget to send replies, reject her work.[486]

Similarly, Howarth offered virtually no early support to Judith. As a student she received no 'special considerations', or none either she or he noted. Imagine if, like Rowbotham, she had been introduced to writers, and set on a writerly career in her early twenties. As a graduate, she received remarkably little attention from Howarth, despite her status as a former student, and despite her Sydney address (Sheridan notes that *Southerly* was 'a very Sydney-centred publication'). In the seven years between the publication of her first non-university, mature poem, under the name 'Judith Wright', and the publication of *The Moving Image* (1946), *Southerly* published just one poem, subsequently titled 'The Hanging Avalanche of Days'. In the same period, she had twenty-five poems published in *Southerly*'s counterparts, mainly *Meanjin* and *The Bulletin*. It was not for want of trying. Judith's letters from the period reveal that she submitted poems to *Southerly* which were either rejected, or not considered for years. Later, she told a correspondent that Howarth was inconsiderate towards writers (though Slessor, Hope, Rowbotham and Coetzee might have disagreed) and, further, that he would be 'eternally disgraced' by his foolish publishing decisions.[487]

Howarth's record on Judith does look foolish. Certainly his judgment as an editor, and as a mentor, could be questioned by the lack of interest he showed in her early work. Admittedly, Howarth never displayed a particular affinity with it. Her poetry was not included in his lectures, and he did not review it, despite giving his views on many Australian poets.[488] Yet it cannot be said that he objected to her poetry inherently. Once she became well known he published her poems in great quantities. Just before the publication of *The Moving Image*, when Judith believed Howarth knew it was imminent, he included the already-published 'Bullocky' in his anthology *Australian Poetry 1944* (1945).[489] She was one of three women published in that anthology, vastly outnumbered by the twenty-one men.

In 1947, with positive reviews of Judith's first collection mounting, Howarth published her again in *Southerly*, after a seven-year break. In the following five years he included six more Judith Wright poems in his magazine. It was *The Moving Image* bandwagon. Staggeringly, this level of support may be the most significant Howarth displayed towards a woman. Sheridan nominates Judith as evidence that Howarth 'championed modernist writing – by women as well as men...Howarth's *Southerly* published some of her earliest poems, from 1946 onwards'.[490] But during those seven years, between the publication of her first *Southerly* poem, in 1940, and her second, in 1947, when his backing would have really made a difference, Howarth did not champion Judith's work.

That Howarth championed modernist writing is another contentious point. Was Howarth really ahead of the pack? After all, excerpts from Howarth's lecture on Sitwell, quoted earlier in this chapter, suggest a more conservative response to modernist writing. His positions on modernist writing and Australian literature framed Judith's first academic encounter. If Judith was exposed to new poetic models and Australian writers in the lecture hall, were they endorsed, treated sympathetically, or ridiculed? The difference is significant. The scholarly online database *AustLit* explains that Howarth 'attracted attention locally for introducing his students to modern writers such as James Joyce and T. S. Eliot'.[491] Certainly, Howarth 'introduced' students to these writers (both Herring and Judith use a similar phrase) but the implication that it was a sympathetic introduction − that the rationale behind their work, not just the work itself, was presented − is hard to justify.

During the 1930s Howarth read experimental writers by the standards of another period. His 1935 extension lecture, on Sitwell, reflected a frustration with contemporary writers at large. This was long held and freely elaborated on. As an undergraduate, in 1929, Howarth won the University Wentworth medal for an essay which was highly critical of Australian poets, including Slessor, whom he accused of lacking 'poetic feeling', and of being overly artful. Eliot and Sitwell also lacked 'feeling', a common early criticism of modern poets, and were 'intellectually extravagant'. Such assessments formed the basis of his early lecturing. In 1935 he was more forgiving of Eliot than Sitwell, but only moderately; Eliot used literary devices 'now with extreme aptness, now ineptly...but his perception is more a matter of intellectual comprehension' than the unfortunate Sitwell's. Howarth's 1938 extension lecture developed a similar theme, declaring that Ezra Pound's *Cantos* did not make sense, and produced no 'meaning'. It was 'bad, dreadfully bad'. In fact, it was 'not poetry'.[492]

In his early editorials for *Southerly* Howarth railed against what he saw as the 'lamentable decline' in Australian poetry. His bugbear was poets who celebrated, and encouraged, a reader's subjective response, who wrote poems 'just as they might prepare entries for a guessing competition'. Responding to accusations that *Southerly* did not publish the 'more unconventional...radical writers, experimentalists, futurists, and the like', Howarth said he did not endorse 'weirdness' and 'novelty'. He could only promise to be 'as liberal as it is possible to be'. Elsewhere, in a 1939 review of Walter Murdoch's essays, he strongly endorsed the writer who, he said, was 'unable to see anything in Joyce, Stein, Edith Sitwell, and the rest...[H]e is apparently cold to Eliot'.[493]

But Howarth's views on modernist writing changed, and this may account for the confusion in historical accounts. *Notes on Modern Poetic Technique* (1949), drawn from lecture notes, marks the beginning of this turn. In it he explained the methodology of modernist writers; they were simply trying to interpret the new world around them, a laudable effort. As an example he quoted approvingly from Eliot's work. Innovative approaches, such as surrealism, enable 'self-expression' and prevent 'propaganda'. Sitwell he described as 'advanced'. There is none of his earlier criticism of these poets for producing a lack of meaning. Ironically, Slessor's worth, as the 'leading Australian modernist', is demonstrated by the fact that he 'was the first to feel the impact of Eliot and Edith Sitwell'. Howarth commends the Australian for his references to her work, principally the poem 'Aubade'.[494]

Although less extreme, Howarth's attitude towards Australian literature also underwent a transformation during the decades in which it became more accepted. Widely remembered as an 'early and enthusiastic advocate' of Joseph Furphy, amongst other Australian writers, in fact he did not begin writing on him, in a published forum, until 1946. Furphy, who died in 1912, was championed by critics from outside the University, including Kate Baker, A. G. Stephens, and Vance and Nettie Palmer, from the point of his death. Miles Franklin, ever alert to double standards, was disgusted by the kudos academics received for discussing Australian writing, pointing out that while Furphy was alive 'not one single solomon simon university person had ever written to him, or taken notice of him whatever'. As for Howarth's 'advocacy', she saw it as neither prescient nor courageous: 'Howarth, and all these little sawflies...are "professing" Furphy now that is he is "safely dead"'. This was a general pattern. In the 1920s and 1930s Australian writing was being discussed, defined and published outside of academia. As late as 1943, Guy Howarth was describing it as a 'dominion literature', a good one at that, but 'comparison with the literature of England is another matter'.[495]

Within the pages of student publications *Hermes* and *The Arts Journal*, during the years 1934 to 1936, modernist writing, and its most influential exponent T. S. Eliot, were the number one topics of discussion. Terms such as 'standardisation', 'tradition', 'expressionism', 'newness' and 'the modern' saturated the pages.

According to Judith, aesthetic conservatism dominated the student body. Australia, she deduced from her experience of trying to get published in student magazines, 'was no place for experimentation'. At university, she said, she 'brooded over Eliot and Gerard Manly Hopkins with real excitement'. These writers shared a desire to capture complex psychological states through indirect imagery. Although Hopkins was born in the mid–nineteenth century, his work, not published until 1918, 'belongs...to the twentieth century', writes Michael Schmidt; its complex syntax alone, which drew attention to the form of the poem, rather than its meaning, made it more consistent with the work of modernists than contemporaries such as Tennyson and Browning. But at the University, Eliot's and Hopkins' work was simply regarded as indirect, recalled Judith. In her enthusiasm for their devices she produced poetry regarded by her peers as unpublishable. Later, Judith was glad it was so: 'this was fortunate in its way'.[496] She was happy to have been moderated.

Was it Howarth, through his influence on students, including student editors, that curtailed Judith's diction, uniquely traditional and modern, as Wallace-Crabbe has described it? What stance did student editors take during Judith's time? And did their publishing record betray a bias towards traditional forms of poetry, as she recalled? Brady offered conflicting assessments, perhaps conscious of the diversity of opinion on campus.[497] In his study of McAuley and Harold Stewart, Michael Ackland argues that although *Hermes* had a 'modernist program', overwhelmingly Sydney students of the late 1930s were 'narrow-minded' on the subject of modernist writing and 'refused to adjust to the tempo'. For Ackland, a small minority of students favoured experimentation and these were the ones most active within student publications. What was published, therefore, did not reflect majority opinion but simply the more avant-garde taste of editors such as McAuley.[498]

A survey of the eight issues of the University's main literary magazine, *Hermes,* published between 1934 and 1936, bears this out. However, the situation depended on who edited the magazine. During these years there were three editors: Beattie, mentioned earlier, who edited four issues; Alan Crawford, who edited one; and Margaret Walkom, who edited three. Both Beattie and Walkom insisted that what they published was determined by what was submitted. Introducing her first issue Walkom said that an editor's 'apparent freedom of choice is largely illusionary' and that the stylistic bent of the magazine would depend 'entirely on the contributions we receive'.[499] Beattie, two years earlier, said much the same and was not at all happy about it given that his literary views were not in keeping with those represented by most submissions.[500] There was always, of course, the option taken by deputy editor Donald Horne when putting together a 1939 issue of *Hermes*. Remembered Horne: 'no one volunteered anything usable, so it was filled with the work of our friends'. He added: 'we did not have enough friends' so the two editors worked at the last moment to 'fill the gaps', writing much of the verse under pseudonyms.[501]

Were Beattie and Walkom right in claiming they had little control over the stylistic bent of the magazine? Taking into consideration their views (Crawford's short-lived reign does not allow such analysis), and what they published, it is clear that, despite the limitations imposed by the submission process, editors did exercise their literary tastes, and this was likely to have influenced Judith's writing style at university. What were these tastes?

Beattie was a strong proponent of experimental and modernist styles. In 1934, he wrote: 'dislike of the new literature means dislike of this day', encouraging students to adapt. They should risk 'clumsy sailing on the deep', unknown territory of the new rather than 'paddling in a backwater'. He believed that the 'most striking innovators' are those who thought a poem could be the 'focus of a cultivated modern consciousness, both in its coherent and incoherent moments'.[502] It seems unlikely then that Judith's poems, with their 'free verse and linguistic entanglements I fondly imagined were Hopkinsian' were not published in her first one and half years of university simply because they were experimental. Beattie was looking for innovation.

He was not alone at the University. In an article responding to the 1935 extension lectures titled 'Modern Literature', it was observed that 'modern poetry has been much talked of, much sneered at, but little understood'.[503] A small cohort of influential Arts students were flag-waving advocates of experimentalism during the 1930s. In *The Arts Journal* of 1936, mentioned in Chapter 5, the editorial committee, which included Judith, argued that negative reactions to new forms of writing disguised a general fear of technological, industrial, social and cultural upheaval:

> We are all frightened of this new land where we have found ourselves dumped with so little warning and ceremony. It will not help us to cling madly to custom: it will not help us to go on pretending that things are the same as they ever were; it will not help us to let our English course stop suddenly at the end of the last century...

And so it went. It was not a clear-cut endorsement of modernist writing; after all, students such as Walkom, who had her reservations, were on the committee with Judith. Nonetheless they proclaimed: 'if your lines of thought do not conform with those of your ancestors, then thank God for it'.[504] It was a celebration of newness, and Judith was part of it.

Roughly, the major influences on student poetry in the period could be grouped into two camps: modernist and Victorian. Of course, identifying and generalising using such terms is a problematic task, but the majority of poems, perhaps aware of the heated context into which they were being thrown, identified themselves quite clearly as 'for' or 'against' twentieth-century forms of experimentation.[505] Over the course of 1934 and 1935 Beattie's *Hermes* included verse of which about one-third had modernist influences, one-third had Victorian influences, and about one-third had other influences. This suggests that Beattie was even handed, but, as Ackland suggests, most students neither liked, nor wrote, modernist poetry. Beattie complained of the submissions he received, believing that amongst students there was a general 'regard for the past and a disregard of the present', which they learnt from their English courses. Because the curriculum did not embrace the 'modern period', it was rare to 'hear mention of work composed in the present century' in the lecture halls, 'no new current catches up students in its swirl'.[506] Students were turned off experimental literature by lecturers such as Howarth.

Beattie's *Hermes* was constructed from a submission pool largely made up of verse with a dominant literary influence unlike that which he favoured, yet he managed to give modernist writing an even weight-ing. Students must have wondered that so few of the poems they liked were published. According to Horne, they did not bother wonder-ing; he testified that throughout the 1930s most students were either 'indifferent' to or 'hated' *Hermes*, believing editors looked down on their tastes. A 1940 *Southerly* review endorsed the persistent accusation that '*Hermes*, so far from being representative of the undergraduate body, tends to become the monopoly of a minority clique'.[507]

It was a point Walkom made in her first editorial. Introducing her editorial 'policy', she noted that although each issue of *Hermes* published 'fragments of "modern" verse', these 'always form the pivot of a controversy which is usually hostile and frequently acrimonious'. This was so, Walkom argued, because students believed modern verse was too demanding. It had, she said tactfully, 'limited appeal'. Very few people actually liked Eliot, Pound, Cummings or Empson and the 'undergraduate recoils with suspicion and dislike' from poetry which sought to intimidate them. Students felt such work was having a joke at their expense. And they concluded that it was not worth 'bothering about'. Walkom distinguished herself from editors who had come before, finding it incredible that '*Hermes* editors continue, year after year, to print such verse, with the faint hope that their efforts will provide encouragement for the discerning and stimulation for the indolent'.[508] She would be a popular editor, and not patronise.

Walkom's record certainly demonstrates an impatience with experi-mental, modernist writing. She tended to publish just one poem each issue which could be categorised as such. About half of the poetry in her *Hermes* had obvious Victorian influences, and the rest had a ragbag of other influences, more nineteenth than twentieth century. Walkom clearly favoured poetry that was highly descriptive of natural landscapes. While she tolerated poems that did not abide by a traditional poetic structure, she clearly did not appreciate that which drew attention to its form, did not make 'sense', or sought to represent the unconscious. Perhaps it was Walkom whom Judith was thinking of when she remembered her Hopkinsian verse being rejected.

Walkom's views were echoed throughout University publications of the period. Students pointed to the crudity of modernist writing, its pretension, and its presumptuous attempts to redefine literature.

In a 1934 article for *Hermes*, 'H. M. S.' explained that Eliot's work was 'the most thoroughgoing piece of intellectual snobbery'. Though it did, at times, demonstrate 'acute perception', it was not poetry of feeling.[509] Margaret Mackie advocated a rejection of expressionism, which she saw in the work of Eliot and Pound, on the grounds that it was impossible for critics to make judgments about it, except on the basis of its popularity.

Like Howarth, Mackie was disturbed by the 'incoherence' of this poetry, by such writers' insistence that what mattered was the reader's experience of the poem. It was well known, after all, that 'in the case of literature an uneducated majority is nearly always wrong'. Even though the majority of students might have felt themselves in her camp, they must have comforted themselves that they did not constitute an '*uneducated* majority'. In the same issue, edited by Walkom, 'J. A. P.' wrote on the superficiality of Eliot's rhetoric, his 'pontifical moralism': the 'empty pretentiousness masquerading as philosophy and as art'. Perhaps it was Howarth's suspicion of new literary techniques, not his enthusiasm for them, as Judith said, that was his most profound influence on the literary conversation that took place amongst students.[510]

What conclusions can we make about Judith's early publishing experience from this discussion? How does it compare with her own account? Given that Beattie edited half the issues of *Hermes* published while Judith was at university, and that he went out of his way to publish experimental writing, it seems unlikely that her more experimental poetry was rejected on this basis alone. Australia *was* a place for aesthetic experimentation, as least if you were a student at the University of Sydney in 1934 and 1935, and you were prepared to look beyond what was taught in the lecture halls. It does, however, seem likely that Judith would have had trouble getting such verse published in 1936. From a distance of fifty years, it may have been hard to distinguish one year from three, and maybe she only worked up the confidence to submit poetry in large quantities during her final year.

So just how did Judith write? Whose sympathies did she tug? The following, and final, chapter of this book seeks to answer this question by nominating eleven poems which I believe were written by Judith and published under pseudonyms between 1934 and 1936. This chapter has shown that students were not completely hostile to modernist writing, or to the notion of a distinct Australian literary tradition, despite doubts about the legitimacy of their current manifestations amongst the student body and the lecturing staff. There was divergence amid the population and a discussion loud and lively enough for the young poet to reconsider the aesthetic and cultural creeds she had grown up with, or to encourage her already developing reassessments of them. The final chapter demonstrates that Judith Wright was already thinking about ways to write a new kind of poetry, a kind officially given birth to a decade later with the publication of *The Moving Image.*

CHAPTER 8

The Poems That Came Before

Emotionally, intellectually, creatively, Judith endured isolation throughout her childhood and teenage years. In Sydney, all this changed. Not
only was she introduced to the intellectual paradigms that would
shape her life, but to the mechanics of publishing and the workings
of a literary community. As discussed over the previous four chapters,
at the University of Sydney Judith gained access to an elite world that
vigorously discussed new developments within and outside the lecture
halls. Student publications were a major forum for this exchange and
Judith participated in them as columnist and editorial member. But
what about Judith as a poet? Did her student poetry demonstrate the
influence of modern Sydney and the intellectual stimulations she
received there? Did it reflect the new modernist style or the older
Victorian one, favoured by most at the University and esteemed by
Ethel Wright? Did it depict something of the young woman who we
see in her passport photo, taken on finishing university, who appears
composed, sophisticated, but also more vulnerable than some of the
images and accounts discussed in this book have conveyed? Did this
poetry foretell the emergence of *The Moving Image* (1946), a collection
that seemed to collapse aesthetic oppositions, and was both self-assured
and tender? What did her student poetry look like?

Until now these questions have been difficult to answer. According
to the digital encyclopaedia of Australian literature, *AustLit*, Judith's
first poem was published in 1939, two years after leaving university.
The Oxford Companion to Australian Literature (1994) marks the beginning of her literary career at 1940. Judith did not identify any poetry

published before 1938, except that written as a child. Over forty years ago, Hugh Anderson, in a one-page review of *Judith Wright: A Bibliography* (1968), asked whether it was proper that no poems were attributed to Judith before 1940 when 'there were *at least* fifteen poems printed prior to that date'. Acknowledging that 'most of them can be termed schoolgirl verse', he provocatively asked: 'can this be said of the four items in *Hermes* ("Nocturne", "The Crucible", "Autumn" and "Ballade of Passion") between 1934 and 1936?' No one had mentioned them before. Since Anderson had no record of research on Judith, it seems unlikely he trawled through old copies of *Hermes* and pounced confidently upon poems published under the signature 'JW'. More likely is that Judith, or a mutual friend, offered the information to Anderson. His notation, 'Judith Wright prefers that the earlier work should not be mentioned', suggested this further.[511]

Judith need not have worried, for Anderson's claim drew little interest, except from Shirley Walker, who has pursued Judith's early poetry more than any other scholar. In her 1977 doctoral thesis, Walker identified and printed sixteen poems Judith had published as a child and teenager in *The Sydney Mail* and the *New England Girls' School Chronicle*, as well as two of those named by Anderson. Of the other two, Walker wrote: 'A search of *Hermes* 1934–1936 has failed to disclose the two other Judith poems which Anderson maintains are there'. In Walker's archive of Judith papers, stored at the University of Queensland library, there is a copy of one other *Hermes* poem, from 1935. This poem was written under a separate signature, 'JMW'. In her interview for the National Library of Australia, Judith recalled revealing some of her university poetry to Walker; perhaps the JMW poem was it?[512]

Walker, however, did not identify any of Judith's university poems in a published forum. Her bibliography *Judith Wright* (1981) lists no poems written between 1932 and 1938, and her critical work *Flame and Shadow* (1991) makes no mention of any university poetry. Remarkably, no discussion of these five poems has been pursued in any literary or biographical study of Judith. Their only mention comes in a one-page review from 1968, an unpublished thesis from 1977, and an archived box of papers.

For her part, Veronica Brady identified one other university poem as discussed in Chapter 4, the poem entitled 'Love' published anonymously in *The Magazine of the Women's College* in 1936. If Judith wrote 'Love' she was pandering to the lighter tone of the magazine. It appeared alongside a column entitled 'It's Moments like these – !' Yet Brady considered the poem typical of Judith's output at the time, and used it to emphasise her poetic immaturity: 'Judith had not found her real voice yet, and most of her poems were fashionably melancholy or about love'. Brady stated that Judith had poems published in *Hermes* but did not identify any. Similarly, a passing assertion made by Jennifer Strauss that 'the first fruits of Sydney writing were not spectacular' is not given weight by reference to any of these first fruits.[513] As stated in the introduction to this book, it has become commonplace to dismiss Judith's early writing but does anyone really know what it looked like?

The only other commentary on Judith's university poetry that exists is that tantalisingly presented by the poet herself. Late in life Judith revealed that 'most' of the poems she had published before she left Australia for Europe in 1937 appeared in *Hermes* and that other University literary magazine, *The Arts Journal*, under pseudonyms 'or otherwise', by which she presumably meant an abbreviated form of her name. She recalled revealing some, 'but not all', of her early poems to Shirley Walker. And added: 'I never divulged to Shirley either what pseudonym I'd been using!' Her amusement, possibly relief, was audible on the tape. Earlier, in 1969, she said she was 'now very ashamed' of her university poetry.[514] Could it really have been so unworthy, given the accomplished poetry she wrote as a child?

And, is it even possible to identify it? Referring to the interview just quoted, Anouk Lang reasoned: 'when these publications for the years in which Judith may have contributed are examined, it is of course impossible to determine which, if any, of the works are hers'. Identifying Judith's university poetry is not a sport many have indulged in. Anderson's avoidance of expansive discussion of his nominated poems, Walker's reluctance to identify them in a published form, and Lang's eschewing of the undertaking, all underline potentially serious complications arising from it. After all, there were eight issues of *Hermes* published while Judith was at university. Each published an average of fifteen poems, meaning there were about 120 poems that could be Judith's. On top of this are poems from *The Arts Journal*, of which there were at least nineteen published during Judith's time. The endeavour to identify Judith's poetry is made more difficult by the inaccessibility of these journals today.[515]

In this final chapter I contend that eleven poems published under pseudonyms at the University between 1934 and 1936 were written by Judith Wright. Six have been either wholly or partially identified before: four are the 'JW' poems identified by Anderson, of which Walker located two; one is the 'JMW' poem which appears in Walker's archive; and one is another 'JMW' which appeared in the same publication. In this chapter their resemblance to Judith's other published work is discussed for the first time. Two new pseudonyms are also identified. These signatures, 'Margaret Jay' and 'JA', are attached to five poems between them. While it cannot be conclusively stated that these were Judith's poems, I believe that the evidence suggests they were. If these were not her poems, someone else at the University of Sydney was producing a distinctive brand of poetry remarkably similar to the one Judith made famous.

These eleven poems provide a fresh and historically attuned frame-work for reading the better-known work of her early publishing career. We see that, even during the mid 1930s, Judith was a serious poet, regularly producing poems using a range of established poetic techniques and forms, many of them elaborate, from the ballade supreme to free verse. We see how open she was to language, embracing and rehearsing elements of both modernist and Victorian aesthetics in an attempt, presumably, to find where she was most comfortable, poetically, and to refine her own abilities. Literary discussion at the University must have influenced Judith, distinguishing her teenage poetry from that which she wrote as a young adult. These were not like the poems she wrote as a child to please her mother, that sentimental verse 'about men going to the war, and babies, and flowers, and eternal love', as she later described it, and they differed from her teenage poems.[516] These poems were different. And yet they could be just as saccharine on topics more mature, such as beauty and self-sacrifice. Most notably, these poems reveal how consistently, and over what a stretch of time, Judith worked to develop the characteristic style and some of the thematic concerns of *The Moving Image*. We see that, in fact, she appears to have been rehearsing the poem that would become her most famous, 'Bullocky', more than a decade before it was published.

We see also, with startling clarity, how important sex was to Judith's poetry; that her early work was fuelled by a desire to put physical intimacy into words. Though this was widely recognised with the publication of Judith's second collection of poetry *Woman to Man* (1949), we see that Judith was writing erotic poetry long before. And, it is argued here, none of that poetry – with its effervescent sexuality, its hybrid diction – would have been possible without the experience of Sydney and the University. Until now, this book has looked at the cultural change Judith was exposed to in coming to university in Sydney. Here we see change mirrored in poetry.

Identifying Judith Wright's university poetry is hard because she used fake signatures. Did she do so to be deliberately mischievous? To protect her future reputation? The significance of these signatures is worth considering before looking at the poems themselves. When asked why she used fake signatures, Judith was clear: she used them because she was a woman and 'women were not regarded very highly'. She felt she 'had a good deal better chance of being published as J. Wright, unknown, than as Judith Wright'.[517] But, of course, she was not published as 'J. Wright' in any University publications; this was just an example. It was a denunciation of the University literary culture, much in the same vein as that she made when describing how she had been 'shunted' on the social column at *Honi Soit*. But, like that claim, this one appears less robust when considered in its historical context.

Between 1934 and 1936 the overwhelming majority of poems published in magazines at the University of Sydney were signed with initials. As Donald Horne commented: 'it was an age of initials'. Even when not seeking anonymity, both student and professorial writers at the University favoured initials for their first and middle names, in the mode of T. S. Eliot. It was a natural extension to abbreviate further for poetry so that only two or three letters stood by a poem. AJM and HD were both truncated forms of real names used by student poets. Horne remembers signing his work in *Hermes* with at least four different versions of his name, all but one of them incorporating initials.[518]

Equally rife was the practice of concocting a fake set of initials or a one-word name, such as 'Ian', or 'Arstaeus', as favoured by Horne. Michael Heyward considered James McAuley's use of fake signatures at university unremarkable (compared to his later, remarkable use of one), writing: 'when James McAuley wasn't 'J. Mc' ('jay muck' his friends pronounced it) he was 'Glaucon' or 'Proteus'.[519] Other students were on the same wavelength, contriving signatures, such as 'Setna', 'Sarge' and 'Artemidorus', that made them seem ever more clever. Others, including DDD, had fun with initials.

As this indicates, men used fake signatures just as enthusiastically, if not more enthusiastically, than women. Amongst the few students who ventured whole, real names between 1934 and 1936 were Adele Bieri and Margaret Walkom. One of the most frequently published poets during the period was Isabel Ellis, a name which appears to be fake. Why would someone invent a female name if it really was harder to be published as a woman? Gender identification appears to have had little to do with the practice. At the University the widespread use of initials was symptomatic of a culture of evasion and game playing. Anonymity generated intrigue and mystique, and insured against outright rejection. Heyward ruminated on the benefits of the practice, noting that, whereas 'a name signals an identity', no name 'denies readers the right to assume anything'. Even more wonderful when exclusivity is a sign of sophistication, anonymity 'projected writing as a higher activity accessible only to those in the know'.[520]

Like most students at the University, Judith probably submitted her poems anonymously because it enabled her to experiment. And it was fun. As well as using her real initials, JW, I argue in this chapter that Judith employed versions of them. 'JA' stood for 'Judith Arundel', her first and middle name; 'JMW' may have been a nod to the woman, May Wright, on whose back she had gone to university in the first place. The final signature identified in this chapter, an obviously female one, 'Margaret Jay', could only be traced back to Judith by those familiar with her family tree. Perhaps Judith was confusing University publications with other magazines, such as the *Bulletin*, in which she published in the following years. There, being identified as a woman may have carried more significance.

∞

JW, the signature which Anderson connected to Judith over forty years ago, was credited with four *Hermes* poems between 1934 and 1936 (see Appendix A). 'Nocturne', which appeared on an unremarkable page twenty-two in a 1934 issue, resembles Judith's early poetry in one very clear way: it is a passionate description of a mountainous landscape which symbolises the female speaker's desire. Throughout *The Moving Image* the land is represented as if a woman's sensuous body, which not only forms beautiful, distinctively female shapes but both feeds and hungers, responding to its changing environment. In 'South of My Days', the tableland is a 'high delicate outline/ of bony slopes wincing under the winter' and 'my blood's country' is 'clean, lean, hungry'. In 'For New England', 'all the hills' gathered waters feed my seas'; 'the long slopes' concurrence is my flesh', and the speaker's 'jealous bones' hoard another earth. The technique worked to imply an innate, emotional and sexual connection between a woman's body and the natural landscape. This alone was not new; what was distinctive was the bold assertion of a woman's active subjectivity. These female bodies were not made purely receptive by comparisons with the land; they became alive, yearning, and even spoke their wishes. The poems of that first collection asserted a taboo subject: female desire.

'Nocturne', which adheres to the traditional characteristics of a poetic or musical nocturne with its dreamy evocation of night, reveals that Judith was working on the technique for at least a decade. Shadows lie sleeping, 'clasped in the arms of the hills'. The moon is a mistress who each evening rises, dressed appropriately for her dalliance with Night; 'her form wrapped round in moon-mist tiffany/ which clothes but to reveal'. Night is excited by the spectacle, becomes desirous, 'hastens their union', and embraces Moon's body, which is white as the 'wave-spent foam'. Once naked, Night disappears into the 'innermost crevice of the hills' and an 'intolerable radiance engulfs the world'. The trees bow their 'plumed heads in prayer' at the scene. As Judith would, JW praises a woman's sexual fulfilment, which is achieved by her active participation; Moon 'flings' her clothes aside and 'ascends the stairways of heaven'. In contrast, coyness, adherence to typically feminine behaviours, gets a woman nowhere. Beauty achieves no sexual satisfaction: 'to be beauteous must be sad'.

'Nocturne' was conventional in other ways, resembling many *Hermes* contributions with its employment of well-established associations between the moon and a woman's body, between male sexuality and the night. Nina Murdoch's poem 'Sybarite', published in *The Wide Brown Land* that same year, also spoke of 'the silver samite of the moon', shadows creeping, air singing and trees which 'bow down' to evoke a corporeal experience.[521] 'Nocturne' speaks of sex and longing in euphemistic, symbolic terms – as did much Victorian and, consequently, *Hermes* poetry. But its emphasis on female desire made it different.

Although the landscape evoked in 'Nocturne' is not identifiably Australian, there is a focus on particular features within it which Judith's first collection of poetry also dwelt on. The opening line of 'Nocturne' ('where the mountains go down to the sea') evokes the dramatic contrast between an elevated, imposing landmass and the relatively flat sea. The meeting place between mountain and river, between river and sea, is a recurring image in Judith's poetry. In 'The Moving Image' Judith wrote of: 'a sweet slope of grass edged with the sea'. In 'For New England', as noted, she wrote: 'all the hills' gathered waters feed my seas'. The description of moon and mist together, and the personification of the moon, as seen in 'Nocturne', is also present in Judith's early writing. In 'Soldier's Farm', she wrote: 'the mist was early and the moon was late'. That poem, although about something quite different, uses the movement of trees to dramatise the sexual encounter; the 'delicate gatherings of dancing trees' responded to his desire such that 'his wife's body answered to his arms'. In 'Nocturne', the folding trees represent the completion of sex ('while wind-swept trees upon a curving hill/ Bow their plumed heads in prayer'), and seem to symbolise a spiritual unity between nature and human.

JW's 'The Crucible', published in the same issue of *Hermes*, was more characteristic of the magazine's output. The poem was grounded neither by its environment nor its historic context. Details, such as the spelling of 'to-morrow', the capitalisation of important words, and the rhyming structure, confirm the influence of Victorian poetry, alive too in the emotions of the poem. About the challenge of sexual postponement, if JW had been recognisably female this would have given the poem a distinctive edge. After all, it was not usual for a woman to describe her lips as 'hungry' or her desire as 'hot' in the pages of *Hermes*. Nowhere, though, does the poem specify the speaker's gender.

'The Crucible' is hard to resist reading biographically. Judith, as we know from Chapter 5, had several boyfriends during these years and described herself as more liberated than her male counterparts. In her memoir she wrote of the doctor boyfriend who wanted to finish university before getting married. By the time he had finished he settled on someone less 'worldly' than Judith.[522] In the poem, the speaker worries that if the lovers do not act on their desire now, 'a kiss which now does seem/ Fulfilment of a lovely dream/ May have become monotony'. Referring to 'when we're old', the speaker reasons that since they had a long future being 'subdued by a more temperate fire', why not enjoy 'the heat of our desire'?

It is a curious thing that, at the same time as 'The Crucible' was published, Jack McKinney, Judith's future husband, was in the process of having his novel published, also titled *The Crucible*. Published by Angus & Robertson in 1935, he most likely came to Sydney in 1934 to discuss the book. Every time and place has its 'it' words and phrases; 'crucible' may have been theirs. The concurrence suggests that Judith and Jack, even before they met one another, were attracted to the same language and ideas.

Almost two years later, in the first term of 1936, JW had two more poems published in *Hermes*. 'Autumn', conventionally, personified the seasons as female; it depicted them seducing a masculine force-of-nature (here, time), not out of sexual desire but out of a desire for power. These were familiar themes in classical Greek literature, and so were favoured by the Victorians and contributors to *Hermes*. 'Autumn' was, in fact, not unlike a number of Judith's lesser-known poems which drew inspiration from European mythology, in contrast to her better-known ones which described nature in new and unique terms. She liked to write of nature's forces as characters, and to capitalise their names. She liked to write of myths and fairytales, and her female characters were more feisty than traditional fairytale ones.[523] Judith wrote about the seasons in poems such as 'Spring After War' and 'The Child', from *Woman to Man*, in 'Song for Winter', from *The Gateway* (1953), and even as a teenager in 1932, when she wrote 'This Spring

Morning'.[524] 'Autumn' may have been more rousing than the average *Hermes* poem with its depiction of carnal hedonism ('and at the door stands Autumn, naked, brown/ Thin-hipped and slender-waisted') but it was male desire that it described frankly. And *this* was a common preoccupation of contributors.

The final JW poem, 'Ballade of Passion', also published in 1936, bore strong resemblance to 'Nocturne'. Like that poem, sex is described in joyful, explicit terms, with nature responding to, even emulating, human actions and emotions. As in 'Nocturne', the trees fold over upon the satisfactory completion of sex, as if tenderly embracing the lovers and also 'spent': 'till I upon the beach recline,/ Spent, on the shore of Paradise,/ For I have drunk of passion's wine./ The trees bend down from their far height/ With vain arms, which would emulate/ Our ecstasy...' As already mentioned, many of Judith's poems depicted tree branches as arms, recalling the sensation of being enclosed within another's embrace. Sometimes this is non-sexual, as in 'Child and Wattle-Tree', from *Woman to Man*, which instructs: 'lock your branches around me, tree;/ let the harsh wooden scales of bark enclose me/ take me into your life and smother me with bloom'. 'My Friend', another teenage poem, introduces 'my lovely, lonely friend who is a tree'. A maternal figure, 'in her kind arms they [birds] build and love and mate'. The speaker beams at the tree, and she 'smiles back at me'.[525] Whereas in Judith's childhood and teenage poetry nature was a comforting presence, in her university poetry we see it rife with sexual energy. 'Ballade of Passion', as with 'Nocturne', uses the moon and the sky, the tides and the sea, to symbolise sex.

'Ballade of Passion', although ambiguous, could easily be read as a conventional depiction of male sexuality. Aspects of the poem are clichéd. The white moon is innocent; the lover has stars in her eyes; waves move in a 'faster rhythm', then they 'beat against the shore' until the lover reclines on the beach, 'spent'. Being in love is described as having 'drunk of passion's wine'. Such metaphors might have appeared in the pages of Ethel's women's journals. Moreover, the poem is a conventional, albeit accomplished, example of the intensely rhythmical, intricate form, ballade supreme. Composed of three ten-line stanzas and an envoi (addressed, as is usual, to the poet's audience), four rhyming sounds are arranged in a strict ababbccdcd scheme throughout. Coupled with an unwavering iambic tetrameter, 'Ballade of Passion' is tight and regular, determinedly pounding its case, encapsulated by the repeating refrain: 'for I have drunk of passion's wine'. JW's poetry suggests that Judith, although interested in finding new ways of writing about desire, had not significantly developed her style; that she was not attempting experimental, modernist aesthetics, and that particularly Australian material had not made its way into her poetry. But this was not the whole story.

In Shirley Walker's archive of Judith Wright papers another *Hermes* poem is listed. Published in 1935 under the signature JMW, it was also titled 'Nocturne' and, like JW's 'Nocturne', is pensive in approach and loosely structured in form, evoking the 'dreaming' referred to in its opening line. Curiously, there is no reference to the other JMW poem published in the same issue and titled 'We Die'. Two things stand out about these poems (see Appendix B). Firstly, they were well received. Published in the only issue edited by Alan Crawford, a prominent figure in the University literary scene, 'We Die' appeared on the first page of poetry and 'Nocturne' on the last. It was *Hermes*' jubilee issue and to commemorate it essayists were asked to consider the past and future of the magazine. When HMS enquired, in his essay, 'who shall say what the next fifty years may bring forth?', he may have done so on the same page as the early work of one of the century's most successful poets.

The second notable feature of the poems was their aesthetic approach. As distinct from JW's poems, JMW's were abstract, succinct and revolved around one striking image. 'We Die' depicts a phenomenon that Judith, and modernist poets such as T. S. Eliot, revisited throughout the 1930s and 1940s. This was a short-lived moment of ecstasy, both preceded and followed by emotional depletion. Writers seemed driven to accept this depleted state as our natural one, while remaining fascinated by the timeless, 'half-recalled', 'flickering' moment, phrases which Eliot would later use in 'Little Gidding' (1942). In that poem, the communication of the dead expresses something we cannot know when alive, and takes place in 'the intersection of the timeless moment'. Similarly, in 'We Die', the moment after death is when we 'float upon the tideless waters of all time'. In both poems, after this moment comes the continuation of time which inspires unrelenting melancholia. JMW writes of waking, seeing all about 'our dead desires, clinging vainly/ to the crumbling greyness of the years'. In 'Little Gidding', the timeless moment is followed by 'ash on an old man's sleeve', a state of numbness where there is 'death of hope and despair'.

Eliot was looking, in his poems, for moments of (some say religious) release and exultation within reality. In 'Little Gidding' he would describe the sounds that are 'not known, because not looked for/ but heard, half-heard, in the stillness/ Between two waves of the sea'. Judith also sought to explicate the 'half-moment'. Two years after finishing university, she had 'Earth' published in *The Australian National Review* (see Appendix E). It described human life as a fleeting, spontaneous moment subsumed by the earth: 'all our thoughts,/ our truths, our lies, our loves, return to her'. One might 'climb for redemption to the curving sky', but the earth 'beats you back...earth in the end will take you back entire'. The poem concludes with a moment much like the one in 'We Die', in which the speaker describes waking 'for a moment'; 'some strange and shifting jet catches the light,/ Changes, and loses power, and sinks again,/ And then becomes the earth.' Both poems raised, for just a moment, the spectre of something beyond the knowable.

JMW, like Judith, was drawn to the rejuvenating potential of nature and the pleasure that could be experienced in mimicking this process by submitting oneself to a greater force. 'Nocturne' centres on the image of a flame, which captures and consumes life. Throughout her work, Judith used flames and flame trees to represent this cyclical process. In 'The Flame Tree' (1953), she described how 'gloriously' the tree shed her blossoms; how 'what the earth takes of her, it will restore'. JMW meditated similarly. 'Nocturne' begins by alluding to a flame's allure with the phrases 'sky spiral' and 'pale ecstasy': how the flame seems to represent passage to something beyond the everyday. A butterfly submits to the flame's pull: 'the flame of the flowers allures,/ The butterfly hovers...and falls,/ Into the heart of the flame'. Despite these similarities, if JMW was Judith, we see again that she was not yet interested in couching her poetry in particularly Australian terms. Larkspur, primrose and lilac; the emphasis on a delicate, transient, even dim pleasure ('pale ecstasy', 'faint scent', 'white mist') all conjure a very different landscape.

In this chapter, the poetry of pseudonyms that others have connected with Judith Wright has been discussed. How do we know Judith used other signatures while at university? In her interview with the National Library of Australia she said that at least one fake signature had never been discovered. Laughing, she said that she would not reveal it even if 'wild horses are harnessed to me'.[526] No doubt there was a pleasure in preserving some mystery, privacy even, about her writing life.

There is one pseudonym which carried special, personal significance for her. 'Margaret Jay' is the name attributed to a short *Hermes* poem published during Judith's first term (see Appendix C). Records show there was no student at the University called 'Margaret Jay'. It was, however, Judith's great-great-grandmother's maiden name. As discussed in Chapter 1, Margaret Wyndham (nee Jay) became an archetype of perfection for May Wright and generations of Wyndham women.

Under the guise of 'Margaret Jay', and like so many other students, this poet focused on a Greek mythological figure. Aphrodite, or Venus, as she was in classical Rome, appealed to a Victorian sense of drama and romance, and resurfaced throughout this poetry. Graceful Aphrodite, goddess of love, mother of many, abandoned her home because she fell in love with Adonis. In rough terms, her life resembled that of Margaret Jay, who left Belgium to marry a man determined to leave Europe, and became a mother to nine. There cannot have been many Hunter Valley women in 1827 who could play the piano and speak several European languages. In her world, she was an Aphrodite.

The final line of 'Aphrodite' might refer to winemaking, Margaret and George's main agricultural interest ('blackberries/ crushed, and running red'), but could also be a reference to a darker feature of their existence, flagged by the mention of blood in the poem's opening. 'Beneath the trees', writes Jay of the twilight, 'the fluid shadow patterns fall'. It was a similar description to that which Judith would use when explaining May's sensation of being watched, in the evening time, by Aboriginal people hiding in the scrub. In *Generations of Men* (1959) she wrote: 'it was often hard to be sure if they were there or not, their bodies melted so strangely into the darkness of the stems'. Judith, like Jay, emphasised how their bodies seemed to blend into the bush and move fluidly, too well hidden for their 'quiet old horse' Bolliver to detect: 'sometimes in the long grass Bolliver would almost step on the body of a child crouching, still and invisible. It would dart out from under him and disappear again in a moment, to go on with the game of watching without being seen'.[527]

And, in the years between, Judith wrote similarly in 'The Invaders' (1950), a poem that remains uncollected. The Aboriginal women dissolved into the bush and watched on, hidden: 'their faces were the faces of the strange lilies/ watching in the forest at the edge of sight'. Their hiding signalled something sinister. The poem describes how 'they were like the black snakes that rear to bite'.[528] In *Generations of Men*, the 'continual surveillance made May a little uncomfortable', a feeling not eased by her display of markswomanship.[529] In 'Aphrodite', the twilight darkens and climbs up the speaker's veins until blood is, metaphorically, spilt in the final lines: 'blackberries/ crushed, and running red...' The phrase 'in my veins' also alludes to the indelible connection of family, as does the fake signature. Judith would be forever tied to such stories. 'Aphrodite' might suggest that Judith, as early as 1934, was looking for the language and imagery to describe her family's colonial history; that she wanted her Australian history to form part of her poetry.

Something else suggests Judith used another signature altogether. When she spoke of being published at university Judith said it was in *The Arts Journal*, as well as *Hermes*. No JW, JMW or Margaret Jay, let alone Judith Wright poems, appeared in *The Arts Journal* in 1935 or 1936 and, as mentioned, either no 1934 issue of the magazine was published or no copies of it exist in a public library. As stated in Chapter 5, in 1936 Judith was on the editorial committee of *The Arts Journal*. It was common practice for those involved in the production of a magazine to publish their own work. Sometimes this was under fake signatures and sometimes not. Looking at the 1936 issue of *The Arts Journal*, only four signatures could be Judith's.[530] One of them, JA, was responsible for four poems in *Hermes* and *The Arts Journal* in 1936, and none in the following year when Judith had graduated. When she revealed her university poems were published 'usually under a pseudonym or otherwise', Judith immediately followed: 'this was why Miles Franklin chose her second name'.[531] Franklin had been an inspiration in other respects, so it might have made sense for Judith to do as she had done and adopt her own second name, Arundel, as part of her signature, creating the initials 'JA'. Yet these are inconclusive arguments; the real proof is in the pudding. The remainder of this chapter will explicate these arguments for these poems being attributed to Judith Wright for the first time, and cast new light on her poetic development.

Published in *Hermes*, and written by JA, 'Poem' (hereafter referred to as 'Poem 1' to distinguish it from JA's other 'Poem', see Appendix D) is a poem about the human search for perfection, which is doomed by the 'fallen' human condition and which creates pain ('the penalties of aspiration') by revealing the gap between the unattainable ideal and the physical, bestial lived reality. In one sense this is a poem with a 'universal' meaning, or at least a narrative that is very recognisable within Western civilisation, evident for example in Milton's lines about the Earth being 'hell' for one, such as Satan, who has seen the perfection of heaven.

Nonetheless the wording, the imagery, the (admittedly limited) characterisation and certainly the 'physical' environment presented, strongly suggest a 'new world' and more specifically an Australian context, within which this 'universal' struggle or desire or lament is being made. Phrases such as 'after-drought rain'; 'hot hands'; 'drag men'; 'pant on hard paths'; 'man stumbles' and 'travelling through twilight to receding day', though not connected in the poem by a straightforward narrative, suggest a specific kind of experience or drama. This is one in which a figure, or figures, is or are physically anguished by a journey. The mention of 'iron bands' and 'brands' suggest coercion and control, indeed the domination of one figure, or species, over another.

In the context of Australia, where the poem was published and which is inclined towards the droughts mentioned in the poem, such imagery seems to allude to one of two figures, which, by the 1930s, figured largely in the nation's literary imagination: the bullocky (portrayed by, amongst others, Joseph Furphy, Henry Kendall, and Katharine Susannah Prichard) and the convict (portrayed by John George Lang, Marcus Clarke, William Hay and many more). Such figures were not typical subject matter for *Hermes*, and this suggests that JA had a particular desire to incorporate Australian history into poetry.

The difference, or lack thereof, between humans and animals is a question which hangs over the poem and, it could be argued, is the only motivation behind two references to beasts. Whereas at the beginning of the poem it is stated that Man is not beast, and thus is unable to achieve 'serenity', the final lines conclude that Man is 'still the beast with the old brands', and ultimately unable to escape 'his' physical struggles. However, that the poem specifically mentions branded animals, together with a kind of travelling which is coerced, suggests that JA wanted the reader to be reminded of the bullock and its driver. While the metaphorical significance of such imagery clearly has 'universal' application, the 'drama' of the poem deserves to be recognised too.

In 'Bullocky' (see Appendix E), first published eight years after 'Poem 1', in *The Bulletin*, Judith was applauded for grounding a story of human struggle in the realities of an Australian pioneering setting. After all, at its core, 'Bullocky' is also about the 'universal' human desire for perfection. Like 'Poem 1' it emphasises the brutish nature of reality and how the struggle for perfection, or aspiration (in this case, for 'the Promised Land'), leads towards greater degradation of human experience, such that there becomes little to separate humans from animals. The cattle, described, as humans might be, as a 'heavy-shouldered team', become, in the bullocky's dream, 'slaves'. In the context of Australia, such a word conjures the figure of the convict, a figure which 'Poem 1' also alludes to with the mention of 'iron bands'. While 'Bullocky' communicates a 'message' which specifically relates to the 'settling' of Australia, both it and 'Poem 1' convey a more fundamental point about the human condition.

In both poems, perfection is represented as a place unseen but promised by God; in 'Poem 1', 'heaven', 'lovely and unreal lands', a place which might 'shine only in the spirit's divination', 'the never-visible rose': in 'Bullocky', 'the Promised Land'. The desire to be released to this place is given voice through prayers in both poems.

To represent perfection as heaven, admittedly, is not unusual. But, taken together with some more unusual similarities, such common features help form a noteworthy list.

In both, the image of perfection becomes more deeply embedded in one's mind as one's reality stretches further from it. The word that both JA and Judith use to describe this is 'etched'. In 'Bullocky', the 'long solitary tracks' are 'etched deeper' with every trip. The lines immediately preceding this suggest repeated physical turmoil has created tracks of thoughts in the bullocky's brain ('he weathered all the striding years/ till they ran widdershins in his brain'), such that further labour compounds these anguished thoughts, which, as the poem tells us, circle on promised tranquillity. Thus, his thoughts of salvation are etched deeper with every physical hardship. In 'Poem 1', JA also uses the words 'brain' and 'etched'. The very same image, created in 'Bullocky', is more straightforwardly communicated in 'Poem 1': 'the heaven etched like torment on the brain'.

In 'Poem 1' and 'Bullocky', the day's end is the time of greatest mental anguish. This is when, in 'Poem 1', the man is 'driven by torment'; when, in 'Bullocky', the man is 'cupped' by darkness and shouts his 'prayers and prophecies'. It is significant, too, that the 'dreams of final peace', referred to in 'Poem 1', are of 'after-drought rain'. The end of drought is a particularly, though not singularly, Australian realisation of peace. It was a preoccupation which Judith famously gave voice to throughout *The Moving Image*, where dust and drought figured centrally. In 'Bullocky', there is also a drought. That 'Poem 1' and 'Bullocky' share a common central figure, in the bullocky, as well as specific wording and imagery, is remarkable enough to warrant strong consideration of their being written by the same person.

In the same 1936 issue of *Hermes* there appeared another 'Poem' by JA (hereafter 'Poem 2', see Appendix D). It presented an unflattering portrayal of university students: they were mindless and emotionless, states which seem to have sprung from them never having felt true pain; of never having fought or died for love. As they sat in lectures they were thrilled by evocations of actual sacrifice. Their response was to analyse these descriptions since they could not really understand them within their 'perfection'. The repetition of the words 'forged' and 'perfect' suggests that the struggle towards a social ideal leads one away from individuality and, ultimately, humanity. In 'Poem 2' perfect human beings become robots.

It was a theme Judith was drawn to throughout her life. In 'Computers' (1966), she began: 'those things make me nervous'. Humans, she said, were becoming more like them: 'we're ashamed to fall in love/ because They don't do it./ We analyse poems instead of reading them/ because that's what computers do'.[532] Such analysis formed knowledge which was cold, inhumane, incomplete. That it was valued so highly in Western societies was a provocation for Jack's philosophy. Similarly, in 'Advice to a Young Poet' (1970), Judith asked her subject: 'your mind's gone electronic/ and your heart can't feel?/ but listen, your teachers tell you,/ it's not to worry'. Even as a young woman Judith believed that feeling pain made us human. In 'Waiting' (1946) she wrote: 'let our weeping…make us whole'. Cities, and the technology on which they relied, encouraged people to deny their emotional response to life, to wear an identical 'mask of stone', as in 'The City Asleep' (1949).

'Poem 2' suggests that Judith, at twenty-one, was already thinking in these terms, that she was developing the language and imagery of such poems decades before they were published. It commences with an image similar to that which opens 'The City Asleep': a white mask is lit up by electricity, that symbol of the industrial metropolis. Whereas in 1966 she would write about computers, in 1936 she referred to their contemporary equivalent, robots.

What became lifelong concerns for Judith were widespread at the University in the 1930s. The effects of 'standardisation', a popular term in the period, were explicated by *Hermes* editor Margaret Walkom, in the same issue in which 'Poem 2' appeared. She described a 'decay' of difference, a loss of idiosyncrasy: 'the more people look alike and speak alike, and the more they see and hear the same things, the more are they bound to think alike'. Walkom evoked a devolution of human beings towards robots. All this change, she said, was the result of 'mechanical development' and 'the mass product'.[533] As discussed in Chapter 4, the immense social change which technology and changing patterns of work and leisure brought to Sydney in the late 1920s had many worried. 'Poem 2' echoed its editor's concerns.

The strongest indication that Judith wrote 'Poem 2' can be found in her first 'Quadrangles' columns, also published in 1936 and discussed in Chapter 5. That column included an original poem whose title, 'University Specimens No. 1: The Perfect Student', echoed JA's ironic employment of the term 'perfect'. In 'University Specimens' the 'perfect student', the 'very model student', is self-satisfied, mindless, superficial, evasive and cowardly – not at all perfect. Like JA, Judith was critical of what her university classmates aspired towards. In both poems, the subject is a student who knows a lot; in 'University Specimens', 'he's aware of current happenings/ And discusses them all day'; in 'Poem 2' the lecturer's words are pinned to the page for future analysis. Both lack emotional and moral depth: in 'University Specimens' the speaker suggests it is impossible to know what the perfect student really thinks; in 'Poem 2' the student has an 'iron heart'.

'University Specimens' was lighter than 'Poem 2'; it was, after all, part of a social column. The latter explicated self-centredness and heartlessness as if its subject was facing final judgment. 'Drink', commands the speaker, 'drink that blood'. The horrific decree is a punishment which offers redemption. The image reminds us of the primary example of pain and self-sacrifice in Western culture, as well as the sacramental performance of it in church. 'Poem 2' directs the subject to drink blood in order that he or she become more human, more aware of the suffering of others. Such enlightenment would bring the person a kind of 'everlasting life'. Whose suffering, specifically, does the poem direct us to consider? It is no more specific than 'those who/ thought and acted/ so many years ago...those who could fight and die for love'. What is being praised is self-sacrifice, physical accomplishment and bravery. JA might have been referring to World War I veterans or early Australian colonialists, both of whom may have featured in 'her' family. Perhaps 'she' was referring to both.

During Judith's childhood, enthusiastic exhortations of self-sacrifice were common. She was born, after all, in the midst of a war that drew on Australian volunteers. As a teenager Judith penned one such exhortation, titled 'A Call to Arms'. Published in the NEGS chronicle, Judith's poem instructed 'children of the Empire' to 'rise up and take your place'.[534] Brady refers to the poem in her biography, viewing it as an aberration from Judith's natural inclination towards non-violence. The poem, wrote Brady, suggests 'she might not have been a radical... for once she seems to have succumbed to imperial feeling'.[535] 'Poem 2' suggests that she succumbed more than once. Crucially, 'A Call to Arms' positioned the self-sacrifice of soldiers as an extension of colonial hardship. She told her classmates: 'remember how your fathers,/ With comforts small and few,/ Fought and died like heroes/ To pave the way for you./ And where they fought their battles/ Was there where now you stand./ Their weapon was the plough-share,/ And their foe the untilled land'.[536]

'Poem 2', published four years after 'A Call to Arms', demonstrates an ongoing concern with public duty and self-sacrifice. In both, experience of hardship is a moral duty and a fulfilment of one's humanity. This fundamental belief – which we might easily trace in Phillip and May's politics, in the Wyndham mythology, in English Protestantism – remained throughout Judith's life; a constant in a life of apparent contradictions and change. No matter what, Judith urged her reader to remember the pain involved in the formation of Australia.

'Poem 2', like 'Poem 1', shows JA experimenting with contemporary literary devices. The affecting use of directives ('drink', 'feel', 'drink') reflects an intimate, confrontational persona which Judith recreated in poems such as 'Country Town'. There, she would explicate exactly who she thought her compatriots should remember: 'Remember Thunderbolt, buried under the air-raid trenches./ Remember the bearded men singing of exile./ Remember the shepherds under their strange stars'. Remember, she might have said, the suffering that has enabled your life. It was the central refrain of her writing life. Later on she would encourage her audience to think of other, more extreme forms of suffering – of Aboriginal populations, and of the decimation of natural landscapes – but the framework through which she viewed these social problems was already set, we can see, in her early twenties. Such problems were always the result of a majority who lived unthinking, sanitised, even greedy lives, ignoring the pain of others.

A third JA poem, published in the final *Hermes* of 1936, may reflect the influence of both Victorian and modernist forms of writing on Judith. 'Haunted House' (see Appendix D) demonstrates an interest in death, ghosts and fear, also seen in Judith's childhood and teenage poetry. As stated elsewhere in this book, this was also a preoccupation of much Victorian poetry, and latter day imitations of it, such as those found in Ethel's women's journals. The dominance of these themes within Judith's juvenilia no doubt reflected her own, intimate experience of death. 'Fear', published just four years before 'Haunted House', began: 'there's fear in my heart to-night,/ And fear chills my hands./ For something walks the house to-night/ From unknown lands'.

Like 'Haunted House', 'Fear' allows that being afraid can be pleasurable. Both poems centre on a ghost. In 'Fear' the ghost is a dead version of the speaker; in 'Haunted House' the ghost is a more complex figure; a memory, perhaps, of 'our dead paradise'. Both are sensual creatures. The 'gold-haired' ghost in 'Fear' smiles before sensuously slipping past the speaker. In 'Haunted House' she puts a 'dazzle over your eyes'. The dead young woman as an affecting, erotic presence was another trope in Victorian literature. Both poems emphasised the inevitability of death. In 'Fear' Judith writes: 'as true as I shall die'; in 'Haunted House', JA concludes: 'you will die'. Both poems make a rhyme out of the word 'stone' (with 'moan' and 'shone') to draw the reader's attention to the matter, a reminder of the ghost's pale perfection and an allusion to her deathly coldness.[537]

And yet other features of 'Haunted House' point to an interest in contemporary literary techniques. Early in 1936, about six months before 'Haunted House' was published, W. H. Auden wrote a short, highly distinctive poem, titled 'IX', which became part of the 'Autumn Song' sequence. It revelled in misery, with apocalyptic directives: 'Stop all the clocks, cut off the telephone…Bring out the coffin, let the mourners come'. Its diction was echoed by 'Haunted House' ('Shatter the windows, stain the stone…Let no lovers inhabit here'), but it is unclear whether Auden's poem would have been seen by Australians in 1936, and so may or may not have been a direct inspiration. Even if JA had not seen 'IX', 'she' was clearly influenced by Auden and Eliot's affecting use of directives throughout their 1930s poetry.

Another image in 'Haunted House' that suggests Judith's authorship is the blooming garden. In the poem JA writes: 'look, how strangely the garden flowers/ each year', despite the house's atmosphere of fear and melancholia. Similarly, when her husband dies, May, in *Generations of Men*, returns to the boarded-up, 'woebegone' house of her grandparents George and Margaret. The house's 'indefinable air of loss' signals the end of something. Perhaps George's dreams of a paradise in Australia are finally confirmed over. The house becomes a ghost like that in 'Haunted House', a 'ghost of our dead paradise'. And yet, strangely, the lavender bush flourishes:

> The house, bereaved as she herself was, had lost its grace and welcoming air; it gathered brooding in stone round the courtyard, where grass grew among the flagstones, and the pump at the well was broken...But the lavender-bush May remembered near the great heavy side-door had multiplied itself and grown riotously.[538]

In both 'Haunted House' and *Generations of Men*, the finality and solemnity of death is underscored through comparison with blooming flowers. Such flowers seem to thrive mysteriously, eerily even, within the tomblike space.

The final JA poem, published in the same issue of *The Arts Journal* which Judith helped edit, was entitled 'Venus to Adonis' (see Appendix D). Venus, the Roman version of Aphrodite, was a familiar subject for Judith. She had, it is argued in this chapter, even written a poem in her name under the 'Margaret Jay' pseudonym. 'Venus to Adonis' brings together many of the themes in Judith's pseudonymous work, as well those in the poetry published under her own name.

The similarities between 'Venus to Adonis' (from here on 'Venus') and 'The Crucible' strongly suggest JA was JW. Both poems establish a dialogue between one lover, who urges 'waiting', and another who submits that they should yield to their passions. Such contests may not have been unusual amongst undergraduates, who were expected to be married before having sex. In poetry pages there were echoes of this argument but almost entirely from the perspective of an obviously male figure who is sexually frustrated. In contrast, 'The Crucible' and 'Venus' portray the lover who advocates delay as wise. Furthermore, in the latter, the sexually frustrated lover is a woman, Venus. She urges: 'forget the tentative violins of thought/ for these deep violoncellos, throbbing low./ This storm has thunder/ to drown all other voices, however wise'. Our desire is so strong, says Venus, it cannot be resisted. Such enthusiasm is expressed similarly in 'The Crucible', where it is argued that 'we should both/ Be happy-hearted, nothing loath/ To watch this Love of ours take form...To see the heat of our desire'. Like the speaker in the 'Ballade of Passion', these advocates had 'drunk of passion's wine'.

'Venus' resembled JW's poetry in a way which emphasises the distinctive quality of what is argued is Judith's pseudonymous poetry. These poems were not, like much student poetry, indirect descriptions of a woman's body. Instead, they were about the satisfactions of sex – for both parties. In 'Venus', desire ('spring's bugle-call') is followed by a 'slow irregular drum' which becomes faster, then 'quicker, quicker hasten until spring is spent'. The following line ('forget the half-seen wonder') might be an allusion to the half moment, mentally achieved, and described in 'We Die'. This physical moment, in contrast, is complete and uncompromised. What follows the semicolon at the end of the line explains how it is so: 'my muffling dark is warm about your eyes'.

In JW's 'Nocturne' there is a similar invocation of oral pleasure: 'darkness', the male figure, is described fleeing 'into the innermost crevice of the hills/ and all is silver glory, a well-nigh/ intolerable radiance'. And again in 'Autumn', the male lover responds to the female lover's call by travelling into the 'dark'. He 'runs down dark'ning ways/ Pursuing strange desire through paths unknown/ 'Neath russet trees that drip with early rain./ Down, down into the woody depths he goes'. His own desire, charged by 'lust-sped feet', is secondary for 'far ahead he hears her laughter ring'. These are the 'sweet, swift-spent hours'. The recurring use of the term 'spent' in what is argued is Judith's pseudonymous poetry (in 'Autumn', 'Venus' and 'Ballade of Passion') is not conclusive evidence of common authorship – after all, the term was widely used. But it does signal the importance of sexual satisfaction to this poetry; specifically, female satisfaction. In 'Autumn', 'Venus' and 'Nocturne', female sexual fulfilment is suggested. In 'Ballade of Passion' the reference to 'our ecstasy' implies mutual fulfilment. It was a distinguishing feature.

'Venus' shares common traits with JW's poetry, and even Margaret Jay's poem, but it is Judith Wright's poetry which it most strongly resembles. An excerpt from 'Nigger's Leap, New England' ('now we must measure/ our days by nights, our tropics by their poles,/ love by its end and all our speech by silence') demonstrates this. The final lines of 'Venus' exhibit similarities in both syntax and meaning: 'now, we know more than we shall ever know,/ And have found more than seeker ever sought'. In both poems the phrase 'now we' is followed by a series of striking paradoxes. More remarkably, both poems allude to the particular experience of understanding more about the world without having sought to, of having one's knowledge expanded in ways one never imagined. In 'Venus' it is love which does it. In 'Nigger's Leap' it is migration. In both there is the juxtaposition of expectation with aftermath. Judith, of course, used paradoxes throughout *The Moving Image* (examples include 'we know the agony we do not know' and she who is 'the gazer and the land I stare on'), as did contemporary writers such as Eliot, but it was a technique not so commonly found in the pages of *Hermes* or *The Arts Journal*.

'Venus', like many of Judith's early poems, is about a woman lover surrendering to her desire, and casts sex as a search for something unknown. In 'Woman to Man' sex represents a collapse of oppositions and the futility of conventional forms of enquiry ('this is our hunter and our chase...this is the question and reply'), in much the same way as the lovers 'know more than we shall ever know...found more than seeker ever sought' in 'Venus'. This theme, of self-sacrifice leading to knowledge, permeates Judith's work and is most succinctly expressed by the line 'in the loss of myself, to find', from 'The Flame Tree', which she calls the 'thanks of lovers'.

Another poem from *The Moving Image*, 'The Company of Lovers' (from here on 'The Company'), resembles 'Venus'. While allusions to war in 'The Company' shape its meaning differently, sex functions similarly in both poems. Indeed, 'Venus' suggests that Judith thought about sex as an escape long before she wrote about it as an escape from war-time tension in 'The Company'. Whereas Venus tells her lover to 'forget...forget' and let 'all other voices' be drowned out by the noise of their desire, in 'The Company' the lovers 'forget/ the night in our brief happiness'. In both poems lovers relinquish control. Sex allows them to transcend their separateness for a short while. They find more in sex, curiously, of that which they sought outside it. From 'Venus': we 'have found more than seeker ever sought'. From 'The Company': 'we who sought many things, throw all away/ for this one thing, one only,/ remembering that in the narrow grave/ we shall be lonely'. In 'Venus', sex will 'warm our chilling blood'; in 'The Company' the lover is instructed to 'lock your warm hand above the chilling heart'.

In 'Venus' the lovers hear the 'slow irregular drum' before it quickens; in 'The Company', 'the dark preludes of the drums begin'. In 'Venus' the poet tested these images; in 'The Company' she perfected them. JA's poems, like those of JW, JMW and Margaret Jay, it is argued here, were Judith Wright's training ground.

∞

It has been said of Judith's first two collections of poetry, *The Moving Image* (1946) and *Woman to Man* (1949), that they broke new ground in Australia. Of the first Walker concluded: 'it is difficult to overstate the impact of this collection'. Here was a woman writing, with skill and assurance, of distinctly Australian themes in a modern diction. 'Bullocky' and 'South of My Days' ensured her prominence within Australian literature and became, Walker says, anthologised more often than any other Australian poems, in Australia and overseas. By any measure *The Moving Image* has been one of the most successful collections of poetry written by an Australian. Why, then, have the early drafts of those poems never been recovered?

The task of unearthing Judith's early poetry has attracted little interest. Does this reflect a latent sexism within Australian literary history? After all, a less successful poet in James McAuley has had his university poetry exhumed at a cracking pace. It is discussed in at least three books.[539] Or is the situation a reflection of Judith's own views? As Anderson said, she preferred that her early poetry was not discussed and, throughout her life, dissuaded biographical investigation.[540] Those that have pursued biographical criticism, chiefly Shirley Walker, Veronica Brady and Fiona Capp, maintained a strong respect for their subject's approach. All had personal connections with the poet and none seemed inclined to go against her wishes. Perhaps, in the end, the situation reflects the traditional delineation between literary studies and history, which has deterred literary scholars from archival research and historians from investigations into poetry.

Certainly, it must be allowed, these eleven poems might not have been written by Judith Wright. If this were the case then, as stated in the introduction to this chapter, different questions need to be asked about them given the strength of their resemblance to poetry published under Judith's name in the succeeding years. If she did not pen them she seems to have been strongly influenced by whomever did. Among the dozens of poems published between 1934 and 1936 in *Hermes* and *The Arts Journal* there may also be others that Judith wrote. Yet no others so closely, or completely, resemble the themes and phrasing of the work we know as Judith Wright's.

If we accept that these were the poems that came before *The Moving Image* then they can be seen to show, most obviously, the length of time it took to create that first collection. A decade before it was published, Judith was experimenting with phrases and images she would use for it. Some poems, especially those written under the 'JW' signature, demonstrate the extent to which Judith was still influenced by her mother's favoured poetry genre, Victorian poetry. Other poems, especially those written under the 'JA' signature, show her experimenting with contemporary techniques, an experimentation which would lead her to become confident in modern diction by the early 1940s.

Following the questions raised in Chapter 7 about the bias of *Hermes* editors, these poems reveal that Judith was published most often by Margaret Walkom, in 1936, who generally did not favour experimental modernist writing. Interestingly, three of the five Judith poems she published were amongst Judith's most stylistically adventurous and modern. A. C. Beattie, who as *Hermes* editor in 1934 and 1935 championed experimental writing, still published Judith's work, but less frequently. It might suggest that, in direct contrast to Judith's own claims, she had a better chance of being published when being daring. Or it might simply suggest that Judith's work got better over the course of three years. Either way, it could not be said that Judith was unsuccessful as a poet at university.

Thematically, the poems demonstrate that Judith was drawn mainly to subject matter familiar in European poetry. Many of the poems use images from nature to explore universal themes of love and love lost. As with Judith's known poetry, nature is personified. The parts of nature on which these poems focus are the same as those in Judith's later work. However, the natural world conjured in these poems is not obviously Australian, as it would be in Judith's later work, and is sometimes even clearly European. The exception to this is 'Poem 1' which not only depicts a drought-stricken landscape (in as much as any landscape is depicted), but also uses images and themes which connect it to Australian history and its portrayal in the nation's literature. At the same time, that poem, like Judith's 'Bullocky', was also about the 'universal' desire for perfection and release from our physical, lived reality. If it is accepted that 'Poem 1' was written by Judith, it shows the length of time that she was working on the poem that would become her most famous.[541]

These eleven poems also challenge the notion that Judith's poetry became more focused on female sexuality with *Woman to Man*, written in the first blush of her relationship with Jack. Walker, who views her first two collections as 'remarkably different...in both tone and theme', contends that 'this new emphasis upon love [in *Woman to Man*] is obviously related to Judith's association with Jack McKinney'. Biographical readings have assumed that it was only through her relationship with Jack that Judith was able to give expression to – indeed, perhaps find – a dazzling, clearly female sexuality. This in turn gave her poetry a distinctive, subversive quality. The notable thing about *Woman to Man*, wrote Walker, was 'the frank sensuality of the woman's response to her lover...it is difficult for a modern reader to imagine the response, in the 'forties, to such a frank confession of female sensuality'. For these poems were, astonishingly, able to 'simulate the sexual act from the woman's point of view in a quite explicit way'.[542]

And yet now we find that more than a decade earlier, and several years before Judith met Jack, she appears to have been writing with that same, sure-footed delight in sex. Even then she was interested in expressing sex from a woman's point of view, and concerned with what sex could teach us intellectually. These early poems, although not as accomplished as those published under the name 'Judith Wright', or as free from cliché, were written by the same woman who concluded: 'all that is real is to live, to desire, to be'. The philosophical importance of desire was something Judith understood a decade before. There can be no doubting that Jack's influence on Judith was profound, and much occurred during the years before *The Moving Image* was published that would shape Judith intellectually, but, we see now, this was a woman who was pushing similar boundaries well before she met Jack, was chilled by the war, or began, in earnest, on that collection of poems that would reshape the Australian cultural landscape.

Postscript

Nobody's perfect. It is an allowance we make for each other's regrettable flaws and inconsistencies. And yet part of us longs for perfection, if not in ourselves, then in others. The aim of this book has been to illuminate unexplored areas of Judith Wright's background and early years in the belief that, by doing so, her life and thought – that necessarily imperfect trajectory that all of us are on – would make more sense. My guiding supposition has been that poets are as much made as born, and that by paying attention to this process – this social composition of selfhood – we might observe broader historical and cultural forces at work. Historical enquiry has long championed the value of such endeavour, for understanding these forces on the individual makes us alert to the precise ways social change unfolds at a particular time – for better and worse – and to how, as in this case, key artworks emerge from and in turn help to shape society.

To more fully understand the extent to which Judith was bound, as both a young and an older woman, to the colonial mythologies within her family, is to attain a better grasp of the pervasive if often unconscious cultural impacts of Whiteness and imperialism, and perhaps of the limits of human psychology. And yet, this political 'imperfection' did not inhibit Judith from championing, and bringing about, important social change – perhaps, in the end, it was the necessary seed for those actions.

To more fully understand the extent to which Judith's refusal of conventional femininity was driven by the differing examples of her mother and grandmother helps illuminate the complexity of gender and of a child's relationship with her guardians. That this refusal to adopt the role of pastoral woman – the 'perfect' female within her society – was necessary to her writing career, and animates the barriers young women faced, and still face, in leading an intellectual life.

Greater understanding of the politics of Australian pastoralism, and the considerable degree to which Judith grew up within them, helps us see the extent of her intellectual development and, conversely, the common attributes between such politics and other, progressive politics, with which she was involved.

And, to more fully understand Judith's social, cultural and intellectual context, as she came to maturation, helps us identify the ingredients, and their origins, that made possible *The Moving Image*: a confident but distinctly Australian female voice; a circumspect interest in aesthetic modernism; a knowledge of Australian history; a familiarity with Western philosophy; a despair about the loss of traditional Aboriginal societies; an impatience with mainstream, metropolitan cultures; and perhaps above all, a writerly poise and self-assurance that could only come from a familiarity with the field – the literary characters, dominant intellectual concerns, and practical mechanics of publishing – into which she delivered her work.

Though there is evidence that Judith was unconventional in some senses before Sydney, could that girl who arrived there and proudly declared her connection with an Australian poetess have imparted the knowing and resolute tone of that monumental first collection? To learn how unworthy the University regarded such literature, what indeed the University and its students regarded as literature, was to begin to learn the voice which she would need to speak to this audience, as well as to the many other poetry audiences that were defined by their relationship with literature as the universities understood it. To observe, react against and sympathise with the postures of her lecturers was to understand the tradition of intellectual enquiry she then shared with her reading public. University was a testing ground for Judith; a place for messy imperfections – on the page and in life – which helps explain, rather than detract from, her more masterly control of language and intellectual subtlety of later years. There was more to *The Moving Image* story than we have known.

∞

In scholarly research, perfection is the end game, and understandably so. In history or biography this means getting the details right and relaying those details as directly and transparently as possible matters. In her final published poem, Judith emboldened younger poets to be a 'prism' through which the world, that 'source of the light', was cleanly reflected: 'Simply stay attentive/ to the source of the light, and/ always/ keep the prism clean'. The biographer, even perhaps the reader, covets the possibility that 'the light' on the page is an accurate reflection of its real-life occurrence. The transmission of factual details seem to offer this promise.[543]

And yet, the further I have ventured, the more I have detected a tension between getting the details right and getting the truth right. This, after all, has been a project in which I have discovered many incorrect details on the public record, leading me to argue for a reconsideration of the life of Judith Wright. But in insisting on such details – some undeniably significant, some just curiosities – there is the danger the bigger truth of this book becomes a story which I know for sure is actually not true: that Judith misrepresented herself, her family and her history in a coordinated, conscious effort to mislead.

My hunch is that some of Judith's inaccuracies were the result of bad memory, and some were of not believing that remembering accurately was always important. Trauma also has a way of dramatically shaping the story one tells about oneself, and Judith had her fair share of that. Other inaccuracies, elisions, or overemphases might have been a result of Judith's unwillingness, or inability, to completely reject the story her family told her from a young age, or reorganise her own story of selfhood. If this is a fault, it must be acknowledged to be a particularly human one, more striking in those who are truly willing to question, whose ability to critically examine seems exemplary.

Judith had little mental space, or desire, to spend time on her own zigzag path, her raggedy story. Ensuring other representations of her life were 'clean' was certainly not her responsibility, though it is inevitably the aspiration of subsequent biographers. Towards the end of her life the Cause mattered more than her life story, and it does not take much imagination – whatever your belief – to see that as an admirable thing. The commitment and energy Judith put into things beyond her own self were remarkable: that was my starting point and, in a roundabout way, is my end point.

For the characteristics that fuelled her activities may have been the same ones that prevented her from readily accepting the 'imperfections' in her personal and family history. Confidence, idealism, commitment, selflessness, effort: they propelled her beyond what anyone might have expected of a pastoral girl; and they made it hard to critically analyse one's own endeavours. Judith respected Carl Jung's belief in the magnetic force of opposites; she might have recognised in herself the way characteristics tended to yield both 'positive' and 'negative' effects.

The ideal of perfection, then, just does not seem to account for these contrary pulls. If Judith were perfect she would not be someone who I would have written about, or you would have read about. For she probably would have done nothing so bold as reshape Australian poetry, just as a starter. Recognising that she was not born a poet, or a prophet, should lead to a greater valuing of what she achieved as an idealistic creator and advocate of beauty and truth.

Striving for perfection, as I have found out, risks creating mistruths. This book is a balancing exercise, an attempt – though I did not set out for it to be one – to give greater weight to stories cast aside in other literature; to fill out a picture. Though I could never understand Judith's belief that, as she told her daughter Meredith, emotion is often truer than fact, at the end of this book I find I do.

Poems by JW

Nocturne

Where the mountains go down to the sea…
There, when the day is over and done
And the shadows lie sleeping,
Clasped in the arms of the hills,
Walks Beauty all alone, by unknown ways,
To greet the coming Night, the one she loves.

But he, false lover, waits the sickle Moon
Who is his mistress. From the seas she rises,
In silver radiance, a pale orb celestial,
Her form wrapped round in moon-mist tiffany
Which clothes but to reveal. Night's black desire
Hastens their union, he receives her body,
White as the wave-spent foam and petal-soft
In Ethiopian arms. While Beauty, sad, must weep
That she fulfil her destiny
For Beauty to be beauteous must be sad…

Then the Moon casts aside her flowing gown
Of silver mist, and flings it on the sea
As she ascends the stairways of the Heaven
In naked splendour; darkness flees

Into the innermost crevice of the hills
And all is silver glory, a well–nigh
Intolerable radiance engulfs the world...

While wind-swept trees upon a curving hill
Bow their plumed heads in prayer.

From *Hermes* (Michaelmas 1934): 22.

The Crucible

I fearing said: 'But we may change –
Within a year, or maybe less,
Our hungry lips, which closely press
Till Time's swift ever-onward stream
Stands still, a kiss which now does seem
Fulfilment of a lovely dream
May have become monotony.'
But you were wiser far than I.
You said: 'All things must suffer change
And we should cull the flowers which lie
About our feet, not seek to range
Within To-morrow's grassy fields
For blossoms which the future yields.'
True, change must come, but we should both
Be happy-hearted, nothing loath
To watch this Love of ours take form
Within Time's flaming crucible;
To see the heat of our desire
(Subdued by a more temperate fire)
Emerge, pure metal, clear of dross,
And love the Love that Time should mould
Out of Youth's passion, when we're old.

From *Hermes* (Michaelmas 1934): 24.

Autumn

Mad Autumn, with her tousled locks,
Her tawny mane of unkempt hair,
Red-gold; her brown and lissom body, knocks
Upon the door of Time. He lies within fair
And pink-fleshed Summer circled in his arms
In sensuous slumber. Down the glades of sleep
He wanders through a dreamland that has been –
Gold-crested cornlands ripe with splendid grain
Beneath the sun; fair fruits and plentiful;
Sweet, swift-spent hours
When he lay basking on a bank of flowers
With Summer by his side, a slender bride and fair;
Of meadows somnolent beneath the sun;
Of waters scintillant beneath the moon
That shone from out a maze of star-drift...
He wakes, roused by the cry of Autumn.
In the eaves
He hears the sparrows whispering, dead leaves
Like little ragamuffin boys
Scurry before the uncouth wind,
And at the door stands Autumn, naked, brown,
Thin-hipped and slender-waisted. At her call
He leaves his love and runs down dark'ning ways
Pursing strange desire through paths unknown
'Neath russet trees that drip with early rain.
Down, down into the woody depths he goes,
With lust-sped feet crushing the violets,
Seeking a flying nymph who mocks his grasp
While far ahead he hears her laughter ring
And Summer is a long-forgotten thing.

From *Hermes* (Lent 1936): 20.

Ballade of Passion

The trees, blind eunuchs of the night,
sway loveless limbs, importunate.
The moon, a white-robed acolyte,
Looks down upon their sorry strait
In innocence immaculate.
Two stars lie drowned within your eyes,
Which, fairer than the studded skies,
Look up with joyful fear to mine,
Look up in fashion young but wise,
For I have drunk of passion's wine.

Your naked limbs are splendid, white,
And indolent in pagan state.
Blue waves which move, moon-bathed with light,
White curves which slowly undulate
Into a faster rhythm. Great
Waves beat against the shore. Sound dies
With each wave-beat, again to rise
Till I upon the beach recline,
Spent, on the shore of Paradise,
For I have drunk of passion's wine.

The trees bend down from their far height
With vain arms, which would emulate
Our ecstasy, as I recite
A hymn of Love, defying Fate
Which would with strictures separate
Us twain, who love though all else lies
In ruin, through the world decries
Fond amore. Heart that beats to mine,
I would not have it otherwise,
For I have drunk of passion's wine.
                    ENVOI.
Beloved, see, the darkness flies,
Dawn should not here our love surprise.

Let us away. All joy is thine,
I care not if the day brings sighs,
For I have drunk of passion's wine.

From *Hermes* (Lent 1936): 25.

Poems by JMW

We Die

We die, and for a little,
Float upon the tideless waters of all
time.
Then for a moment wake,
And see where all about us
Flock our dead desires, clinging vainly
To the crumbling greyness of the years.

From *Hermes* (Michaelmas 1935): 8.

Nocturne

A white butterfly and dreaming
flowers
Flaming pale upon the wind.
Sky spiral of larkspur,
Pale ecstasy of primrose.
A butterfly swaying moth-like
To the flower-flame,
Drawn by the faint scent of lilac,
A white mist of perfume.
The flame of the wind burns clear,
The flame of the flowers allures,
The butterfly hovers...and falls,
Into the heart of the flame,
Into the flame of the flowers.

From *Hermes* (Michaelmas 1935): 26.

Appendix C

Poems by Margaret Jay

Aphrodite

Indigo twilight, darkening my blood
climbs in my veins
with the voluptuous mutations
of full tides.
Beneath the trees
the fluid shadow patterns fall,
like blackberries
crushed, and running red...

From *Hermes* (Lent 1934): 20.

Poems by JA

Poem ('Poem 1' in this book)

These are the penalties of aspiration;
      The heaven etched like torment on the brain,
      The dreams of final peace, after-drought rain,
These will evade for ever the hot hands,
Shine only in the spirit's divination.

The lights of lovely and unreal lands
Drag men from the serenity of the beast
To pant on hard paths, pray for a glimpse at least
Of what he shall never perfectly attain,
Though logic lead him in its iron bands.

This tension of the nerve, this restless pain
To rise ever a semitone, complete the chord
That never will ring true, temper the sword
To further strength — who dares come out and say
If this is loss to man at last, or gain?

Travelling through twilight to receding day,
Perhaps away from day, there is none knows,
Hungering to find the never-visible rose,
Man stumbles, still the beast with the old brands,
Driven by torment on the doubtful way.

From *Hermes* (Trinity 1936): 19.

Poem ('Poem 2' in this book)

A round white mask hovers about the desk.
Under the glaring electric lights its mouth
Opens and shuts.

All the bent automata on the benches
Catch the meaningless words, pin them to the page.
Foolish words, war, death, action,
Blood such as robots never could contain
Spilt on the naked page to be analysed.
Drink it, robots, drink that blood.

Who knows, suddenly breath may come to you,
Suddenly your forged perfect iron hearts
May receive life and beat, your forged and perfect
          arteries
Feel the blood course down them of those who
          thought and acted
So many years ago: and you will feel the pains
Of those who could fight and die for love,
Thrilling your cold intricate brains and nerves.
Drink this, and receive everlasting life.

From *Hermes* (Trinity 1936): 13.

Haunted House

Through all the house let the wind moan
  in years to be.
   Shatter the windows, stain the stone,
but in it stays this ghost of ours,
this memory.

Let no lovers inhabit here
but wind and rain,
Lock the door for very fear,
but look, how strangely the garden flowers
each year, again.

The ghost of our dead paradise,
should you pass by,
Will put a dazzle over your eyes
as when the sun leaps out in showers,
and you will die.

From *Hermes* (Michaelmas 1936): 11.

Venus to Adonis

Let us discuss no longer.
In winter evenings such a time will come,
We shall be glad of matter for argument
To warm our chilling blood to quiet heat.
Spring's bugle-call grows stronger,
And in our ears the slow irregular drum
Will hasten soon its beat,
And quicker, quicker hasten until spring is spent
Forget the half-seen wonder;
My muffling dark is warm about your eyes.
Forget the tentative violins of thought
For these deep violoncellos, throbbing low.
This storm has thunder
To drown all other voices, however wise.
Now, we know more than we shall ever know,
And have found more than seeker ever sought.

From *The Arts Journal* 1 (1936): 11

Selected Poems by Judith Wright

Earth

Men breed the marvellous, but earth breeds man.
We build as she directs; and all our thoughts,
Our truths, our lies, our loves, return to her.
The mould is rich, it smells of dreams decayed.
All knowledge feeds it. No there is no hope
To renounce the earth; men find no grip on air,
Water and fire repel them. Answer this,
The eternities you create and contemplate,
What are they built of but a little earth?
Climb for redemption to the curving sky,
It beats you back; the stars are leagued against you,
Earth in the end will take you back entire,
For she is proud and has not known defeat.
You must accept the bargain she compels,
See men and women, coloured, lit and shadowed;
See trees with burning fruit, and hear the song,
The futile laughter, the senseless bravery
Of life in the hawker's cry along the road.
The flame-tree there leaps among iron roofs,
And the poinsettia spins its crimson discs.
From the silent seed awhile some fountain plays,
Some strange and shifting jet catches the light,
Changes, and loses power, and sinks again,
And then becomes the earth.

From *The Australian National Review* 4, no. 22 (1938): 53–4.

Bullocky

Beside his heavy-shouldered team,
thirsty with drought and chilled with rain,
he weathered all the striding years
till they ran widdershins in his brain:

Till the long solitary tracks
etched deeper with each lurching load
were populous before his eyes,
and fiends and angels used his road.

All the long straining journey grew
a mad apocalyptic dream,
and he old Moses, and the slaves
his suffering and stubborn team.

Then in his evening camp beneath
the half-light pillars of the trees
he filled the steepled cone of night
with shouted prayers and prophecies.

While past the camp fire's crimson ring
the star-struck darkness cupped him round,
and centuries of cattlebells
rang with their sweet uneasy sound.

Grass is across the wagon-tracks,
and plough strikes bone beneath the grass,
and vineyards cover all the slopes
where the dead teams used to pass.

O vine, grow close upon that bone
and hold it with your rooted hand.
The prophet Moses feeds the grape,
and fruitful is the Promised Land.

From *Collected Poems 1942–1985* (Sydney: HarperCollins, 1994), 17.

Notes

Introduction

1   I refer to the central characters of this book – Judith, Phillip, May, for example – by their first names. To do otherwise would seem overly formal. According to Laurie Oaks, when Gough Whitlam and his staff 'racked their brains, trying to think of a woman sufficiently prominent and respected to be acceptable in the role' of Governor-General, they came up with one name: Judith Wright. L. Oaks, *Crash Through or Crash: the Unmaking of a Prime Minister*, Drummond, Richmond, VIC, 1976, p. 162.

2   Judith began to lose her hearing in her mid twenties so her deafness does not help us understand her childhood or early adult years.

3   According to her daughter, Meredith McKinney, Judith believed that the writing of biographies distracted people from more important work that needed to be done in the Humanities. M. McKinney, interview with the author, 8 August 2008.

4   S. Walker, *Flame and Shadow: A Study of Judith Wright's Poetry*, 2nd edn, University of Queensland Press, St Lucia, QLD, 1996 (1991), p. 2.

5   V. Brady, 'After Life With Judith Wright', *Meanjin*, vol. 64, no. 3, 2005, p. 110.

6   On Brady seeking Judith's direction in the writing of *South of My Days*, see for example: V. Brady to J. Wright, 6 January 1997 and J. Wright to V. Brady, 11 December 1996, Judith Wright papers, box 83, folder 596, National Library of Australia, Canberra; J. Wright to T. Lister, 19 May 1995, in P. Clarke & M. McKinney (eds), *With Love and Fury: Selected Letters of Judith Wright*, National Library of Australia, Canberra, 2006, p. 517.

7   For the relationship between Brady and Wright, see Judith Wright papers, box 83, folder 596, National Library of Australia, Canberra; J. Wright, 'Judith Wright: Corrections to Biographical Errors', *Australian Literary Studies*, vol. 19, no. 4, 2000, p. 438; P. Hill, interview with the author, 28 April 2008; J. Wright to P. Sherman, 26 August, 1998, Judith Wright papers, MS Acc08.078, National Library of Australia, Canberra.

8   V. Brady, *South of My Days: A Biography of Judith Wright*, Angus & Robertson, Sydney, 1998, p. 5.

9   ibid., p. 4.

10   ibid., pp. 11, ix.

11   Clarke & McKinney (eds), *With Love*, p. 3.

12   McKinney, interview.

13   Throughout this book I note inaccuracies in Brady's work. Many could be explained by the fact that Brady did not use a recorder when interviewing Judith and did not properly source archival works. Regarding not recording interviews, P. Bundred, interview with the author, 20 March 2007. When citing Judith's interviews with Heather Rusden for the National Library of Australia, Brady used two numbers, for example 'OH [Oral History] ii/3'. The interview, however, should be referred to using three numbers: tape number, tape side, and page number, for example '1 2/10'. This would refer to material found on tape one, side two, and on page ten. Since Brady is heavily reliant on this source, and her citations are not illuminating, it is difficult to verify many of her quotations.

14   Walker, p. 2; Jennifer Strauss, *Judith Wright*, Oxford University Press, South Melbourne, VIC, 1995, p. 44.

15   Brady, *South*, p. 55.

16   Strauss, p. 1.

17   P. Mead, 'Veronica Brady's Biography of Judith Wright', *Australian Literary Studies*, vol. 19, no. 2, 1999, pp. 163–75.

18   P. Mead, *Networked Language: Culture and History in Australian Poetry*, Australian Scholarly Publishing, North Melbourne, VIC, 2008, pp. 269–72.

19   B. Rooney, *Literary Activists: Writer–Intellectuals and Australian Public Life*, University of Queensland Press, St Lucia, QLD, 2009, pp. 5–8.

20   S. Sheridan, *Nine Lives: Postwar Women Writers Making Their Mark*, University of Queensland Press, St Lucia, QLD, 2011, pp. 7, 19, 25–49.

21   P. Clarke & M. McKinney (eds), *The Equal Heart and Mind: Letters Between Judith Wright and Jack McKinney*, University of Queensland Press, St Lucia, QLD, 2004, p. 1.

22   D. Horne, *The Education of Young Donald*, Angus & Robertson, Sydney, 1967, p. vii.

23   B. Caine, *Biography and History*, Palgrave Macmillan, London, 2010, p. 3.

Chapter 1: The Wyndham World

24   White quoted in D. Marr, *Patrick White: A Life*, Random House, Sydney, 1991, p. 4; 'Judith Wright: A Written Interview', interview with C. Masel & M. Schmidt, 1992, Judith Wright papers, MS 5781, box 71, folder 513, National Library of Australia, Canberra.

25   J. Wright & J. McKinney in P. Clarke & M. McKinney (eds), *Equal Heart*, pp. 26–8.

26   J. Kociumbas, *Oxford History of Australia*, vol. 2, *1770–1860: Possessions*, Oxford University Press, Melbourne, 1992, p. 126.

27   J. Wright, *The Generations of Men*, Oxford University Press, Melbourne, 1965 (1959), p. 9.

28   C. M. Wright, introduction, *Extracts from Dinton-Dalwood Letters: From 1827 to 1853*, C. M. Wright (ed.), 1927, p. 3. Duplicated by D. E. Wilkinson, 1964, Judith Wright papers, MS 5781, box 70, folder 504, National Library of Australia, Canberra.

29   J. Wright, *Generations*, p. 5.

30   ibid., p. 4.

31   ibid., p. 5.

32   J. Wright, 'For a Pastoral Family', *Australian Verse: An Oxford Anthology*, J. Leonard (ed.), Oxford University Press, Melbourne, 1998, pp. 212–16.

33   Judith was still content with *Generations of Men* in 1980 when she had discussions with screenwriter Frank Harvey about a television series based on the book. J. Wright to F. Harvey, 21 August 1980; F. Harvey to J. Wright, n.d., Judith Wright papers, box 37, folder 285, National Library of Australia, Canberra; J. Wright to A. Miller, 14 September 1993, *With Love*, pp. 505–6.

34   J. Wright, *Half a Lifetime*, Text Publishing, Melbourne, 1999, p. 3.

35   Judith's papers at the National Library of Australia, Canberra, include correspondence between her and the Dalwood Restoration Association. Judith explained that she did not want to be a financial member or on their list of steering committee members, but she did provide them with historical sources where relevant. Box 48.

36   P. A. Wright, *Memories of a Bushwhacker*, reprint with afterword by B. Mitchell, The University of New England, Armidale, NSW, 1982 (1972), p. 115.

37   ibid., p. 2.

38   Judith Wright initially suggested that George Wyndham studied at Oxford, but later confirmed that it was Cambridge. *Generations*, p. 5; J. Wright, *Cry for the Dead*, reprint by new publisher, API Network, Perth, 2004 (1981), p. 32.

39   J. Wright, *Cry*, p. 32.

40   ibid., p. 33.

41   D. Seton Wilkinson, 'The Importance of Dalwood', document prepared for the Dalwood Restoration Society, 2010, unpaged.

42   C. M. Wright, pp. 4–5.

43   Judith referred to the vessel as the 'George Horne' in her 1967 entry on George Wyndham for the *Australian Dictionary of Biography*. J. Wright McKinney, 'Wyndham, George (1801–1870)', National Centre of Biography, accessed 5 February 2016, adb.anu.edu.au/biography/wyndham-george-2824/text4049. Newspaper reports and shipping intelligence, which include details of passengers, dates and cargo, show it was called the 'George Home'. Untitled article, *The Hobart–Town Courier*, 1 December 1827, p. 2, accessed 13 January 2016, nla.gov.au/nla.news-article4225675, 'Shipping Intelligence', *The Sydney Gazette and New South Wales Advertiser*, 28 December 1827, p. 2, accessed 13 January 2016, nla.gov.au/nla.news-article2189657; G. Wyndham, 'On the Land Policy of New South Wales', pamphlet, H. Thomas, West Maitland, NSW, 1866?, p. 2; J. Wright, *Cry*, p. 33.

44   C. M. Wright, pp. 2–3; J. Wright, *Generations*, p. 5; J. Wright, 'G. W. Australia 1827', *Meanjin*, vol. 6, no. 3, 1947, p. 173; M. A. Wyndham to M. Wyndham, undated, C. M. Wright (ed.), p. 25. As this letter is undated, George Wyndham's position on the British Prime Minister cannot be definitively stated. However, it is likely that M. A. Wyndham was referring to the Tamworth Manifesto, in which British conservative politicians endorsed modest reform, including on the issue of Catholic Emancipation.

45   J. Wright, *Half*, unnumbered page.

46   F. McInherny, introduction, in G. Wyndham, *The Diary of George Wyndham 1830–1840: A Pioneer's Record*, A. Wyndham & F. McInherny (eds), on behalf of the Dalwood Restoration Association, Parkes the Printer, Armidale, NSW, 1987, p. 7.

47   Kociumbas, p. 123.

48   J. Wright, *Half*, p. 12; J. Wright, *Cry*, p. 31; C. M. Wright, p. 3; S. Macintyre, *A Concise History of Australia*, Cambridge University Press, Cambridge, 1999, p. 75.

49   Tasmanian Archive and Heritage Office, 'Wyndham, Given Name Not Recorded', Record IDs 629653 and 629652, Departures, Names Index, accessed 12 December 2015, www.linc.tas.gov.au.

50   Seton Wilkinson, unpaged.
51   R. Milliss, *Waterloo Creek: The Australia Day Massacre of 1838, George Gipps and the British Conquest of New South Wales*, McPhee Gribble, Ringwood, VIC, 1992, pp. 48–51.
52   J. Ferry, *Colonial Armidale*, The University of Queensland Press, St Lucia, QLD, 1999, p. 73.
53   Seton Wilkinson, unpaged.
54   J. Wright, *Generations*, p. 4.
55   G. Wyndham, 'Diary', pp. 15, 17, 20, 29, 54, 69.
56   Sending workers to the police station, ibid., pp. 15, 48, 71; flogging a worker, ibid., p. 15.
57   J. Wright, *Half*, p. 7.
58   McInherny in G. Wyndham, 'Diary', p. 7.
59   Kociumbas, p. 135.
60   'Colonial Secretary's Office, Sydney, April 30, 1829', *The Sydney Gazette and New South Wales Advertiser*, 5 May 1829, p. 1, accessed 13 January 2016, nla.gov.au/nla. news-article2192371.
61   G. Wyndham, 'Diary', p. 43.
62   J. Wright, *Cry*, p. 43.
63   Macintyre, p. 77; M. A. Wyndham to G. Wyndham, 12 October 1828, C. M. Wright (ed.), p. 23; G. Wyndham, 'Diary', p. 95.
64   A. Wyndham in G. Wyndham, 'Diary', p. 4.
65   J. Wright, *Generations*, p. 5.
66   Seton Wilkinson, unpaged; L. Wyndham to M. Wyndham, 30 December 1833, C. M. Wright (ed.), p. 66.
67   C. M. Wright, p. 8.
68   P. A. Wright, p. 101.
69   L. Wyndham to G. Wyndham, 18 July 1828, C. M. Wright (ed.), pp. 19–20.
70   Seton Wilkinson, unpaged.
71   J. Wright, *Generations*, pp. 2–3.
72   C. M. Wright, p. 3.
73   J. Wright, *Generations*, pp. 3–4.
74   J. Wright, *Half*, p. 21.
75   J. Wright, *Generations*, p. 4.
76   Ferry, p. 22.
77   J. Wright, *Generations*, p. 5.
78   G. Farwell, *Squatters' Castle: The Saga of a Pastoral Dynasty*, Angus & Robertson, Sydney, 1983, p. 9.
79   J. Wright, *Generations*, pp. 6, 233.
80   The website of the Wonnarua Nation Aboriginal Corporation, 'Strategic Report 2009–2012', accessed 7 August 2012, wonnarua.org.au/projects.php.
81   This is the approximate road distance between Singleton, Maitland and Wollombi. A much larger estimation of Wonnarua territory was performed by J. W. Fawcett, whose early descriptions of the tribe were influential, but has since been contested: 'their tribal district had an area of upwards of 2000 square miles, and included all the country drained by the Hunter River and its tributaries'. 'Notes on the Customs and Dialect of the Wonnah-Ruah Tribe', *Science of Man and Journal of the Royal Anthropological Society of Australasia*, vol. 1, no. 7, 22 August 1898, pp. 152–4.
82   C. M. Wright, p. 3.
83   McInherny in G. Wyndham, 'Diary', p. 8.

84 J. Wright, *Generations*, pp. 4, 7, 11.

85 J. Wright, *Cry*, p. 1; T. Griffiths, 'Truth and Fiction: Judith Wright as Historian', *Australian Book Review*, August 2006, no. 283, p. 29.

86 Milliss, p. 23.

87 James Miller, a Wonnarua historian, argues that there were several distinct tribes in the Hunter Valley, and that there was conflict between the Wonnarua and Kamilaroi. J. Miller, *Koori: a Will to Win: The Heroic Resistance, Survival and Triumph of Black Australia*, Angus & Robertson, Sydney, 1985, pp. 12, 10. Fawcett was amongst the first Europeans to write about the Wonnarua (see note above). I avoid using the terms 'upper' and 'lower' Hunter Valley because they are imprecise, do not correlate with tribal boundaries, and the use of them has furthered the false impression that there were two distinct territories in the Hunter with markedly different histories.

88 Judith notes, late in Chapter 2 of *Cry for the Dead*, that the Wyndhams did not occupy Kamilaroi territory until 1839, when they claimed land further north. She mentions the Wonnarua only twice in the same chapter, once when discussing life in the Valley before European invasion, and once when noting Major Mitchell's observation of 'a remnant of the Wonnarua people…eking out life in a last refuge' on the rocky ranges. *Cry*, pp. 53, 31, 40.

89 J. Wright, *Cry*, pp. 35–7, 42.

90 'Fight Amongst the Aborigines', 3 June 1843, *The Maitland Mercury and Hunter River General Advertiser*, p. 2, accessed 19 January 2016, nla.gov.au/nla.news-article660579; 'Maitland', 1 January 1852, *Freeman's Journal*, p. 11, accessed 20 January 2016, nla.gov.au/nla.news-article114835137; 'Latest Intelligence', 27 April 1861, *The Armidale Express and New England General Advertiser*, p. 3, accessed 20 January 2016, nla.gov.au/nla.news-article192530832; 'Telegraphic Intelligence', 12 November 1867, *Empire*, p. 5, accessed 20 January 2016, nla.gov.au/nla.news-article60846955.

91 Fawcett, p. 152.

92 James Miller was raised in Singleton in the 1950s. Many Wonnarua moved to Singleton in the 1870s. Miller, pp. xv, 14. See www.wonnarua.org.au for more information about the Wonnarua today.

93 Most Hunter Valley landowners did not live there in the period. For information on David Maziere, 'Free Settler or Felon?', accessed 15 January 2016, www.jenwilletts.com/george_wyndham.htm

94 See George Wyndham's description of Australia before European settlement as a 'waste land', G. Wyndham, 'Land Policy', p. 1.

95 Miller, p. 1; J. Laffan & C. Archer, *Aboriginal Land Use at Tocal: The Wonnarua Story*, NSW Agriculture, Paterson, NSW, 2004, p. 7.

96 Millis, p. 54.

97 ibid.; Miller, pp. 33–4.

98 J. Connor, *Australian Frontier Wars, 1788–1838*, UNSW Press, Sydney, 2002, p. 62; Milliss, p. 55. Regarding incidents near Annandale/Dalwood, late in 1825 members of the Dharuk, Darkingung and Wonnarua killed two European men near Putty, about 30 kilometres west of the property. In 1826 another violent encounter occurred, this time in Maitland, also less than 30 kilometres from Annandale/Dalwood. Miller, pp. 36, 40.

99 Millis, pp. 58–61; 'R. Scott Esq., to Mr McLeay', document 11, 'Original Documents on Aborigines and Law, 1797–1840', Macquarie Law School, accessed 21 December 2015, www.law.mq.edu.au/research/colonial_case_law/nsw/other_

features/correspondence. James Miller argues violence between Europeans and Wonnarua was common and overt until 1830, p. 42.

100   J. Wright, *Cry*, pp. 52, 36.

101   Australian Dictionary of Biography, 'Scott, Robert 1799–1844', accessed 9 March 2016, adb.anu.edu.au/biography/scott-robert-2642; W. Wyndham to G. Wyndham, 8 August 1828, C. M. Wright (ed.), p.15.

102   L. Wyndham to G. Wyndham, 28 October 1829, C. M. Wright (ed.), p. 24; C. Wyndham to M. Wyndham, 29 October 1829, C. M. Wright (ed.), p. 26; L. Wyndham to G. Wyndham, 28 November 1830, C. M. Wright (ed.), p. 42; Millis, footnote 12, p. 848.

103   'R. Scott Esq., to Mr McLeay', document 11 & 'Attorney General to R. Scott Esq', document 16, 'Original Documents on Aborigines'; Miller, p. 41; 'G. Clavis to R. Scott Esq.', document 19 & 'R. Scott Esq. to Col. Sec.', document 25, 'Original Documents on Aborigines'.

104   Milliss, p. 406.

105   J. Wright, *Cry*, p. 38. Judith suggests that the reason why George armed himself when travelling to Mahngarinda was because he feared conflict with other Europeans (convicts, 'bolters and bushrangers'), rather than Aborigines.

106   Miller, p. 42.

107   Family historians believe that the correspondence between the Wyndhams was 'heavily censored' by George and Margaret's granddaughter, May Wright. C. Wyndham, interview, 10 November 2010. George's side of the correspondence was destroyed; according to May Wright this was done with no ill intent.

108   G. Wyndham, 'Diary', pp. 22, 54, 70, 29; Connor, p. 58; A. Wyndham, introduction, in G. Wyndham, 'Diary', p. 5.

109   Scott stated that the 'Black' had been 1.4 kilometres from his homestead, a curious admission on face value given that in 1816 Governor Macquarie had declared that Aborigines were not allowed to be armed within one mile of a White man's settlement. 'R. Scott Esq. to Col. Sec.', document 33, 'Original Documents on Aborigines'.

110   'Fight Amongst the Aborigines', *The Maitland Mercury and Hunter River General Advertiser*, 3 June 1843, p. 2, accessed 19 January 2016, nla.gov.au/nla.news-article660579. Given that Scott, by his own estimation, was not an 'unprejudiced witness' on matters to do with Aborigines, it is difficult to know how to interpret the account. It does suggest the men used Aborigines to guard their properties – and that they needed protecting. As Judith emphasised, the Wyndhams might have been the target of aggression from other Europeans; on one occasion Margaret defended herself against a servant using a carving knife. J. Wright, *Cry*, p. 38.

111   'Threlkeld's handwritten report for 1837', document 56, 'Original Documents on Aborigines'.

112   Miller, pp. 42, 51; 'G. Bowman to R. Scott', document 102, 'Original Documents on Aborigines'.

113   J. Wright, *Half*, p. 7; G. Wyndham, 'Diary', p. 74; 'Hunter's River', *The Sydney Gazette and New South Wales Advertiser*, 24 August 1833, p. 2, accessed 13 January 2016, nla.gov.au/nla.news-article2213584.

114   Untitled article, *The Sydney Monitor*, 25 July 1835, p. 2, accessed 13 January 2016, nla.gov.au/nla.news-article32149407; G. Wyndham, 'Diary', p. 35; 'Classified Advertising', *The Sydney Gazette and New South Wales Advertiser*, 28 May 1839, p. 4, accessed 13 January 2016, nla.gov.au/nla.news-article2551131.

115 G. Wyndham, *The Impending Crisis*, R. Jones for the Mercury Office, Maitland, NSW, 1847, pp. 12, 10; G. Wyndham, 'Land Policy ', pp. 4–5.

116 J. Wright, *Cry*, p. 37.

117 In *Cry for the Dead* Judith describes the phenomenon of crossing territorial boundaries as an 'illegal exodus' (37), 'lawlessness' (39), a 'lawless and womanless invasion' (40); she refers to 'the illegal squatting region' (43) and points to 'the illegality of the invasion' (38). 'Sage advice' quote, *Cry for the Dead*, p. 43.

118 J. Wright, *Cry*, p. 58. In the Bathurst area, one landowner and magistrate believed that all Aborigines should be shot, with their bodies used as fertiliser. Miller, p. 38.

119 A. Wyndham in G. Wyndham, 'Diary', p. 24; G. Wyndham, 'Diary', p. 19; C. Wyndham to G. Wyndham, 8 August 1830, C. M. Wright (ed.), p. 36; Miller, p. 25.

120 Judith, acknowledging George's likely association with the group in *Cry*, stated that if the group's membership 'was ever fully known, [it] cannot be ascertained now'. She rightly surmised that George, as a 'wealthy member of the "Pure Merinos"…must have at least been under pressure to join the association', p. 53; R. Reece, *Aborigines and Colonists: Aborigines and Colonial Society in New South Wales in the 1830s and 1840s*, Sydney University Press, Sydney, 1974, p. 147; Millis, p. 403.

121 Reece, p. 148; 'Vox Populi, Vox Del', *Australian*, 20 November 1838, p. 2.

122 J. Wright, *Cry*, pp. 43–5, 64; Scott in Reece, p. 30.

123 George's sister Ella wrote to him: 'Your poor Mr. Scott was too active in mind to last long. The mind will kill the body…' His sister Charlotte wrote: 'our dear old friend, Robert Scott'; 'the constant anxiety of body and mind that he underwent exhausted him at last… He appeared to me always to wish to do a little more than could be done'. E. Wyndham to G. Wyndham, May 1845, p. 115; C. Wyndham to G. Wyndham, n.d., p. 116; J. Wright, *Generations*, p. 7; C. M. Wright, p. 2; Reece, p. 28.

124 J. Wyndham to G. Wyndham, 7 November 1845, pp. 118–19.

125 E. Wyndham to G. & M. Wyndham, 30 December 1845, pp. 120–1; C. Wyndham to G. Wyndham, 31 March 1846, p. 121; J. Wyndham to G. Wyndham, 9 April 1846, p. 122

126 J. Wyndham to G. Wyndham, 9 April 1846, p. 122; A. Wyndham to G. Wyndham, 15 April 1846, p. 123.

127 J. Wyndham to G. Wyndham, 4 November 1846, p. 124.

128 J. Wright, *Cry*, pp. 38, 70–1; C. M. Wright, p. 2.

129 J. Wright, *Cry*, p. 71.

130 C. Wyndham to G. Wyndham, 27 November 1850, p. 130; J. Wright, *Half*, p. 7.

131 J. Wright to K. Inglis, 8 April 1994, *With Love*, pp. 514–15; J. Wright, *Half*, p. 16.

132 Jan Kociumbas cites the Wyndhams as an example of the difference family wealth made to pastoralists in the 1840s depression. It was because such families were 'less dependent on borrowed capital', she writes, that they 'emerged from the depression even wealthier than before', p. 211.

133 Brady, p. 20.

Chapter 2: The New England Wrights

134 Family historian Cedric Wyndham (a cousin of Phillip's) recalled that this is what Phillip Wright said when conferring an honorary doctorate on Judith at the University of New England. C. Wyndham, interview with the author, 10 November 2010.

135 J. Wright to M. Robertson, 18 October 1968, *With Love*, p. 194; F. Capp, *My Blood's Country*, Allen & Unwin, Crows Nest, NSW, 2010, p. 78.

136 Masel & Schmidt.

137 J. Wright, *Generations*, p. 232.

138 Ferry, p. 4; A. Atkinson, 'What is New England?', in A. Atkinson, J. S. Ryan, I. Davidson & A. Piper (eds), *High Lean Country: Land, People and Memory in New England*, Allen & Unwin, Crows Nest, NSW, 2006, p. 14.

139 The website of the University of New England, 'Indigenous Information', accessed 18 August 2012, www.une.edu.au/eeo/indigenous/indigenous.php; R. Walker, *Old New England: A History of the Northern Tablelands of New South Wales 1818–1900*, Sydney University Press, Sydney, 1966, p. 172; Ferry, p. 18.

140 Ferry, pp. 7, 25–6; Atkinson, p. 17.

141 J. Croft, 'Imagining New England', in Atkinson et al., p. 280.

142 J. S. Ryan, 'Uplands Always Attract', 'Stories and Prose', in Atkinson et al., pp. 5, 307; Ferry, pp. 20–6.

143 J. Wright, *Generations*, p. 200.

144 J. Wright, *Half*, p. 25.

145 P. Wright, p. 15; J. Wright, *Half*, p. 26; C. Wyndham, interview.

146 Horne, p. 20.

147 Ferry, pp. 74–6.

148 J. Wright & H. Rusden, 'An Interview with Judith Wright McKinney', transcript of tape-recording. 1987–88, TRC 2202, National Library of Australia, Canberra, Oral History and Folklore collection, tape 1, side 1, p. 20; P. Wright, pp. 69, 72.

149 P. Wright , p. 72.

150 J. Wright, *Generations*, pp. 232–3.

151 C. Wyndham, interview; J. Wright, *Generations*, pp. 62–6.

152 J. Wright, *Generations*, p. 144.

153 ibid., p. 213.

154 J. Wright, *Half*, p. 63; P. Wright, pp. 6, 24–6; Clarke & McKinney, *With Love*, p. 3.

155 J. Wright, *Half*, p. 50; P. Wright, pp. 7, 13.

156 J. Wright & Rusden, tape 1, side 1, p. 10; P. Wright, pp. 31–2.

157 Masel & Schmidt.

158 J. Wright, *Generations*, pp. 181–5.

159 J. Wright, *Generations*, p. 201; J. Wright, *Half*, p. 88; J. Wright & Rusden, tape 1, side 1, p. 10.

160 Hill, interview.

161 J. Wright, *Generations*, p. 180.

162 J. Wright & Rusden, tape 1, side 1, p.19; C. Wright, interview with the author, 28 April 2008.

163 J. Wright & Rusden, tape 1, side 1, p. 19.

164 B. Mitchell, afterword, *Bushwhacker*, p. 118; Macintyre, p. 161.

165 Mitchell, p. 118; Macintyre, p. 161.

166 P. Wright, p. 39–40; Mitchell, p. 119; J. Wright, *Half*, p. 26.

167 P. Wright, pp. 40–2.

168 V. Burgmann, *Revolutionary Industrial Unionism*, Cambridge University Press, Cambridge, 1995, pp. 174–5.

169 U. Ellis, *The Country Party: A Political and Social History of the Party in New South Wales*, F. W. Cheshire, Melbourne, 1958, p. 13; J. Wright, *Half*, p. 253.

170 P. Wright, pp. 83–6; J. Wright to T. Lister, 28 May 1995, *With Love*, p. 518.

171 L. Overacker, *The Australian Party System*, Oxford University Press, Oxford, 1952.
172 D. Aitkin, *The Country Party in New South Wales: A Study of Organisation and Survival*, Australian National University Press, Canberra, 1972, p. 8; Ferry, p. 57.
173 Aitkin, p. 8.
174 Ellis, pp. 1–2. As anthropologists have speculated, Aborigines probably chose not to practice sedentary agriculture because it did not suit the climate and was uneconomical to do so.
175 ibid., pp. 179, 226.
176 P. Wright, pp. 95, 99; J. Wright to M. Robertson, 18 October 1968, *With Love*, p. 194.
177 P. Wright, p. 90.
178 U. Ellis, *New England, the Seventh State*, The New States Movement, Armidale, NSW, 1957, p. 2.
179 P. Wright, p. 90
180 J. Wright to B. Blackman, 23 September 1976, *With Love,* p. 295.
181 Capp, p. 78.
182 J. Wright to J. Blight, 1 August 1984, *With Love*, p. 385.
183 J. Wright, 'City Rain', *Australian National Review*, no. 28, 1939, pp. 51–2.
184 J. Wright & Rusden, tape 1, side 1, p. 17; J. Wright to B. Scott, 3 August 1998, *With Love*, p. 551; J. Wright to J. Bradhurst, 4 May 1985, *With Love*, p. 402.

Chapter 3: A Childhood Unravelled

185 P. Wright, p. 35; Marr, p. 4; J. Wright, *Half*, p. 13.
186 J. Wright, *Half*, pp. 18–20, 58.
187 ibid., pp. 51, 50.
188 ibid., p. 31.
189 ibid., pp. 46, 34.
190 ibid., pp. 49, 29.
191 J. Wright, *Tales of a Great Aunt*, ETT Imprint, Bondi Junction, NSW, 1998, p. 12; Ferry, p. 8.
192 J. Wright, *Cry*, p. 44.
193 J. Wright, *Half*, p. 33.
194 P. Wright, pp. 59–60.
195 J. Wright, *Half*, pp. 45–8.
196 ibid., p. 30.
197 ibid., pp. 35, 89; J. Wright to V. Brady, 11 December 1996, Judith Wright papers, box 83, folder 596, National Library of Australia, Canberra; J. Wright to C. Mitchell, 6 June 1996, *With Love*, p. 531.
198 J. Wright, *Great Aunt*, pp. 10–12; J. Wright, *Half*, pp. 85–8, 35.
199 ibid., p. 11.
200 J. Wright, 'The Colour of Death', in *The Nature of Love*, Sun Books, Melbourne, 1966, p. 98.
201 J. Wright & Rusden, tape 1, side 1, p. 2.
202 J. Wright, *Half*, p. 38.
203 ibid., pp. 39–40.
204 K. M. Reiger, *The Disenchantment of the Home: Modernizing the Australian Family 1880–1940*, Oxford University Press, Melbourne, 1985, p. 37; J. Wright to T. Lister, 28 May 1995, *With Love*, p. 518.
205 J. Wright & Rusden, tape 1, side 1, p. 8; Hill, interview.
206 J. Wright, *Half*, p. 43.

207   ibid., pp. 44, 53, 99.
208   B. Falk in *The Half-Open Door: Sixteen Modern Australian Women Look at Professional Life and Achievement*, P. Grimshaw & L. Shrahan (eds), Hale & Iremonger, Sydney, 1982, p. 21.
209   J. Wright & Rusden, tape 1, side 1, p. 8.
210   J. Wright, *Half*, pp. 53–4.
211   ibid., p. 38.
212   J. Wright to D. Hart, 30 September 1989, *With Love*, p. 448; J. Wright, *Half*, p. 54; Judith Wright papers, MS 5781, box 65, folder 474, National Library of Australia, Canberra. All juvenile poetry quoted comes from here, unless otherwise stated.
213   J. Wright to T. Lister, 19 May 1995, *With Love*, p. 517.
214   J. Wright, *Half*, pp. 103–4.
215   ibid., p. 104; J. Wright & Rusden, tape 1, side 1, p. 22.
216   J. Wright to C. Mitchell, 6 June 1996, *With Love*, p. 531.
217   Bundred, interview.
218   Hill, interview.
219   J. Wright to M. Robertson, 18 October 1968, *With Love*, p. 195; Hill, interview.
220   J. Wright to C. Mitchell, 6 June 1996, *With Love*, p. 531.
221   J. Wright & Rusden, tape 1, side 1, p. 1; J. Wright, *Half*, pp. 103–5; P. Wright, p. 94.
222   P. Wright, pp. 36, 93.
223   K. Grose & J. Newall, *So Great a Heritage*, New England Girls' School in association with Allen & Unwin, Sydney, 1990, p. 116.
224   J. Wright, *Half*, p. 112; Grose & Newall, p. 97; Hill, interview.
225   J. Wright, 'Save the First Dance', Judith Wright papers, MS 5781, box 65, folder 474, National Library of Australia, Canberra.
226   G. Blomfield, 'Judith McKinney Wright – Rough Draft Only', n.d., Judith Wright papers, MS Acc08.078, National Library of Australia, Canberra.
227   New England Girls' School, *Prospectus*, c. 1928, microform, N 2225, National Library of Australia, Canberra; A. Mackinnon, *Women, Love and Learning: The Double Bind*, Peter Lang AG, Bern, Switzerland, 2010, p. 34.
228   J. Wright, *Half*, p. 106; J. Wright, 'First Dance', Judith Wright papers.
229   J. Wright, *Half*, p. 110; J. Wright in P. Clarke & M. McKinney (eds), *Equal Heart*, p. 24.
230   J. Wright, *Half*, p. 111.
231   J. Wright to The Principal, Correspondence School, c. 1985, *With Love*, pp. 406–7.
232   J. Wright, *Half*, p. 114; *The Armidale Express and New England General Advertiser*, 6 July 1931, p. 4, viewed 29 January 2016, http://nla.gov.au/nla.news-article192999248.
233   P. Clarke & M. McKinney, *Equal Heart*, p. 4; J. Wright to T. Lister, 19 May 1995, *With Love*, p. 517.

Chapter 4: Becoming Modern

234   Capp, pp. 92–3.
235   Brady, p. 47.
236   J. Wright & Rusden, tape 1, side 1, p. 27.
237   University of Sydney, 1934 Calendar, p. 757, 'Calendar Archive', accessed 31 March 2011, calendararchive.usyd.edu.au/index.php; C. Turney, U. Bygott & P. Chippendale, *Australia's First: A History of the University of Sydney, vol. 1, 1850–1939*, the University of Sydney in association with Hale & Iremonger, Sydney, 1991, p. 642.

238   H. McQueen, *Social Sketches of Australia*, 2nd ed., Penguin Books, Ringwood, VIC, 1991, p. 140. This depiction is challenged by Dymphna Cusack's report to Florence James that the Broken Hill library, in the 1920s, was 'excellent'. F. James in D. Cusack, *Jungfrau*, Penguin, Ringwood, VIC, 1989, p. viii.

239   Turney et al., p. 199; J. Shipp, ed., *The Fisher Library Centenary 1909–2009*, the University of Sydney Library, Sydney, 2009, pp. 8–13.

240   J. Wright & Rusden, tape 1, side 2, pp. 4–5; 1934 Calendar, pp. 114–18; Hill, interview.

241   J. Wright, *Half*, pp. 119–20; J. Wright & Rusden, tape 2, side 1, pp. 18–20.

242   In its list of former students, the 1934 University of Sydney Calendar shows that none of the descendants of Weeta and Arthur Mackenzie studied there. Descendants' names are taken from a family tree provided by D. Seton Wilkinson, secretary of the Dalwood Restoration Association; C. Wyndham, interview.

243   The website of the Nobel Prize, 'The Nobel Prize in Literature 1973: Patrick White', accessed 27 August 2012, www.nobelprize.org/nobel_prizes/literature/laureates/1973/white-autobio.html#; Marr, p. 16.

244   D. Seton Wilkinson, email to the author, 15 March 2011.

245   J. Wright, *Half*, p. 23; J. Wright to V. Brady, 11 December 1996, Judith Wright papers, MS 5781, box 83, folder 596, National Library of Australia, Canberra.

246   J. Wright & Rusden, tape 1, side 1, p. 25; Aitkin, p. 18; McQueen, p. 126; B. Kingston, *A History of New South Wales*, Cambridge University Press, Port Melbourne, VIC, 2006, p. 148; J. Wright, *Half*, p. 121.

247   Kingston, p. 149; Ellis, *Country Party*, p. 164.

248   Turney et al., pp. 598, 501.

249   P. Wright, p. 95.

250   In 1927 parliamentary member for the Northern Tablelands, David Drummond, who backed a rural university, became Minister for Public Education. His work led to the creation of the Armidale Teachers' College in 1928. Kingston, p. 152. The university building, Booloominbah, and 74 hectares of surrounding land were donated by Patrick White's family. Phillip donated 300 acres of land. Ellis, *Country Party*, p. 178.

251   When the University of New England College (UNEC) finally opened, in 1938, pragmatic reasons were cited for its creation; it was apparently motivated by a 'growing realisation' that 'scientific and economic research would assist the rural, industrial and manufacturing sectors of the community'. And yet its first curriculum demonstrated a different concern. With a timetable made up almost entirely of European languages, Literary Studies and Philosophy classes, it appears UNEC was actually designed for Judith's NEGS classmates and trainee teachers, who favoured Arts courses. Indeed, UNEC became known as a place to send rural daughters being as it was 'free of the moral danger that accompanied student life in Sydney'. Turney et al., pp. 615–18; Atkinson, 'What is New England?', p. 19.

252   K. Leopold, *Came to Booloominbah: A Country Scholar's Progress 1938–1942*, J. Ryan (ed.), University of New England Press, Armidale, NSW, 1998, pp. 6–23.

253   J. Matthews, *Dance Hall and Picture Palace: Sydney's Romance with Modernity*, Currency Press, Strawberry Hills, NSW, 2005, pp. 14–15.

254   ibid., p. 18; P. Wright, p. 7.

255   Matthews, p. 19.

256   ibid., p. 26.

257   J. Wright, *Half*, p. 118.

258   *The Argus*, 18 January 1941, p. 15; *The Sydney Morning Herald*, 4 July 1936, p. 11.

259   J. Wright, *Half*, p. 118.
260   ibid.
261   Horne, p. 199.
262   J. Wright & Rusden, tape 1, side 1, p. 25; McKinney, interview.
263   J. Wright to P. Wright, 20 August 1972, Judith Wright papers, MS 5781, box 101, folder 731, National Library of Australia, Canberra.
264   K. Price & J. Wing, 1987, NSW Bicentennial Oral History collection, National Library of Australia, Canberra.
265   N. Christesen, 'A Russian Migrant', in Grimshaw & Strahan, p. 66.
266   L. Edmonds in W. Lowenstein, *Weevils in the Flour*, Scribe, East Brunswick, VIC, 1981, p. 189.
267   J. Wright, *Half*, pp. 122–3.
268   University of Sydney, 1934 Calendar, pp. xi, 354. Another unspecified but 'relatively large number' of students attended the University on private bursaries and scholarships. In 1934 the annual average wage for men was £213, 4 shillings. Women's wages were pegged at approximately 52 per cent of the male rate. Website of the Australian Bureau of Statistics, 'Labour Report, 1934 (6101.0)', accessed 28 February 2011, www.abs.gov.au/AUSSTATS/abs@.nsf/DetailsPage/6101.01934?OpenDocument; Price, interview.
269   J. Wright & Rusden, tape 1, side 2, p. 5. Only two-thirds of Australia's wool stock was bought in 1929, at a price two-thirds of that achieved in 1928. McQueen, p. 128.
270   In 1931 funding from the New South Wales government was cut from £70,000 to £58,000. Turney et al., pp. 460, 492; University of Sydney, 1934 Calendar, p. xi.
271   Macintyre, p. 134; Matthews, pp. 75, 90; J. Wright, *Half*, p. 121.
272   McQueen, p. 122; J. Wright, *Half*, p. 122.
273   Quoted in Matthews, p. 66; J. Allen, *Rose Scott*, Oxford University Press, Melbourne, 1994, p. 242.
274   A. Summers, *Damned Whores and God's Police: The Colonisation of Women in Australia*, Penguin, Blackburn, VIC, 1975, pp. 407–8; E. Freeman, 'Towards Happier Parenthood', *Woman Today*, no. 1, 1937, p. 10.
275   J. Matthews, 'Dancing Modernity', in *Transitions: New Australian Feminisms*, B. Caine & R. Pringle (eds), Allen & Unwin, St Leonards, NSW, 1995, pp. 74–87.
276   Editorial, *The Arts Journal of the University of Sydney*, no. 1, 1936, p. 9.
277   M. McKinney told the author in an email that the photo was taken when Judith was working for J. Walter Thompson in Sydney.
278   J. Wright, *Half*, pp. 124–5, 145.
279   *Honi Soit*, no. 8, 1935, p. 2; *Honi Soit*, no. 24, 1935, p. 2.
280   J. Wright & Rusden, tape 2, side 1, p. 21.
281   Price, interview.
282   J. Wright, *Half*, pp. 125–6.
283   ibid., p. 107. A notice in *Honi Soit* announced that people wishing to attend an athletics club party should contact its secretary, Judith Wright. *Honi Soit*, no. 2, 1936, p. 3; S. Lilienthal, *Newtown Tarts: A History of Sydney University Women's Sports Association*, Allen & Unwin, St Leonards, NSW, 1997, pp. 34, 96.
284   J. Wright, 'Surfer', *Poet's Choice 1974*, Island Press, Sydney, 1974, pp. 30–1.
285   J. Wright & Rusden, tape 2, side 1, p. 20.
286   Sheridan, p. 13.
287   J. Matthews, 'Erotic Modernities', in *The Impact of the Modern: Vernacular Modernities in Australia 1870s–1960s*, R. Dixon & V. Kelly (eds), Sydney University Press, Sydney, 2008, p. 7.

288 P. Spearritt, *Sydney's Century: A History*, University of New South Wales Press, Sydney, 2000, p. 68.

289 J. Wright, *Half*, pp. 120–1.

290 J. Wright & Rusden, tape 2, side 1, pp. 19, 25; T. Irving & R. Cahill, *Radical Sydney: Places, Portraits and Unruly Episodes*, University of New South Wales Press, Sydney, 2010, pp. 5–6, 168–9, 199.

291 J. Wright, *Half*, p. 126.

292 D. Modjeska, 'Rooms of Their Own', in *Women, Class and History: Feminist Perspectives on Australia 1788–1978*, Elizabeth Windschuttle (ed.), Fontana and Collins, Melbourne, 1980, p. 347.

293 The Glebe house was unlikely to have been licensed by the University; the operations of licensed managers were monitored carefully and licences were awarded or revoked annually. University of Sydney, 1934 Calendar, pp. 16–17; J. Wright, *Half*, p. 126.

294 In this letter Judith termed Dora a 'schizo…in a minor way'. J. Wright to V. Brady, 21 November 1996, Judith Wright papers, MS 5781, box 83, folder 596, National Library of Australia, Canberra.

295 Horne, pp. 271–2.

296 J. Wright to T. Lister, 28 May 1995, *With Love*, pp. 518–19.

297 J. Wright, *Half*, p.132; J. Wright & Rusden, tape 2, side 2, p. 8.

298 J. Wright, *Half*, pp. 140–1.

299 ibid.

300 ibid., p. 127; J. Wright & Rusden, tape 1, side 1, p. 25.

301 J. Wright & Rusden, tape 1, side 1, p. 25.

302 E. Macken, 'The World of Women: Women's Colleges Within the University of Sydney', *The New Nation*, 15 October 1934, p. 41.

303 W. Hole & A. Treweeke, *The History of the Women's College Within the University of Sydney*, Angus & Robertson, Sydney, 1953, p. 160.

304 Hole & Treweeke, pp. 134, 160; *The Women's College Within the University of Sydney Calendar 1935*, Australasian Medical Publishing Company, Glebe, NSW, 1936; D. Wetherell & C. Carr-Gregg, *Camilla: A Life of C. H. Wedgwood*, NSW University Press, Kensington, NSW, 1990, p. 86.

305 J. Wright & Rusden, tape 1, side 1, p. 26.

306 Hole & Treweeke, p. 136; Wetherell & Carr-Gregg, p. 85.

307 *The Magazine of the Women's College University of Sydney*, no. 21, 1935, pp. 16, 22; Hole & Treweeke, p. 136; Wetherell & Carr-Gregg, pp. 84, 102.

308 Hole & Treweeke, p. 137; Wetherell & Carr-Gregg, p. 87; J. Wright & Rusden, tape 2, side 1, p. 19.

309 J. Wright & Rusden, tape 1, side 1, p. 26; Hole & Treweeke, pp. 128, 166; *Magazine of the Women's College*, no. 22, 1936, p. 9.

310 *Magazine of the Women's College*, no. 21, 1936, p. 11; *Magazine of the Women's College*, no. 22, 1936, p. 13. Another anonymous poem from magazine number 2, in 1936, 'New Words to an Ancient Theme', may also have been written by Judith.

311 J. Wright & Rusden, tape 1, side 1, p. 26.

Chapter 5: A Very Model Student

312 J. Wright, *Half*, pp. 122–7; J. Wright & Rusden, tape 3, side 1, pp. 1–2; tape 2, side 1, p. 17; tape 2, side 2, pp. 4–5.

313 ibid, tape 3, side 1, p. 20; Brady, *South*, pp. 49, 4, 56. Brady writes: 'her opinions "turned many of the family into firecrackers"'. Her reference is to Rusden's

interviews with Judith, specifically tape 2. There is no such quote on that tape and none has been found by the author on any tape. Judith may have said it to Brady, who incorrectly attributed it. J. Wright, *Half*, p. 124.

314 J. Wright, *Half*, p. 3.

315 Turney et al., p. 583; Horne, p. 200.

316 Turney et al., p. 583; Women's College Archivist, conversation with author, 30 November 2010; Kingston, p. 137; Horne, p. 200; J. Wright & Rusden, tape 2, side 1, p. 25.

317 J. Wright & Rusden, tape 2, side 1, p. 20; Turney et al., p. 516; J. Wright, *Half*, p. 125.

318 A. Barcan, *Radical Students: The Old Left at Sydney University*, Melbourne University Press, Melbourne, 2002, pp. 42, 90, 68–9, 84.

319 *Honi Soit*, no. 17, 1935, p. 2; *Honi Soit*, no. 5, 1936, p. 2; *Honi Soit*, no. 1, 1936, p. 2.

320 Barcan, pp. 71, 80. In 1936, 2,500 copies of *Honi Soit* were printed each week. The total number of students enrolled was just over 3,000. The editors claimed that the standard printing run was sometimes not enough. *Honi Soit*, no. 8, 1936, p. 1; J. Wright & Rusden, tape 2, side 1, pp. 9–10.

321 Turney, et al., p. 583; *Honi* Soit, no. 12, 1935, p. 1; *Honi Soit*, no. 25, 1935, p. 2.

322 J. Wright, *Half*, p. 125; J. Wright & Rusden, tape 2, side 1, p. 12; Brady, p. 55.

323 Horne, pp. 250–1, 269–71.

324 Very few women became editor of *Honi Soit* until the 1970s. The website of the University of Sydney, 'About *Honi Soit*', accessed 12 June 2012, www.src.usyd.edu.au/honisoit. *Honi Soit*, no. 1, 1936, p. 2; 1935 Calendar, p. 878; *Honi Soit*, no. 10, 1936, p. 2.

325 Barcan, p. 73.

326 *Honi Soit*, no. 14, 1936, p. 3; *Honi Soit*, no. 25, 1935, p. 2; *Honi Soit*, no. 6, 1935, p. 5.

327 *Honi Soit*, no. 1, 1936, p. 2.

328 *Honi Soit*, no. 25, 1936, p. 2; M. Stell, *Half the Race: A History of Australian Women in Sport*, Angus & Robertson, North Ryde, NSW, 1991, pp. 73, 48–9.

329 Allen, p. 243.

330 *Honi Soit*, no. 5, 1933, p. 1.

331 In 1937 New Zealand feminist Elsie Freeman described an 'international movement for birth control' that was 'sweeping every country in the world (except the fascist countries)'. Freeman, p. 2; *Honi Soit*, no. 6, 1936, p. 3.

332 *Honi Soit*, no. 11, 1935, p. 2; Wetherell & Carr-Gregg, p. 103; *Honi Soit*, no. 24, 1934, p. 4.

333 Barbara Falk, mentioned in Chapter 4, who attended the University of Melbourne a few years before Judith, explained that her 'self-consciousness' towards her appearance at university led her away from academia and towards the 'helping professions'. Falk in Grimshaw & Shrahan (eds), p. 28. Kathleen Fitzpatrick, who also attended the University of Melbourne a few years before Judith, makes the useful point that it is difficult to show 'evidence' for the sexism that women experienced at university, yet it existed. Fitzpatrick in Grimshaw & Shrahan (eds), p. 132.

334 *Honi Soit*, no. 11, 1935, p. 2; *Honi Soit*, no. 15, 1935, p. 1.

335 J. Wright & Rusden, tape 2, side 1, p. 12; Brady, p. 55; J. Wright, *Half*, p. 125.

336 For the first half of 1935 the social editress was Miss Nella Withers. For the second half of 1935 Miss J. Knight was social editress and Miss E Corrigan was assistant social editress. For the first half of 1936 Miss Robin Curtis was the social editress.

All of these names are listed in the University Calendars for their respective years, meaning they were real students. The only name in the 1935 staff list which does not also appear in the 1935 Calendar is 'A. Jeffrey Hill'. Hill was a real person; he was born in 1916, attended the University of Sydney, and became a military historian. *Honi Soit*, no. 14, 1936, p. 3.

337 A. Lang, 'Judith Wright and Frank Scott: Gendering Networks in Australia and Canada', *Australian Literary Studies*, no. 4, 2006, p. 409.

338 *Honi Soit*, no. 20, 1935, p. 2; *Honi Soit*, no. 17, 1935, p. 2.

339 *Honi Soit*, no. 14, 1936, p. 3.

340 ibid.

341 J. Wright, *Half*, p. 126.

342 R. Molesworth, 'University Settlement', *Sydney University Alumni*, Spring 2006, p. 25.

343 Hole & Treweeke, pp. 133, 140.

344 *Honi Soit*, no. 16, 1936, p. 3.

345 *Honi Soit*, no. 17, 1936, p. 3.

346 *Honi Soit*, no. 18, 1936, p. 3.

347 *Honi Soit*, no. 17, 1936, p. 3. The joke in this passage is a reference to the Fisher Library, which was largely funded by the will of shoemaker Thomas Fisher, as detailed in Chapter 4.

348 *Honi Soit*, no. 15, 1936, p. 3; J. Wright, *Half*, p. 125.

349 *Honi Soit*, no. 18, 1936, p. 3.

350 ibid.; J. Wright, *Half*, p. 124.

351 *Honi Soit*, no. 16, 1936, p. 3; *Honi Soit*, no. 17, 1936, p. 3; *Honi Soit*, no. 22, 1936, p. 3.

352 *Honi Soit*, no. 17, 1936, p. 3; *Honi Soit*, no. 21, 1936, p. 3.

353 *Honi Soit*, no. 20, 1936, p. 3.

354 *Honi Soit*, no. 15, 1936, p. 3; *Honi Soit*, no. 23, 1936, p. 3.

355 *Honi Soit*, no. 15, 1936, p. 3; *Honi Soit*, no. 25, 1936, p. 2; *Honi Soit*, no. 23, 1936, p. 3.

356 *Honi Soit*, no. 21, 1936, p. 3.

357 *Honi Soit*, no. 25, 1936, p. 3.

358 J. Wright, *Half*, p. 122.

359 Matthews, p. 66.

Chapter 6: The Shaping of an Intellect

360 J. Wright & Rusden, tape 2, side 1, p. 24.

361 Hill, interview.

362 J. Wright to S. Walker, 10 August 1975, in Walker, p. 211; J. Wright to J. Blight, 27 August 1968, *With Love*, p. 191; J. Wright to J. Blight, 24 October 1977, *With Love*, p. 303.

363 J. Wright & Rusden, tape 2, side 1, pp. 1, 16.

364 Brady, pp. 49, 50, 52.

365 Students working towards a Bachelor of Arts at the University of Sydney needed to pass at least ten courses, which usually took three years. Various rules governed course selection. However, since Judith had not matriculated and was therefore not studying for a degree, many of these rules did not apply. In first year, she chose subjects from only two discipline groups, rather than the usual three. J. Wright, *Half*, p. 123.

366 Brady, p. 50.

367 The reference Brady gives for this quote is 'OH II/2'. As discussed in the Introduction, such references to this interview with Heather Rusden are

inadequate. The quote does not appear anywhere on tape one or two, when Judith discusses her time at university. Brady also incorrectly asserts that Judith was taught by Roberts. In 1934 Roberts did not lecture in first-year history; his underling F. L. Wood did. Admittedly, whether or not Roberts taught Judith, his approach guided all teaching in the three-person department.

368 J. Wright to B. Blackman, 14 June 1977, *With Love*, p. 300; notes on *History of Land Settlement* found in Judith Wright papers, box 8, folder 56, National Library of Australia, Canberra; J. Wright, 'Critics, Reviewers and Aboriginal Writers', in *Born of the Conquerors: Selected Essays by Judith Wright*, Aboriginal Studies Press, Canberra, 1991, pp. 91–3.

369 E. Scott, introduction, in S. Roberts, *History of Australian Land Settlement: 1788–1920*, reissued edition, The Macmillan Company of Australia, South Melbourne, VIC, 1968, p. xii; K. Hancock, review, *The English Historical Review*, no. 158, 1925, p. 290.

370 R. Selleck, 'Empires and Empiricism: The Teaching of History at the University of Melbourne 1855–1936', in *Life of the Past: the Discipline of History at the University of Melbourne*, F. Anderson & S. Macintyre (eds), The Department of History, University of Melbourne, Melbourne, 2006, p. 29.

371 M. Stuckey, 'Not by Discovery But by Conquest: The Use of History and the Meaning of "Justice" in Australian Native Title Cases', *Common Law World Review*, no. 1, 2005, pp. 19–38.

372 Roberts, *Land Settlement*, p. xiv.

373 S. Roberts, *The Squatting Age in Australia 1835–1847*, Melbourne University Press, Carlton, VIC, 1935; reprint with corrections, 1975, pp. 1, 8–9.

374 ibid., p. 10. Though this description of Australian colonisation comes from Roberts' 1935 book, published when Judith was in her second year, the version produced in his 1924 book was similarly unsympathetic to settlers/squatters. He most likely instructed his department to teach according to his latest research.

375 H. Reynolds, 'The Mabo Judgment in the Light of Imperial Land Policy', *University of New South Wales Law Journal*, no. 1, 1993, p. 28.

376 Roberts, *Land Settlement*, p. 178.

377 J. Wright, *Conquerors*, p. 92; Roberts, *Squatting*, p. 19.

378 Roberts, *Squatting*, pp. 87, 332–5, 314–15; J. Wright, *Conquerors*, p. 92.

379 Selleck, p. 29; Roberts, *Land Settlement*, p. 3; D. Schreuder, 'An Unconventional Founder' in *The Discovery of Australian History 1890–1939*, S. Macintyre & J. Thomas (eds), Melbourne University Press, Carlton, VIC, 1995, pp. 127–8.

380 Turney et al., p. 514.

381 Susan McKernan has argued that 'Nigger's Leap, New England' demonstrates that Judith's poetry gave expression to the history of 'specific places'. The poem was, she said, about 'a particular place in the New England ranges where an Aborigine leapt to death'. *A Question of Commitment*, Allen & Unwin, 1989, p. 144. The specific circumstances of the leap, including why the person leapt, are not explained in the poem.

382 J. Wright, scrapbook of juvenile poetry, Judith Wright papers, box 65, folder 474, National Library of Australia, Canberra.

383 Philip Mead has suggested that the final scene of the movie *Jedda* might have been inspired by 'Nigger's Leap, New England'. Mead, *Networked Language*, p. 509. The producers may have been influenced by Judith's depiction of the 'half-caste' girl more broadly.

384 Mead, p. 280.
385 A. McCann, 'The Literature of Extinction', *Meanjin*, vol. 65, no. 1, 2006, pp. 52–4.
386 ibid., p. 52.
387 P. Mead, 'Veronica Brady's Biography of Judith Wright', *Australian Literary Studies*, no. 2, 1999, p. 174.
388 J. Wright, foreword, *Collected Poems 1942–1985*, HarperCollins, Sydney, 1994, n.p.; J. Wright to S. Murray-Smith, 1 June 1986, *With Love*, p. 411.
389 P. Wright, p. 69.
390 J. Wright to D. Green, 7 April 1963, *With Love*, p. 152.
391 J. Wright to S. Murray-Smith, 1 June 1986, *With Love*, p. 411. In the mid 1980s Judith also told Meredith McKinney that she wrote 'Bullocky' based on Ted, who was 'a religious maniac'. J. Wright to M. McKinney, 27 October 1985, *With Love*, p. 409.
392 McCann, pp. 48, 54.
393 Quotes in this paragraph are from 'South of My Days' and 'For New England'.
394 Walker, p. 8; J. Wright to S. Walker, 10 August 1975, ibid., p. 213; Clarke & M. McKinney (eds), *Equal Heart*, p. 11.
395 Walker, p. 8; 1935 Calendar, p. 239.
396 J. Wright, *Half*, pp. 193–4; McKinney, interview.
397 Fitzpatrick, p. 124.
398 Turney et al., p. 501; Ellis, *New England*, pp. 2–3.
399 Mark Weblin does not include any women in a long list of public figures influenced by Anderson. M. Weblin, introduction, *A Perilous and Fighting Life: The Political Writings of Professor John Anderson*, Pluto Press, North Melbourne, VIC, 2003, p. 9; Turney et al., p. 515; Horne, p. 205.
400 J. Wright, *Half*, pp. 127, 192; for McAuley quote, see C. McLean Cole, interview, *All In the Mind*, Radio National, 10 September 2007.
401 J. Wright, *Half*, pp. 223–4; J. Anderson, *Lectures on Greek Philosophy 1928*, C. McLean Cole (ed.), Sydney University Press, Sydney, 2008, cover blurb; J. Wright to S. Walker, 10 August 1975, in Walker, p. 211.
402 J. Wright & Rusden, tape 2, side 1, p. 17.
403 J. Wright & Rusden, tape 2, side 1, p. 16; J. Wright to T. Errey, 3 May 1988, *With Love*, p. 433.
404 Turney, et al., p. 516; Weblin, pp. 12, 15.
405 J. McLaren, *Writing in Hope and Fear: Literature as Politics in Postwar Australia*, Cambridge University Press, Cambridge, 1996, p. 27.
406 J. Wright to J. Blight, 20 October 1952, *With Love*, p. 78; C. Christesen to J. Wright, 4 November 1954, Judith Wright papers, box 70, folder 505, National Library of Australia, Canberra; J. Wright to C. Christesen, 15 January 1944, *With Love*, p. 12.
407 McClaren, p. 28; J. Wright to C. Christesen, 7 November 1954, *With Love*, pp. 92–3.
408 J. Wright to V. Brady, 6 November 1996, Judith Wright papers, box 83, folder 596, National Library of Australia, Canberra.
409 Barcan, p. 90; M. Ackland, *Damaged Men*, Allen & Unwin, Crows Nest, NSW, 2001, pp. 31, 131.
410 J. Wright, *Half*, p. 192.
411 Judith remembered that she 'dropped philosophy at university to move into psychology and anthropology', but her enrolment card shows that she studied both Philosophy and Psychology concurrently in her first two years. Psychology

was a prerequisite for Anthropology. Judith received a mid-class pass in Oriental Studies. In Anthropology she scored a pass in both years, but the subject did not publish lists in order of merit. J. Wright, *Half*, p. 192; Turney et al., p. 517; Price, interview.

412   J. Wright & Rusden, tape 2, side 1, p. 1; J. Wright, *Half*, p. 192; 1934 Calendar, p. 237.

413   J. Wright, scrapbook of juvenile poetry; J. Wright & Rusden, tape 2, side 1, p. 8.

414   J. Wright & Rusden, tape 2, side 1, p. 9; J. Wright to P. Wright, 7 June 1973, p. 250.

415   J. Wright & Rusden, tape 2, side 1, p. 5. In the 1970s Bill Stanner was a co-member, with Judith, of the Aboriginal Treaty Committee. When he died, in 1987, she said she missed him 'more than almost any of my friends'. J. Wright to L. & D. Webb, 1 December 1987, *With Love*, p. 427; 1935 Calendar, p. 247.

416   First-year Anthropology attracted only twenty-seven students in 1934, but fifteen of these were women. Student lists for Anthropology ceased being published in 1935, Judith's first year in the subject. This was at a time when women accounted for only one-fifth of students overall. In 1935 seven of the ten second-year recipients and six of the twelve third-year recipients of the Frank Albert Prize for Anthropology were women, which roughly reflected the genders of award recipients from its inauguration in 1927. 1936 Calendar, p. 472. The only other disciplines in which women did so well, as determined by their success in academic prizes, were the related fields of Geography, Zoology, Psychology and History.

417   The 1936 University budget shows that Anthropology received a statutory endowment from both the Commonwealth and State governments. Elkin's fieldwork was also supported by the Australian National Research Council from 1926 until the beginning of World War II. In 1936 eighteen people undertook special training, only three of whom were women, and only one of whom had matriculated from secondary school. When Judith said that she had considered pursuing anthropological work at the end of her degree she may have been thinking of this course. A. P. Elkin, *The Australian Aborigines*, Angus & Robertson, London, 1938; reprint with revisions, 1981, p. ix, viii; J. Wright & Rusden, tape 2, side 1, pp. 3–4; Turney et al., p. 524; 1936 Calendar, pp. 60, 815, 955.

418   Elkin, p. vi; Macintyre, *Concise History*, p. 186; J. Wright & Rusden, tape 1, side 2, p. 5.

419   J. Wright & Rusden, tape 1, side 2, p. 6.

420   J. Wright, *Half*, p. 33; J. Wright, foreword to Bill Cohen's manuscript, 1986, Judith Wright papers, MS 5781, box 44, folder 331, National Library of Australia, Canberra; J. Wright & Rusden, tape 1, side 2, p. 5.

421   J. Wright, *Conquerors*, p. xi.

422   J. Wright, *Half*, p. 164; J. Wright, *Conquerors*, p. x.

423   Brady, p. 54.

424   References to Aboriginal people in Phillip Wright's memoir, *Bushwhacker*, pp. 56–60. Phillip Wright first showed his daughter Albert Wright's diaries in 1946. J. Wright & Rusden, tape 3, side 2, p. 6.

425   J. Wright, *Conquerors*, p. xi; J. Wright, *Half*, p. 192.

426   Brady, p. 54; J. Wright to L. Webb, 14 February 1977, *With Love*, p. 297; J. Wright, *Cry*, p. 304; J. Wright & Rusden, tape 2, side 1, pp. 1, 6.

427   Elkin, p. vi.

428   J. Wright, *Cry*, p. 19.

429   Elkin, pp. 140, 32.

430   J. Wright to K. Inglis, 8 April 1994, *With Love*, p. 514.

Chapter 7: Campus Literary Discussion

431   T. S. Eliot, 'Tradition and the Individual Talent', *Twentieth Century Literary Criticism*, D. Lodge (ed.), Longman, London, 1972, p. 73.

432   Chris Wallace-Crabbe describes Judith's early poetry as 'at once regionally traditional and modernist in diction', 'Poetry and Modernism', *The Oxford Literary History of Australia*, B. Bennett & J. Strauss (eds), Oxford University Press, Melbourne, 1998, p. 226. David Brooks argues that Judith was influenced by the 'imagist' style of European modernists, 'Judith Wright and the Image', *Poetry and Gender*, D. Brooks & B. Walker (eds), University of Queensland Press, St Lucia, QLD, 1989. Shirley Walker believes several poems in *The Moving Image* 'show the influence of T. S. Eliot', *Flame and Shadow* 2nd ed., University of Queensland Press, St Lucia, QLD, 1996, p. 35. Susan Sheridan describes Judith's early work as 'modernist', 'Gentlemen's Agreements: *Southerly*'s First Editors', *Southerly*, vol. 67, no. 1–2, 2007, pp. 334–5.

433   Patrick Buckridge argues that Judith's early poetry was a 'Romantic-idealist assertion' which opposed nationalist literature and modernism, 'Clearing a Space for Australian Literature 1940–1965', *The Oxford Literary History of Australia*, p. 179. Philip Mead agrees with Buckridge in *Networked Language*, p. 283. Veronica Brady says although Judith experimented with free verse while at university, 'her feeling for the natural world marked her poems out from most of the others who were more modishly influenced by Eliot's *The Waste Land* and urban themes'; earlier she quotes Judith who attested to 'brood[ing] over Eliot...with real excitement', Brady, pp. 55, 51.

434   Mead, p. 269.

435   Wallace-Crabbe, p. 226.

436   J. Wright & Rusden, tape 2, side 1, p. 12.

437   1934 Calendar, p. 226; J. Wright & Rusden, tape 2, side 1, p. 16.

438   1934 Calendar, p. 225; J. Damousi, '"The Filthy American Twang": Elocution, the Advent of American "Talkies", and Australian Cultural Identity', *The American Historical Review*, no. 2, 2007, pp. 16–17; H. M. Symonds, 'Australian Pronunciation', a review, *Southerly*, no. 4, 1940, p. 37.

439   Horne, p. 201; J. Wright & Rusden, tape 2, side 1, p. 18.

440   L. Dale, *The English Men: Professing Literature in Australian Universities*, Association for the Study of Australian Literature, Toowoomba, QLD, 1997, pp. 29, 65.

441   ibid, pp. 67, 72; J. Wright & Rusden, tape 2, side 1, p. 16; the website of the Australian Dictionary of Biography, 'Ernest Rudolph Holme', accessed 9 July 2012, adb.anu.edu.au/biography.

442   J. Wright & Rusden, tape 2, side 1, p. 16; J. Wright, *Half*, p. 123. I disagree with Anouk Lang, who believes that Judith was 'satirising' Waldock in this description; if anything, she was satirising herself. Lang, p. 410.

443   J. Wright, *Half*, p. 123.

444   ibid., p.121; 'Sybarite', in *The Wide Brown Land*, J. S. Mackaness & G. Mackaness (eds), Angus & Robertson, Sydney, 1934, p. 171.

445   J. Wright, *Half*, p. 121.

446   ibid., pp. 121, 123; D. Bird, R. Dixon & C. Lee (eds), *Authority and Influence*, University of Queensland Press, St Lucia, QLD, 2001, p. 30.

447 Dale, p. 32.

448 P. R. Stephensen, 'The Foundations of Culture in Australia: An Essay towards National Self-Respect', *The Writer in Australia: A Collection of Literary Documents 1856–1964*, J. Barnes (ed.), Oxford University Press, Melbourne, 1969, p. 210; Dale, p. 46; J. Wright, *Half*, p. 121.

449 J. Strauss, 'Literary Culture 1914–1939: Battlers All', *The Oxford Literary History of Australia*, p. 118.

450 Dale, p. 83.

451 W. H. Wilde, J. Hooton & B. Andrews (eds), *The Oxford Companion to Australian Literature*, 2nd edition, Oxford University Press, Melbourne, 1994, p. 384; R. G. Howarth, 'Foreword by the Editor', *Southerly*, no. 1, 1939, pp. 3–4.

452 ibid.

453 Dale, pp. 149–50, 225; *Honi Soit*, no. 19, 1935, p. 4.

454 H. M. Green, untitled article, *The Australian National Review*, vol. 5, no. 28, 1939, p. 56; H. M. Green, 'What is Australian Literature?', *Southerly*, no. 2, 1940, pp. 15–17.

455 Green, *National Review*, p. 56; A. L. McLeod, *R. G. Howarth: Australian Man of Letters*, New Dawn Press, New Delhi, India, 2005, p. 141.

456 Strauss, p. 128.

457 J. S. Neilson, 'The Land Where I Was Born', *The Wide Brown Land*, p. 179.

458 Although McAuley is not named as the author of this article, it is written from the perspective of the *Hermes* production team, then headed by McAuley. 'Less of It', *Hermes*, Lent 1937, pp. 37–8; S. Scalmer, 'Charles Gavan Duffy's Ministerial Tour: Oratory, Electioneering and the Meaning of Colonial Democracy', *Australian Journal of Politics & History*, vol. 57, no. 2, 2011, p. 163; Horne, p. 237.

459 *Hermes*, Lent 1937, p. 38.

460 ibid.; *Hermes*, Lent 1937, p. 12.

461 *Hermes*, Lent 1937, p. 38.

462 *Honi Soit*, no. 15, 1935, p. 1.

463 *Hermes*, Trinity 1935, p. 13.

464 *Honi Soit*, no. 15, 1935, p. 1.

465 *Hermes*, Trinity 1935, p. 7.

466 ibid.

467 Dale, p. 72.

468 J. Croft, 'Responses to Modernism', *The Penguin New Literary History of Australia*, Laurie Hergenhan (ed.), Penguin, Ringwood, VIC, 1988, pp. 414–17.

469 J. Wright, *Half*, pp. 123–4; McLeod, p. 37.

470 J. Wright, *Half*, p. 123.

471 E. R. Holme, preface, in R. G. Howarth, E. J. Dobson and A. J. A. Waldock, *Some Recent Developments in English Literature: A Series of Extension Lectures on James Joyce, Edith Sitwell, T.S. Eliot*, The University Extension Board of Sydney University, Sydney, 1935; Dale, p. 73; Waldock, *Recent Developments*, p. 7.

472 Howarth, *Recent Developments*, pp. 24–5.

473 ibid., p. 32.

474 ibid.

475 McLeod, pp. xvi, 41, 140; M. Schmidt, *Lives of the Poets*, Alfred A. Knopf, New York, 2000, p. 697.

476 Dobson, *Recent Developments*, pp. 38, 51–2.

477 H. F. R, 'Concerning Poetry', *The Arts Journal*, no. 1, 1936, p. 19.

478   A. L. McLeod writes: 'following his departure from Australia for South Africa, Howarth's name virtually disappeared from studies of the national literature', pp. xiii, xvi.

479   McLeod does not document any former student who became a writer, other than himself, who appreciated Howarth's encouragements. He does document numerous writers who did not appreciate them. ibid., p. xi.

480   J. M. Coetzee, *Youth*, Vintage, London, 2003, p. 27.

481   McLeod, p. xi.

482   D. Rowbotham, 'From *The Fight for Sydney: A Memoir*', *Southerly*, vol. 59, no. 3–4, 1999, pp. 94–5.

483   Rowbotham, p. 95; G. Howarth, 'Along the Trail', *Southerly*, vol. 59, no. 3–4, 1999, p. 135; Sheridan, 'Gentlemen's Agreements', p. 345.

484   Sheridan, 'Gentlemen's Agreements', p. 345; R. G. Howarth, *Notes on Modern Poetic Technique*, Angus & Robertson, Sydney, 1949, pp. 6–7.

485   McLeod, p. xvi.

486   Sheridan, p. 334.

487   ibid.; J. Wright, untitled poem, *Southerly*, vol. 1, no. 4, 1940, p. 24; J. Wright to J. McKinney, n.d. [1945?], *With Love*, p. 20; J. Wright to J. Blight, 16 April 1951 & 20 October 1952, *With Love*, pp. 61, 77.

488   That Howarth did not lecture on Judith's poetry is difficult to state conclusively. However, *Notes on Modern Poetic Technique*, which Howarth said was 'prepared as a basis for lectures and discussion in the University of Sydney on the technique of modern poetry as exemplified by English and Australian writers' includes only one brief and unflattering mention of Judith. Dozens of other Australian poets are discussed in greater detail. Howarth, *Notes On*, pp. iii, 61.

489   J. Wright to J. McKinney, n.d. [1945?], *With Love*, p. 20.

490   Sheridan, 'Gentlemen's Agreements', pp. 334–5.

491   The website of Austlit, 'R. G. Howarth', *Austlit: The Australian Literature Resource*, accessed 21 July 2012, www.austlit.edu.au.

492   McLeod, pp. 25, 42; Howarth, *Recent Developments*, p. 27.

493   R. G. Howarth, 'The Stuffed Mopoke' & editorial, *Southerly*, vol. 1, no. 3, 1940, pp. 15, 3–4; R. G. Howarth, review of *Collected Essays of Walter Murdoch*, *Australian National Review*, vol. 5, no. 28, 1939, pp. 80–1.

494   Howarth, *Notes On*, pp. 5–22.

495   McLeod, pp. xiii, 53; M. Franklin, undated letter, in Dale, p. 196; Howarth, notes, *Southerly*, vol. 4, no. 2, 1943, p. 38.

496   J. Wright, *Half*, p. 124; Schmidt, pp. 493–4, 497.

497   Brady argued that 'most' student poetry published at the university was 'modishly influenced by Eliot's *The Waste Land* and urban themes'. Judith's poetry, which displayed 'her feeling for the natural world marked her poems out from most of the others'. Four pages earlier Brady said that Judith *was* influenced by Howarth's lectures on modernist writing – not because he was anti-modernist, but because he was *for* such experimentation. Brady, pp. 55, 51.

498   Ackland, pp. 44, 30.

499   *Hermes*, Lent 1936, p. 8

500   Hermes, Michaelmas 1934, p. 3.

501   Horne, p. 261.

502   *Hermes*, Trinity 1934, p. 4.

503   Anonymous, 'Modern Literature', *Honi Soit*, no. 14, 1935, p. 2.

504   *The Arts Journal*, no. 1, 1936, p. 10.

505   For the purposes of this survey, verse has been classified as 'modernist' when it does one or more of the following: experiments with form in ways similar to contemporary poets; abandons traditional metrical, rhyming or line structures; uses everyday or informal language; comments on, and seems resigned to, the limits of language, tradition, religion and life; seeks to communicate the unconscious, perhaps using stream of consciousness; relishes irony or speaks about the modern world, often introducing references to modern culture. These are recurring themes in experimental student poetry of the period. Poems, on the other hand, have been classified as 'Victorian' when they do one or more of the following: use a dramatic voice, often in monologue form, to develop psychological complexity; pursue the 'big' themes of love, beauty, nature, death and time; are strongly descriptive, often reverential, especially when considering art, women, natural landscapes and the other worldly; express a fascination with the past and other societies, particularly ancient and primitive ones; tend to rhyme or use established verse forms to generate musicality. Browning and Tennyson's work might have been their models. There were poems with literary influences not so easy to categorise. These miscellaneous poems do not constitute a discernible group, though it can be said that many of them were poetic forms of the painterly still life, which sought simply and directly to describe something, often a natural scene.

506   *Hermes*, Michaelmas 1934, p. 4.

507   Horne, p. 241; H. L. McLoskey, 'Plus Ca Change...', *Southerly*, vol. 1, no. 4, 1940, p. 33.

508   Editorial, *Hermes*, Lent 1936, p. 8.

509   H. M. S., 'T. S. Eliot and the New World', *Hermes*, Trinity 1934, p. 11.

510   M. Mackie, 'Expressionism and Modern Art', *Hermes*, Trinity 1936, pp. 14–15; J. A. P, 'The Progress of Poetry', *Hermes*, Trinity 1936, pp. 17–19.

Chapter 8: The Poems That Came Before

511   *AustLit: The Australian Literature Resource*, accessed 7 February 2012, www.austlit. edu.au; Wilde et al., p. 828; H. Anderson, 'A Bibliography of Judith Wright', *Australian Literary Studies*, vol. 3, no. 4, 1968, pp. 312–13.

512   S. Walker, 'The Search for Unity in Judith Wright's Poetry', doctorial thesis, University of New England, 1977; S. Walker, papers relating to Judith Wright, box 2097517x, University of Queensland Library, Brisbane; J. Wright & Rusden, tape 2, side 1, p. 14.

513   *The Magazine of the Women's College University of Sydney*, no. 22, 1936, p. 24; Brady, pp. 51, 55; Jennifer Strauss, *Judith Wright*, Oxford University Press, Melbourne, 1995, p. 44.

514   J. Wright & Rusden, tape 2, side 1, p. 14; M. Macdonald, 'Judith Wright: "a Damn good thing"', *Daily Telegraph*, 27 November 1969, p. 33.

515   Lang, pp. 408–9. The Fisher Library at the University of Sydney is the only library to hold a complete collection of *Hermes*. More dishearteningly, only two libraries hold the 1935 and 1936 issues of *The Arts Journal*, of which there were only two, and no public library holds a 1934 issue. Given this, it is possible that Judith had poems published in a 1934 issue of the magazine that will never be discovered. Another possibility is that a 1934 issue was never produced.

516   J. Wright, *Half*, p. 54.

517   J. Wright & Rusden, tape 2, side 1, pp. 12–13.

518   Horne, pp. 258, 261; 'AJM' was A. J. Melville and 'HD' was Howard Daniel.

519   M. Heyward, *The Ern Malley Affair*, Faber and Faber, London, 1993, pp. 48–9.

520 ibid. The University Calendars for the years 1934 to 1936 do not include 'Isabel Ellis' in any student lists.

521 Mackaness & Mackaness, p. 171.

522 J. Wright, *Half*, pp. 127, 141.

523 J. Wright, 'Transformations: 1. Fairytale', *Collected Poems 1942–1985*, Angus & Robertson, Sydney, 1971; reprint, 1994, p. 76.

524 J. Wright, *New England Girls' School Chronicle*, Armidale, NSW, June 1932, p. 17.

525 J. Wright, 'My Friend', ibid., p. 29.

526 J. Wright & Rusden, tape 2, side 1, p. 11.

527 J. Wright, *Generations*, p. 90.

528 J. Wright, 'The Invaders', *The Bulletin*, 12 July 1950, p. 21.

529 J. Wright, *Generations*, p. 90.

530 The following signatures are the only ones from *The Arts Journal* 1936 that could belong to Judith: Setna, JA, HFR, LHB. The other poets published in that issue are J. Mc (James McAuley); C.E.C, most probably C. Carloss, who was on the editorial committee, and who the Calendar confirms had a middle name beginning with 'e'; and Adele Bieri, who was a student. It is highly unlikely Judith used the name 'Setna' as it was credited with poems published before and after she attended university. HFR and LHB were not published in *Hermes* during these years. 1936 Calendar, pp. 538, 547.

531 J. Wright & Rusden, tape 2, side 1, p. 12.

532 J. Wright, 'Computers', *Sydney Morning Herald*, 18 June 1966, p. 15.

533 'Type and Stereotype', *Hermes*, Trinity 1936, pp. 7–8.

534 J. Wright, 'A Call to Arms', *New England Girls' School Chronicle*, Christmas, 1932 Armidale, p. 25.

535 Brady, p. 44.

536 J. Wright, 'A Call'.

537 J. Wright, 'Fear', *New England Girls' School Chronicle*, Christmas, 1932, Armidale, p. 25.

538 J. Wright, *Generations*, pp. 202–3.

539 L. McCredden, *James McAuley*, Oxford University Press, Melbourne, 1992. McAuley's student poetry is also discussed in two books referred to earlier in this book, by Michael Heyward and Michael Ackland.

540 J. Wright to A. Hope, 1 January 1980; J. Wright to B. Blackman, 19 November 1993; J. Wright to Tina Lister, 19 May 1995, *With Love*, pp. 324, 510, 517.

541 'Bullocky' was first published when Judith was twenty-nine (in 1944). When she was seventy years old she told Meredith McKinney that she wrote it when she was twenty-six (in 1941). In 1946 Judith referred to the poem as 'my old hack Bullocky', suggesting that she wrote it some years before it was first published. J. Wright to M. McKinney, 27 October 1985, *With Love*, p. 409; J. Wright to C. Christesen, 18 September 1946, Judith Wright papers, box 70, folder 505, National Library of Australia, Canberra.

542 Walker, pp. 40–1.

Postscript

543 J. Wright, 'To Younger poets', *Overland*, no. 154, 1999, p. 4.

Select References

Ackland, Michael. *Damaged Men*. Crows Nest, NSW: Allen & Unwin, 2001.

Aitkin, Don. *The Country Party in New South Wales: A Study of Organisation and Survival*. Canberra: Australian National University Press, 1972.

Allen, Judith A. *Rose Scott*. Melbourne: Oxford University Press, 1994.

Anderson, Fay and Stuart Macintyre. *Life of the Past: The Discipline of History at the University of Melbourne*. Melbourne: The Department of History, University of Melbourne, 2006.

Anderson, Hugh. 'A Bibliography of Judith Wright.' *Australian Literary Studies* 3, no. 4 (1968): 312–13.

Anderson, John. *A Perilous and Fighting Life: The Political Writings of Professor John Anderson*. Ed. Mark Weblin. North Melbourne, VIC: Pluto Press, 2003.

Anderson, John. *Lectures on Greek Philosophy 1928*. Ed. Creagh McLean Cole. Sydney: Sydney University Press, 2008.

Annable, Rosemary, ed. *Biographical Register: The Women's College Within the University of Sydney*, vol. 1: 1892–1939. Sydney: the Council of the Women's College, 1995.

Atkinson, Alan, J. S. Ryan, Iain Davidson and Andrew Piper, eds. *High Lean Country: Land, People and Memory in New England*. Crows Nest, NSW: Allen & Unwin, 2006.

Barcan, Alan. *Radical Students: The Old Left at Sydney University*. Melbourne: Melbourne University Press, 2002.

Barnes, John, ed. *The Writer in Australia: A Collection of Literary Documents 1856–1964*. Melbourne: Oxford University Press, 1969.

Bennett, Bruce and Jennifer Strauss, eds. *The Oxford Literary History of Australia*. Melbourne: Oxford University Press, 1998.

Bird, Delys, Robert Dixon and Christopher Lee, eds. *Authority and Influence*. St Lucia, QLD: University of Queensland Press, 2001.

Blyton, Greg, Deirdre Heitmeyer and John Maynard. *Wannin Thanbarran: A History of Aboriginal and European Contact in Muswellbrook and the Upper Hunter Valley*. Muswellbrook, NSW: Muswellbrook Shire Aboriginal Reconciliation Committee, 2004.

Brady, Veronica. 'After Life With Judith Wright.' *Meanjin* 64, no. 3 (2005): 109–113.

Brady, Veronica. *South of My Days: A Biography of Judith Wright*. Sydney: Angus & Robertson, an imprint of HarperCollins, 1998.

Brooks, David and Brenda Walker, eds. *Poetry and Gender*. St Lucia, QLD: University of Queensland Press, 1989.

Bundred, Pip. Interview by the author. Tape recording. Red Hill, VIC, 20 March 2007.

Burgmann, Verity. *Revolutionary Industrial Unionism*. Cambridge, UK: Cambridge University Press, 1995.

Caine, Barbara. *Biography and History*. New York: Palgrave Macmillan, 2010.

Caine, Barbara and Rosemary Pringle. *Transitions: New Australian Feminisms*. St Leonards, NSW: Allen & Unwin, 1995.

Capp, Fiona. *My Blood's Country*. Crows Nest, NSW: Allen & Unwin, 2010.

Clarke, Patricia and Meredith McKinney, eds. *With Love and Fury: Selected Letters of Judith Wright*. Canberra: National Library of Australia, 2006.

Clarke, Patricia and Meredith McKinney, eds. *The Equal Heart and Mind: Letters Between Judith Wright and Jack McKinney*. St Lucia, QLD: University of Queensland Press, 2004.

Coetzee, J. M. *Youth*. London: Vintage, 2003.

Connor, John. *Australian Frontier Wars, 1788–1838*. Sydney: UNSW Press, 2002.

Cusack, Dymphna. *Jungfrau*. With a new introduction by Florence James. Ringwood, VIC: Penguin, 1989.

Dale, Leigh. *The English Men: Professing Literature in Australian Universities*. Toowoomba, QLD: Association for the Study of Australian Literature, 1997.

Damousi, Joy. '"The Filthy American Twang": Elocution, the Advent of American "Talkies", and Australian Cultural Identity.' *The American Historical Review* 112, no. 2 (2007): 16, 17.

Dixon, Robert and Veronica Kelly, eds. *The Impact of the Modern: Vernacular Modernities in Australia 1870s–1960s*. Sydney: Sydney University Press, 2008.

Elkin, A.P. *The Australian Aborigines*. London: Angus & Robertson, 1938; reprint with revisions, 1981.

Ellis, Ulrich. *New England, the Seventh State*. Armidale, NSW: The New State Movement, 1957.

Ellis, Ulrich. *The Country Party: A Political and Social History of the Party in New South Wales*. Melbourne: F. W. Cheshire, 1958.

Farwell, George. *Squatter's Castle*. Sydney: Angus & Robertson, 1983.

Fawcett, J. W. 'Notes on the Customs and Dialect of the Wonnah-Ruah Tribe.' *Science of Man and Journal of the Royal Anthropological Society of Australasia* 1, no. 7 (1898): 152–4.

Ferry, John. *Colonial Armidale*. St Lucia, QLD: The University of Queensland Press, 1999.

Green, H. M. Untitled article. *The Australian National Review* 5, no. 28 (1939): 56.

Green, H. M. 'What is Australian Literature?' *Southerly* 1, no. 2 (1940): 15–17.

Grimshaw, Patricia and Lynne Strahan, eds. *The Half-Open Door: Sixteen Modern Australian Women Look at Professional Life and Achievement*. Sydney: Hale and Iremonger, 1982.

Grose, Kelvin & Jean Newall. *So Great a Heritage*. Sydney: New England Girls' School in association with Allen & Unwin, 1990.

H. M. S. 'T. S. Eliot and the New World'. *Hermes* (Trinity 1934): 9–11.

Hart, Kevin. 'Darkness and Lostness: How to Read a Poem by Judith Wright.' *Imagining Australia: Literature and Culture in the New New World*. Eds. Judith Ryan and Chris Wallace-Crabbe, 305–319. Cambridge, Massachusetts: Harvard University Press in association with the Committee on Australian Studies, 2004.

Head, Brian and James Walter. *Intellectual Movements and Australian Society*. Melbourne: Oxford University Press, 1988.

Hergenhan, Laurie, ed. *The Penguin New Literary History of Australia*. Ringwood, VIC: Penguin, 1988.

Heyward, Michael. *The Ern Malley Affair*. London: Faber and Faber, 1993.

Hill, Pollyanne. Interview by the author. Tape recording. Perth, WA, 28 April 2008.

Hole, W. Vere and Anne H. Treweeke. *The History of the Women's College Within the University of Sydney*. Sydney: Angus & Robertson, 1953.

Horne, Donald. *The Education of Young Donald*. Sydney: Angus & Robertson, 1967.

Howarth, Geoff. 'Along the Trail.' *Southerly* 59, no. 3–4 (1999): 131–6.

Howarth, R. G. *Notes on Modern Poetic Technique*. Sydney: Angus & Robertson, 1949.

Howarth, R. G. 'The Stuffed Mopoke.' *Southerly* 1, no. 3 (1940): 15–21.

Howarth, R. G., E. J. Dobson and A. J. A. Waldock. *Some Recent Developments in English Literature: A Series of Extension Lectures on James Joyce, Edith Sitwell, T. S. Eliot*. Sydney: The University Extension Board of Sydney University, 1935.

Irving, Terry and Rowan Cahill. *Radical Sydney: Places, Portraits and Unruly Episodes*. Sydney: University of New South Wales Press, 2010.

J. A. P. 'The Progress of Poetry.' *Hermes* (Trinity 1936): 17–19.

Kingston, Beverley. *A History of New South Wales*. Port Melbourne, VIC: Cambridge University Press, 2006.

Kociumbas, Jan. *Oxford History of Australia*, vol. 2, *1770–1860: Possessions*. Melbourne: Oxford University Press, 1992.

Laffan, Jennifer and Cameron Archer. *Aboriginal Land Use at Tocal: the Wonnarua Story*. Paterson, NSW: NSW Agriculture, 2004.

Lang, Anouk. 'Judith Wright and Frank Scott: Gendering Networks in Australia and Canada.' *Australian Literary Studies* 22, no.4 (2006): 403–16.

Leonard, John, ed. *Australian Verse: An Oxford Anthology*. Melbourne: Oxford University Press, 1998.

Leopold, Keith. *Came to Booloominbah: A Country Scholar's Progress 1938–1942*. Ed. J. S. Ryan. Armidale, NSW: University of New England Press, 1998.

Lilienthal, Sonja. *Newtown Tarts: A History of Sydney University Women's Sports Association*. St Leonards, NSW: Allen & Unwin, 1997.

Lodge, David, ed. *Twentieth Century Literary Criticism*. London: Longman, 1972.

Lowenstein, Wendy. *Weevils in the Flour*. East Brunswick, VIC: Scribe, 1981.

Macintyre, Stuart. *A Concise History of Australia*. Cambridge: Cambridge University Press, 1999.

Macintyre, Stuart & Julian Thomas, eds. *The Discovery of Australian History 1890–1939*. Carlton, VIC: Melbourne University Press, 1995.

Mackaness, Joan S. & George, eds. *The Wide Brown Land*. Sydney: Angus & Robertson, 1934.

Mackie, Margaret. 'Expressionism and Modern Art.' *Hermes* (Trinity 1936): 14–15.

Mackinnon, Alison. *Women, Love and Learning: The Double Bind*. Bern, Switzerland: Peter Lang AG, 2010.

Marr, David. *Patrick White: A Life*. Sydney: Random House, 1991.

Matthews, Jill Julius. *Dance Hall and Picture Palace: Sydney's Romance with Modernity*. Strawberry Hills, NSW: Currency Press, 2005.

McCann, Andrew. 'The Literature of Extinction.' *Meanjin* 65, no. 1 (2006): 48–54.

McCredden, Lyn. *James McAuley*. Melbourne: Oxford University Press, 1992.

McKernan, Susan. *A Question of Commitment*. Sydney: Allen & Unwin, 1989.

McKinney, Meredith. Interview by the author. Tape recording. Braidwood, NSW, 8 August 2008.

McLaren, John. *Writing in Hope and Fear: Literature as Politics in Postwar Australia*. Cambridge: Cambridge University Press, 1996.

McLeod, A. L. *R. G. Howarth: Australian Man of Letters*. New Delhi, India: New Dawn Press, 2005.

McLoskey, H. L. 'Plus Ca Change…' *Southerly* 1, no. 4 (1940): 33.

McQueen, Humphrey. *Social Sketches of Australia*, 2nd edition. Ringwood, VIC: Penguin Books, 1991.

Mead, Philip. *Networked Language: Culture and History in Australian Poetry*. North Melbourne, VIC: Australian Scholarly Publishing, 2008.

Mead, Philip. 'Veronica Brady's Biography of Judith Wright.' *Australian Literary Studies* 19, no. 2 (1999): 163–75.

Miller, James. *Koori: A Will to Win: The Heroic Resistance, Survival and Triumph of Black Australia*. Sydney, NSW: Angus & Robertson, 1985.

Milliss, Roger. *Waterloo Creek: The Australia Day Massacre of 1838, George Gipps and the British Conquest of New South Wales*. Ringwood, VIC: McPhee Gribble, 1992.

Modjeska, Drusilla. *Exiles At Home: Australian Women Writers 1925–1945*. North Ryde, NSW: Angus & Robertson, 1981; reprint, 1991.

New England Girls' School. *Prospectus*. [1928?]. National Library of Australia, Canberra, 2004. Microfiche.

Oaks, Laurie. *Crash Through or Crash: The Unmaking of a Prime Minister*, Richmond, VIC: Drummond, 1976.

Overacker, Louise. *The Australian Party System*. Oxford: Oxford University Press, 1952.

Price, Kathleen. Interview by Judy Wing. Tape recording. 1987, the NSW Bicentennial Oral History collection, digital collections, National Library of Australia, Canberra.

Reece, R. H. W. *Aborigines and Colonists: Aborigines and Colonial Society in New South Wales in the 1830s and 1840s*. Sydney: Sydney University Press, 1974.

Reiger, Karreen M. *The Disenchantment of the Home: Modernizing the Australian Family 1880–1940*. Melbourne: Oxford University Press, 1985.

Reynolds, Henry. 'The Mabo Judgment in the Light of Imperial Land Policy.' *University of New South Wales Law Journal* 16, no. 1 (1993): 27–44.

Roberts, Stephen H. *History of Australian Land Settlement: 1788–1920*. Reissued edition. South Melbourne, VIC: The Macmillan Company of Australia, 1968.

Roberts, Stephen H. *The Squatting Age in Australia 1835–1847*. Carlton, VIC: Melbourne University Press, 1935; reprint with corrections, 1975.

Roe, Jill, ed. *Twentieth Century Sydney: Studies in Urban and Social History*. Sydney: Hale and Iremonger, 1980.

Rooney, Brigid. *Literary Activists: Writer–Intellectuals and Australian Public Life*. St Lucia, QLD: University of Queensland Press, 2009.

Rowbotham, David. 'From *The Fight for Sydney: A Memoir*.' *Southerly* 59, no. 3–4 (1999): 94–101.

Scalmer, Sean. 'Charles Gavan Duffy's Ministerial Tour: Oratory, Electioneering and the Meaning of Colonial Democracy.' *Australian Journal of Politics & History* 57, no. 2 (2011): 155–73.

Schmidt, Michael. *The Lives of the Poets*. New York: Alfred A. Knopf, 2000.

Sheridan, Susan. 'Gentlemen's Agreements: Southerly's First Editors.' *Southerly* 67, no. 1–2 (2007): 333–47.

Sheridan, Susan. *Nine Lives: Postwar Women Writers Making Their Mark.* St Lucia, QLD: University of Queensland Press, 2011.

Shipp, John, ed. *The Fisher Library Centenary 1909–2009.* Sydney: The University of Sydney Library, 2009.

Spearritt, Peter. *Sydney's Century: A History.* Sydney: University of New South Wales Press, 2000.

Stell, Marion K. *Half the Race: A History of Australian Women in Sport.* North Ryde, NSW: Angus & Robertson, 1991.

Strauss, Jennifer. *Judith Wright.* South Melbourne, VIC: Oxford University Press, 1995.

Stuckey, Michael. 'Not by Discovery But by Conquest: The Use of History and the Meaning of "Justice" in Australian Native Title Cases.' *Common Law World Review* 34, no. 1 (2005): 19–38.

Summers, Anne. *Damned Whores and God's Police: The Colonisation of Women in Australia.* Blackburn, VIC: Penguin, 1975.

Turney, Clifford, Ursula Bygott and Peter Chippendale. *Australia's First: A History of the University of Sydney, vol. 1, 1850–1939.* Sydney: The University of Sydney in association with Hale & Iremonger, 1991.

University of Sydney. 'Calendar Archive.' http://calendararchive.usyd.edu.au/index.php

Waldock, A. J. A., R.G. Howarth and E.J. Dobson. *Some Recent Developments in English Literature: A Series of Extension Lectures.* Sydney: Australasian Medical Publishing Company for the University Extension Board, 1935.

Walker, R. B. *Old New England: A History of the Northern Tablelands of New South Wales 1818–1900.* Sydney: Sydney University Press, 1966.

Walker, Shirley. *Flame and Shadow: A Study of Judith Wright's Poetry.* St Lucia, QLD: University of Queensland Press, 1991; reprint, 1996.

Walker, Shirley. Papers relating to Judith Wright. University of Queensland Library, Brisbane.

Walker, Shirley. 'The Search for Unity in Judith Wright's Poetry.' Doctoral thesis. University of New England, 1977.

Wetherell, David and Charlotte Carr-Gregg. *Camilla: A Life of C. H. Wedgwood.* Kensington, NSW: New South Wales University Press, 1990.

Wilde, William H., Joy Hooton and Barry Andrew, eds. *The Oxford Companion to Australian Literature,* 2nd edition. Melbourne: Oxford University Press, 1994.

Wilkinson, Donald. 'The Importance of Dalwood.' Document prepared for the Dalwood Restoration Society, Sydney, 2010.

Windschuttle, Elizabeth. *Women, Class and History: Feminist Perspectives on Australia 1788–1978.* Melbourne: Fontana and Collins, 1980.

Women's College Within the University of Sydney Calendar 1935, The. Glebe, NSW: Australasian Medical Publishing Company, 1936.

Wright, Catherine. Interview by the author. Tape recording. 28 April 2008, Perth, WA.

Wright, Charlotte May, comp. 'Extracts from Dinton-Dalwood Letters: From 1827 to 1853.' 1927. Duplicated by D. E. Wilkinson. 1964. Papers of Judith Wright, MS 5781, box 70, folder 504. National Library of Australia, Canberra.

Wright, Judith. 'An Interview with Judith Wright McKinney.' Interview by Heather Rusden. Transcript of tape recording. 1987–88, TRC 2202. Canberra: National Library of Australia, Oral History and Folklore collection.

Wright, Judith. *Born of the Conquerors: Selected Essays by Judith Wright*. Canberra: Aboriginal Studies Press, 1991.

Wright, Judith. *Collected Poems 1942–1985*. Sydney: Angus & Robertson, an imprint of HarperCollins, 1971; reprint, 1994.

Wright, Judith. *Cry for the Dead*. Oxford: Oxford University Press, 1981; reprint, Perth: API Network, 2004.

Wright, Judith. *Half a Lifetime*. Melbourne: Text Publishing, 1999; reprint, 2001.

Wright, Judith. *Judith Wright: A Written Interview*. Interview by Carolyn Masel and Michael Schmidt. Transcript. 1992. Papers of Judith Wright, MS 5781, box 71, folder 513, Canberra: National Library of Australia.

Wright, Judith. 'Judith Wright: Corrections to Biographical Errors.' *Australian Literary Studies* 19, no. 4 (2000): 438.

Wright, Judith. Papers, 1944–2000, MS 5781. National Library of Australia, Canberra.

Wright, Judith. *Tales of a Great Aunt*. Bondi Junction, NSW: Imprint, a division of ETT Imprint, 1998.

Wright, Judith. *The Generations of Men*. Oxford: Oxford University Press, 1959; reprint, 1982.

Wright, Judith. *The Nature of Love*. Melbourne: Sun Books, 1966; reprint 1968.

Wright, Phillip A. *Memories of a Bushwhacker*. Armidale, NSW: The University of New England, 1972; reprint with afterword by Bruce Mitchell, 1982.

Wyndham, George. 'On the Land Policy of New South Wales.' Pamphlet. West Maitland, NSW: H Thomas, 1866?.

Wyndham, George. *The Diary of George Wyndham 1830–1840: A Pioneer's Record*. Eds. Alward Wyndham and Frances McInherny on behalf of the Dalwood Restoration Association. Armidale, NSW: Parkes the Printer, 1987.

Wyndham, George. *The Impending Crisis*. Maitland, NSW: R. Jones for the Mercury Office, 1847.

Wyndham, Cedric. Interview by the author. Email. 10 November 2010.

Index

CPSIA information can be obtained
at www.ICGtesting.com
Printed in the USA
FSOW02n0454160916
24992FS